973.0451
Voices of the daughters

VOICES

of the

DAUGHTERS

VOICES

of the

DAUGHTERS

Connie A. Maglione

and

Carmen Anthony Fiore

TOWNHOUSE PUBLISHING

Princeton, New Jersey

Published by
Townhouse Publishing
301 N. Harrison Street
Building-B, Suite 115
Princeton, NJ 08540

Manufactured in the United States of America

First Printing

Cover photo: Nicola and Concetta Maglione, circa 1911

Library of Congress Cataloging-in-Publication Data

Voices of the daughters / [recorded by] Connie A. Maglione
and Carmen Anthony Fiore.
    p. cm.
  ISBN 0-939219-05-0 (alk. paper) : $14.95
  1. Italian American women. 2. Italian American
women—Interviews.
I. Maglione, Connie A., 1940–   . II. Fiore, Carmen
Anthony, 1932–   .
E184.I8V65   1989
973'.0451'0082—dc20
                                          89-5031
                                          CIP

I dedicate this book to my daughters,
CONNIE FAYE and **DIANE**,
and to my granddaughter,
AMANDA KELLY,
whose voices are a reflection of the past
and a hope for the future.

Connie A. Maglione

For my grandmothers,
ROSA FIORE & MARIA NICOLE CAPPELLO,
who gave me America.

For my mother,
MARGARET CAPPELLO FIORE,
who gave me life.

For my aunt,
CARMELA RUBERTI CAPPELLO,
my second mother, who gave me my name.

Carmen Anthony Fiore

ACKNOWLEDGMENTS

We are grateful to all the participants for their enthusiastic support, and for their time and effort in completing the questionnaires, and for persevering through the interviews and the telephone follow-up calls, for without their cooperation and help there would be no *Voices of the Daughters*.

And we must thank Penny Johnson Ferri, our editor, whose editorial vigilance was instrumental in bringing the project to a satisfactory completion within the allotted time span.

Also, we wish to thank Janice Piccinini for allowing us to include her three moving speeches in "Voices," which added another dimension to the book.

Much gratitude to Carol Bonomo Ahearn for her continued enthusiasm, as well as her poignant and important written and visual contributions.

The photo collection submitted by Julia and Louis Lombardo enhanced the visual aspect of our book, and we thank them for allowing us to "pick and choose" without reservation.

Finally, we thank our loved ones for providing the support and encouragement necessary to bring *Voices of the Daughters* to fruition.

Contents

Introduction

Foreword

Letter from Ann Seale

BOOK ONE

ETHNICITY

Photographs

BOOK TWO

FAMILY

BOOK THREE

SELF

Photographs

BOOK FOUR

WOMEN IN AN ETHNIC ENCLAVE

Photographs

INTRODUCTION

Voices of the Daughters is a compilation of the thoughts, feelings, attitudes and interests of Italian-American women spanning all ages and geographic areas of the United States.

Questionnaires, face-to-face interviews, telephone interviews, as well as oral histories were employed from 1984 to 1989. Questions on the topics of ethnicity, family, education, religion and politics were asked to elicit participant responses.

Two personal aspects were explored: How being Italian-American may have affected life choices; and when did the self-awareness of being Italian-American occur?

Personal interviews were tape recorded to preserve the information in context and to capture the participants' intonations and expressions. Upon completing, and during, data collection, the recorded interviews were completely transcribed.

Requests for interested women to participate in this project were placed in selected journals, newspapers and newsletters, eliciting unanticipated responses such as letters and speeches written by the individuals for possible inclusion in the book.

After a thorough review of the data, we divided the material into three categories: Ethnicity, Family and Self. The fourth section portrays women who live in an ethnic enclave, which is part of a study of an

Italian-American community, located in a major New Jersey city, that has maintained its ethnic identity for over 100 years.

Voices explores the beliefs and attitudes of more than 100 women who chose to be recognized by either their real names or pseudonyms.

Regarding the topic of ethnicity, the women express pride in their Italian heritage as well as the conflicts associated with assimilation. For some there was a dichotomy of being Italian and being American. And it is interesting to note that many participants speak about being descendants of ethnic groups other than Italian, but their Italian background was dominant. They talk with reverence of their parents, yet relate that parental expectations often limited their life choices.

The fathers of the women are described as powerful and authoritarian; the mothers as quiet influencers and dominant forces.

In regard to the *men* in their lives, respondents discuss Italian and non-Italian males as husbands and mates. Many speak of divorces and remarriages.

The centrality of the family is a dominant theme throughout the book. Family is all-encompassing, supportive and fulfilling, yet—at times—may limit personal choice, creating stress and possible dissension among its members. The women tell about educational restrictions caused by this excess of loyalty to the family taking precedence over personal goals, thus having to choose professions and careers that were considered acceptable for women.

The women in the ethnic enclave express solidarity in regard to their generational occupancy in the community, and they are portrayed as maintaining the southern Italian tradition of allegiance to the family. The residents of this community have sanctioned the

centrality of the family and the concept of the neighborhood as an extension of the family throughout the
generations.

It is also interesting to note that this inter-
generational continuity of family allegiance and loyalty is expressed by enclave girls who attend a
suburban Catholic high school as well as the women
interviewed.

Voices of the Daughters provides a forum for
Italian-American women to have their say in print. It
takes its place among Italian-American literature, and
it will be a resource for study in regard to ethnicity
and women in general. It will serve, we hope, as an
impetus for future similar works.

The women depicted here run the gamut of house-
wives, career women, religious women, superwomen.
They are mothers, daughters, grandmothers—but
they are *all* Italian-Americans—and they speak for
themselves.

Connie Maglione

April 29, 1989
Princeton, N.J.

FOREWORD

I didn't know my grandmothers, Rosa Fiore and Maria Nicole Cappello, but they did influence my future life long before I was born. They were part of the great migration from Europe at the turn of the century. And my father's anecdotal relating of how his family came to America is an eyeopener that has to put down the myth about Italian women being "completely" subservient to their men. Because it was his mother who spearheaded the family's move to America from southern Italy, not his father. "There's no future for us here," my father remembered his mother saying. And she was so right. Southern Italians are still leaving that harsh wasteland. Completely abandoned hilltowns are the stark witnesses to that. So it was my father's mother who made the gutsy decision to travel to America after her son, Angelo, came back to Italy from America after one of his scouting trips to the "land of plenty" where streets were reported to be "paved with gold." My father told me that his father wanted to stay in Italy, but that he ended up *tagging* along with the rest of the family on its ocean voyage to America—not *leading* it to the promised land. So much for the subservient Italian woman myth.

In my teen years, I was told by a distant cousin on my mother's side, that I had a resemblance around my brow and eyes to my grandmother, Maria Nicole, whose husband, Antonio, never addressed her by name. My mother told me that her father always called her mother, *mala'uri* in his southern Italian dialect, which translates loosely to *bad luck*. I think this speaks volumes about the male-female relationship at that time between married Italian immigrants.

And I remember a story my Aunt Carmela told me about my grandmother Rosa, when she was an aging invalid confined to her bed in a side room downstairs in our old house on Centre Street in Trenton. Aunt Carmela, the wife of my mother's brother, Joe, was visiting my mother. She went into the bedroom to pay her respects to my grandmother, who, during the visit, kept cursing up at a large picture of her husband hanging on a nearby wall. Occasionally, she would expectorate at the picture to emphasize her disdain for the deceased husband. And during one of her more active displays, she fell out of bed. After helping my grandmother get back into bed, Aunt Carmela scolded her: "See, God punished you for cursing and spitting at your husband's picture." Again I think this brief anecdote speaks volumes about the "oldtimers" and their marital relations.

This type of *trench warfare* has carried over through the decades of this century, emphatically brought out during the interviews with the Italian-American women interviewed for *Voices of the Daughters*. Time and again they mentioned not wanting to marry Italian men, or if planning to do so, that they not be the "old fashioned" type. The modern Italian-American woman, obviously, wants to be a wife and not just an unpaid house servant, and to have the man in her life *be* a part of her life—which is not too much to ask for in a marriage. But it took the fortitude of those early immigrant Italian women to carry off, usually with silent dignity, the burden of being a wife to their men in a strange land with an unfamiliar language, while making their homesteads secure to nurture their children, in order to prepare them as future adults and Americans.

I believe that the Italian immigrant women and the Italian-American women of the present have always carried the heavier load in America than the Italian male immigrant or the present-day Italian-American male. They have had not only to be wife and mother, responsible for keeping the home clean, the clothes washed and ironed, the children presentable, the food prepared, but often had to help support the family as well. They did what was necessary. If they stayed home, it was sewing for a local clothing factory, or taking in laundry; if they had to, they left their homes to work in sweatshops, whatever it took to make money to help keep the family together—survival as a unit. The woman was the heart and soul of the family. Yes, the man of the house was its titular head, and he received his respectful due, but it was *she* who built the solid foundation for keeping the family intact in a sometimes hostile environment. And her children knew who really ran the "show" in the house.

As a youngster, I witnessed the relationships of the marriages—in my immediate family and in the families of my relatives. I never saw any weak and subservient Italian women—such as the kind that are usually portrayed in the media. The women, who were important to me in my milieu, were assertive, even feisty. They were the *bosses* in their households. Yet, I never sensed any resentment on anyone's part. We accepted it, the men and the children, that *Mom* was the real "First Sergeant" of our houses. Yes, the men were the breadwinners, and, yes, they provided the necessary male strength as protectors, and, yes, when they spoke, we listened, but it was the women in our families who provided the nurturing that made us all better human beings. The women civilized us, as they have in other times and other places. They provided the needed balance in our lives.

And I want to go on record as saying that I can look back on my youth with nostalgic fondness and feel lucky that I not only had a good mother and father, whom I loved, but that I had good aunts and uncles, whom I loved, also. How fortunate I was to have all those caring adults surrounding me, whom I could trust with my life. And I'm sure that my brother and sister and all my cousins feel the same way. Today's America could use a good dose of filial solidarity as one of the answers to its teenage drug problem and broken home dilemma.

Voices of the Daughters has been a vivid growing experience for me. I learned even more about my own family as well as about the families of other Italian-Americans across this country. And I found it amazing how the experiences related by these interesting and honest Italian-American women, whether they lived in ethnic enclaves or in non-Italian neighborhoods, revealed that their Italian background couldn't be denied, that the similarities affected them, overtly or subtlely, but still there—always there. As a poignant example, even now in the eighties, Italian-American college women reported how they stay home and commute to college, rather than leave their homes and families to live on campus, while their friends from different backgrounds couldn't wait to get away from theirs. That in itself reveals how strong a hold, how strong an influence our Italian background has on us, male or female, whether we want to admit it or not.

But I think I am typical when it comes to today's ethnic-American rediscovering his heritage, after meeting so many others who are doing the same thing, joining historical groups and studying Italian culture through academic or social endeavors, plus taking trips to Europe to visit Italy. I think this is healthy. We should know our roots and be proud of them. Forget the media and their stereotyped negative images of *our* people—just follow your heart and be the best at what you are—YOU!

C. A. Fiore

April 26, 1989
Hamilton, N.J.

July 24, 1988

To whom it may concern,

My interest in participating in your book is of excitement. My maiden name is Antonina Avocato. My mother's maiden name is Josephine Bevalacqua. I feel I am qualified for participation in your book. I was raised in a grocery store until I was 16. I'm a hairdresser and I own a small salon. I've lived as an Italian princess until I was 16. I rebelled against it to be my own person, and I have succeeded in overcoming my Italian upbringing. I have a lot of information about Italian girls. I did not want to live out my family's thoughts of women. I'm independent of my family and I am very happy for becoming a real person in this world. I feel very sorry for the millions of Italian princesses in this world that have never quite found out who they are.

Well, I hope I hear from you to participate in your book.

Yours sincerely,

Ann Seale

BOOK ONE

ETHNICITY

I am my grandparents' granddaughter, so to speak. I am the reverse immigration. I have gone back a generation, not ahead. I have returned to Europe.

Margaret Rose

When our parents arrived from Italy, they wanted to become Americans. I was born in America and always wanted to be an Italian.

Catherine M.

I was ashamed for a very short time to be considered the little Italian girl with the pierced ears.

Dolores

I think they were afraid for us to make waves. The more we could blend in the safer it would be.

Jane

As a young girl, I was ashamed of my Italian name, of my beautiful custom-made, hand-knitted woolen dresses, of the delicious sandwiches made with Italian bread, and of the oil-stained bag holding my lunch.

Jennie

COMMENTS BY JANICE A. PICCININI UPON RECEIVING THE AMERITAN AWARD FROM THE MARYLAND, ORDER OF SONS OF ITALY OCTOBER 10, 1983

VICE PRESIDENT BUSH, JUDGE VALLE, HONORED GUESTS, SONS AND DAUGHTERS OF ITALY:

MY GRANDFATHER, CAESAR, WOULD BE SO PROUD TONIGHT TO KNOW THAT HIS GRAND-DAUGHTER—A FIRST-GENERATION AMERICAN—WOULD HAVE THE PRIVILEGE OF SITTING DOWN TO DINNER WITH THIS DISTINGUISHED GATHERING AND THE VICE PRESIDENT OF THE UNITED STATES OF AMERICA. IT WAS WITHIN THE LIFETIME OF SOME OF YOU HERE, THAT MY GRANDFATHER CAME TO THIS COUNTRY, A PENNILESS PILGRIM IN SEARCH OF A BETTER LIFE. HE CAME WITH NO KNOWLEDGE OF EN-GLISH, WITH NO RELATIVES OR FRIENDS TO GREET OR HELP HIM IN A FOREIGN LAND. HE BROUGHT WITH HIM ONLY HIS YOUNG FAMILY AND WITH THEM A VISION AND A DETERMINA-TION TO CREATE A NEW AND BETTER LIFE—A LIFE WITH HOPE AND OPPORTUNITY—FOR HIS CHILDREN AND HIS CHILDREN'S CHILDREN.

I THANK HIM TONIGHT AND THE COUNT-LESS OTHER PIONEERS FROM ITALY WHO WORKED IN THE STEEL MILLS, IN THE FACTO-RIES, ON THE RAILROADS; WHO PERSEVERED DESPITE LANGUAGE BARRIERS, POVERTY AND DISCRIMINATION. I THANK THEM NOT ONLY

FOR CREATING OPPORTUNITIES BUT ALSO FOR INSTILLING IN THEIR CHILDREN THOSE VALUES FROM THE OLD COUNTRY WHICH WOULD SERVE THEM WELL IN THE NEW. WHETHER AS LABORERS, CRAFTSMEN OR ARTISANS, ITALIANS AS AMERICANS HAVE APPROACHED THEIR WORK WITH PRIDE. AND THEY PASSED ON TO THEIR CHILDREN THIS SAME SENSE OF PRIDE IN WHATEVER THEY DO,WHETHER IT BE WORK WITH THE HANDS OR OF THE MIND. ITALIAN-AMERICANS HAVE MADE SIGNIFICANT CONTRIBUTIONS TO VIRTUALLY EVERY TECHNOLOGICAL AND CULTURAL ACHIEVEMENT FOR WHICH THE UNITED STATES IS RECOGNIZED WORLD-WIDE.

I HAVE CHOSEN EDUCATION AS MY FIELD OF ENDEAVOR. YOU HONOR ME THIS EVENING, BUT IN DOING SO YOU HONOR MORE MY FAMILY. IT IS MY FAMILY WITH THEIR COMMITMENT TO EDUCATION—A COMMITMENT THAT IS DEEP IN ITALIAN TRADITION—WHO MADE IT POSSIBLE FOR ME TO BE HERE TONIGHT. IT IS ALSO A TRIBUTE TO AMERICA. FOR WHERE ELSE BUT IN THIS GREAT COUNTRY COULD THE SONS AND DAUGHTERS OF IMMIGRANTS HAVE SUCH ACCESS TO EDUCATIONAL OPPORTUNITIES? WHERE ELSE BUT IN THIS COUNTRY COULD A PEOPLE FLOURISH AS CITIZENS WHILE MAINTAINING THEIR PRIDE IN THE TRADITIONS AND CULTURE OF THE "OLD COUNTRY."

I AM PROUD TO BE AN ITALIAN-AMERICAN, AND I'M PROUD TO BE AN EDUCATOR. I URGE ALL OF YOU TO TEACH YOUR CHILDREN AND GRANDCHILDREN THE VALUES THAT HAVE MADE OUR CULTURE STRONG—THE VALUES OF EDUCATION, OF HARD WORK, OF INTEGRITY AND OF FAMILY. THAT IS OUR HERITAGE AND

PASSING IT ON IS OUR PAYMENT OF DEBT TO
AN ILLUSTRIOUS PAST AND OUR GUARANTEE
OF SUCCESS FOR FUTURE GENERATIONS.

ON A PERSONAL NOTE, I WANT TO MENTION
MY GRANDMOTHER, ROSA PICCININI. SHE
SHARED THE DEPRIVATION AND HARDSHIP
WITH HER HUSBAND AND RAISED AND NUR-
TURED HER FAMILY WITH A QUIET STRENGTH
BORN OF LOVE AND DEVOTION. THE ROLE OF
WOMEN AS PIONEERS IS SELDOM FULLY REC-
OGNIZED, AND I WOULD LIKE TO BELIEVE THAT
I AM HERE TONIGHT, RECEIVING THIS PRESTI-
GIOUS AWARD AS A STAND-IN FOR HER AND
FOR ALL ITALIAN-AMERICAN WOMEN, WHOSE
STRENGTH, DEDICATION AND LOYALTY BUILT
THE FOUNDATION AND FRAMEWORK OF THE
ITALIAN-AMERICAN CULTURE.

* * * *

Stephanie

I've always known I'm an Italian-American, because my parents taught me from when I was little.
And I hope to carry on as many traditions as possible
to present and future generations so they will know
what part they play in the world.

Rosemarie W.

My Italian-American background affects my professional relationships, but in a positive way—Italians
are warm by nature, gregarious and dependable. It

also has had a positive effect on my social life—present and past—except during high school, when we Italians were put down.

Lucia Chiavola Birnbaum

I became an independent scholar when Governor Ronald Reagan's appointee fired me at San Francisco State during the campus strike of 1968–69.

In my bookish childhood in Kansas City, Missouri, my nonconformity was expressed in withdrawal from the flamboyance, the yelling across porches, and the full-decibel Italian opera of my neighborhood. I fled to immersion in school and a scholarship to the University of Kansas City. Not until several decades later would I appreciate my Sicilian peasant heritage.

Marie

I was aware of being an Italian-American from the day I was born.

Theresa Amato Di Buono

My ethnic background was only a problem living in an Irish neighborhood. My children suffered the most, but with our Italian warmth and hospitality, we won them over. It took years, but it finally worked out.

I was always aware of being an Italian-American. It all started in growing up with an Italian background. In my family we spoke Italian before we spoke English. We came home with English words, sat down with our parents, and passed on what we knew. My parents (God bless them) spoke English well.

I intend to carry on traditions of past generations. My parents had great-grandchildren, and they understood Italian well, because someone took the time to tell them about Italy, the different customs and the struggles. Today we run tapes of my parents speaking Italian. The grandchildren, etc., love to listen to them. I'm very proud of my Italian heritage.

Cathy

I swore I would never marry an Italian. But I eventually married an Italian. And he's typical. Macho, conceited, spoiled by his mother, but good to me, good to his family.

Did being from an Italian-American background restrict your goals in education?

I was encouraged, but if I didn't go to school, it didn't matter. My children had to be dying, before they could stay home. My husband made sure they got to school every day. I was married to a husband who had an education. Being male, he had an education. They were pushed for education. They were going to be the breadwinners in the family. But the females weren't.

Did being Italian-American have an effect on your social mobility?

When I was growing up, you couldn't go when you wanted to or where you wanted to like the young girls do today. They have more freedom. If we went on vacation by ourselves the way they do today, we would be considered a *putana,* a whore.

Any effect on childhood and teenage years?

Yes, because you come from a different culture. Other kinds of Americans think differently. If you were with other kinds of people, they didn't understand the way your family thought. It created a conflict with any friend I had who wasn't Italian. When I was a kid I had to help clean and do all kinds of things. My one friend, who wasn't Italian, didn't have to help clean. So I'd get beat up if I wanted to go downtown, because I had to do certain things, before I could· do anything else. Also, they used to make fun of me, of us, what we ate. Spaghetti was referred to as worms. But what was funny, now that I think back, they ate spaghetti, too. More than we did. I didn't eat spaghetti that much when I was a kid.

Did you hear any name calling in school?

Oh, yes, they'd call me wop or dago in school. And to be honest, I was getting to the point that I resented being Italian, because you weren't accepted by the non-Italians. I swore that I would never marry an Italian, because I felt the same way. I guess it stayed with me. I didn't want to go out with Italians, but I eventually married one. And he's typical. Macho, conceited, spoiled by his mother, but good to me, good to his family.

How did being an Italian-American affect your courtship?

If I were going out with someone who wasn't Italian, my parents weren't too crazy about it. If I had a date with an Italian, that was okay. I think they wanted me to marry an Italian, because an Italian man can understand the role of an Italian woman in an Italian family. The way they stick together in a family. Let's face it, Italian parents don't want to let go of their children. And only an Italian man could understand that. An American-type man wouldn't put up with it.

Did you consciously try to select a non-Italian man?

No, I just looked for somebody I was more comfortable with. And to be honest, I was more comfortable with Italians. If you're not married to an Italian, they can call you ethnic-type put-down names. It's a lot easier if you're both Italian and both Catholic.

Did being Italian-American restrict you in finding a suitable mate?

No, I dated other kinds. I only dated three Italians and married one of them.

Friends?

A mixture, but the same economic status.

Work?

I did meet some prejudice in the form of ethnic jokes that are basically put-downs. No matter where you go, you still get the anti-Italian jokes in the disguise of humor. People put too much emphasis on what you are rather than on who you are. I never ask anybody what their nationality is. It doesn't matter to me. If I like them, I like them.

How did you choose your present occupation?

I just fell into it. I had quit school and my aunt knew an insurance agent. Being an Italian-American didn't have any real effect either way.

Any effects with your relationship with your husband?

It had a big effect, our both being Italian-Americans. Being brought up in an Italian family a woman is told that your husband is the law. I don't think that you were considered to be equal. Not when I was married. Not like now with all this equality between the sexes. His mother waited on him and I was expected to wait on him. You've got sixteen jobs to do, but you still have to get his meal on the table. Today the Italian-Americans are a little different. Men will come home and help their wives. And if you helped out at home financially, they didn't mind that, but they weren't about to give in. So it does have an effect on your marriage. You were taught to look up to this male image. You were supposed to do what he says. You don't dare question. You don't dare talk back. And you don't dare voice your opinion.

Do you feel resentment looking back?

No, because I think at that particular time that was the way things were. That's the way everybody managed. You know, years ago. You didn't have all this talk about sex and living freely with someone you weren't married to. When I was getting married, you didn't

dare do what they're doing now. Could you see me living with my husband before I was married to him? If
you did, you were a *putana*. And you did have a name.
It would be all over the place. I don't resent it. It's the
way you were brought up to be. If I could have changed
it, I think I would have. Other people who are married
can talk to their husbands. But I find it difficult to
communicate with my husband.

In what way?

I just do. I always found it difficult.

What about raising your children?

In certain respects I didn't want them living the way I
did. I wanted something better for them. I wanted
them to be educated. I wasn't as strict with my daughter. I let her go. I didn't put any guilt on her. At least I
don't think I did. Italians feel that if you don't call
your mother every day, or if you don't go see them at
least once a week, you don't love them. They put all
this emphasis on it. So I tried not to do that to them.
They're old enough to make their own decisions. But
now that I'm not in the mother role, I think we're good
friends, which I think is a bond that is important.

Any pet peeves?

Yes. Anytime you see anything on TV about Italians,
it's always they're screaming at the dinner table and
slapping one another around and being portrayed as a
loud, crude, monstrous family. There was never any
screaming at our table. Every conversation was normal. We didn't scream. So I don't think the images of

Italians on TV or in the movies portray Italian-Americans as to what they really are. It's what the media people think we are. And it's irritating. Because people think that every Italian acts that way at home, and that every Italian is somehow connected to the Mafia, which we all know isn't true. Italians are hard-working people. I guess that's one of my pet peeves.

Italian background influence religion?

I went to church. I had to receive my sacraments and all that. I went to Saint James. I went to catechism classes taught by the nuns. I think it was more fear of sin and a large guilt trip, than getting anything out of it that was supposed to be religious. The nuns put the fear of God into you, not love of God, the way Jesus wanted you to feel about religion. You couldn't get married in church if you didn't receive the sacraments. If everybody followed the ten commandments, I think everybody could get along. The Catholic Church has its rules and you have to do everything according to their way, and I sort of resented that as I got older, because you lived in fear all the time. If you didn't go to church, you were going to drop dead and go straight to hell. If you ate meat on Friday, lightning was going to come out of the sky and hit you. Yet, later on in years, it was okay to eat meat on Friday. So what happened to all those sins you committed when you ate meat? It's contradictory, when you think about it. But when you're little, you don't understand that. It's when you grow up that you start thinking for yourself, and you start to question all the heavy guilt-making rules. When you're little, you don't dare question. You're afraid of committing a mortal sin. You'll drop dead and go straight to hell and burn forever.

Rosemarie B.

How does my ethnic background affect my social life? I'm proud to be an Italian and I let everyone know this.

Katherine

My ethnic background is not a topic that I talk about constantly, nor has being of Italian descent ever affected my social life.

Sofia

My spouse is deceased, but he was of Italian parentage. I didn't consciously select him because of it. But I was attracted to him more so, because he was Italian. It enhanced the relationship because of the common background and culture.

And my being Italian affects my parenting, because of the traditions which we perpetuate through our children, such as education, social behavior, religion, food, dress.

Alba

I am proud to be an Italian—I can take ethnic jokes. And I wish Cuomo would have run for president.

But I feel that Italians are worried about being linked with the Mafia. This problem may not be solved so easily.

Rosina Raggio

I was aware that I was Italian at a very early age. We lived in an Irish-Catholic neighborhood in Chicago. People often remarked about our name, about the big family gatherings on Sunday afternoons, about the good smells coming from our kitchen. We lived next to an immigrant Polish family and they, too, had some of the same experiences. People really didn't discriminate against us, they just thought we were different.

Being an Italian in Chicago in the thirties meant that you would be reminded of the "Black Hand," Mussolini, the Mafia and Al Capone. My father felt very strongly about that and made every attempt to show people what great American-Italians we were.

Outside the home, we underplayed our Italian ways. But at home we were very Italian. We always ate Italian food. We celebrated Italian feasts and holidays. We kept the traditions, and my parents spoke Italian, though they did not want us to answer in Italian.

For a brief while, so the family folklore goes, I tried to change my name. I was in fifth grade and I tired of all the remarks about my name and the difficulty of pronouncing it. So I told my friends that I was changing it to CRAIG REARDON. I must have felt that would make me suitably acceptable to my WASP friends. Also, at this time, I was into the romance of becoming a famous writer, and I remember very clearly that I thought I had to change my name because I had never heard of a great American writer with an Italian name.

Although I became a nun and not a famous writer, I have published several plays and my Italian name has certainly not presented any difficulty. But in fifth grade . . . what did I know?

Though I have no children and actually live far away from my Italian family, I join my sister and her children in keeping up our family traditions. I am in charge of the yearly family picnic, and I often give gifts that have some Italian relevance. My sister is adamant on maintaining family traditions, and her children continue them, too.

Her children and grandchildren, though only "part-Italian," tell their friends they are Italian. None of her children has married an Italian, so they don't have Italian last names, but they claim they are Italian. And I know that's because as a family, we keep reminding them of that and doing the things that continue our traditions.

My adopted nephew, whose red hair, fair skin and freckled face indicate that he may come from Irish background, says he is Italian—of course he is—he belongs to us, doesn't he?

As far as my interests in theatre and literature are concerned, I think that my parents were typical, almost stereotypical in their Italian flamboyance, which directed me to choose the arts for my career and to choose to be active and contributing to that career.

My parents were active in parish life and even participated in parish variety shows and dramas. We always had season tickets to the Chicago Civic Opera. My parents' idea of entertainment was to take the "L" to Grant Park and have a picnic while listening to a concert at the lake front.

They were not shy or withdrawn and were well known in the parish for their "outgoingness." We lived in a non-Italian neighborhood and the neighbors thought we were different—with a lot of excitement, noise and spontaneous activity in our house. My friends loved to come to my house. It was so different from theirs.

Being Italian has, in general, been a plus in my career. People who don't know me very well seem to relate to me rather quickly, because "everybody likes Italian things—art, food, language." And, surprisingly, my very Italian name is almost always remarked upon when I meet and work with peers in my field. "What a beautiful name!" "You must be Italian." "I've never forgotten that beautiful name." I have met colleagues and business associates after several years who still remember "that musical Italian name."

My colleagues expect me to be the one to come up with a new idea or with a playful approach or imaginative direction in our projects. They are a little surprised that I am not temperamental, since their expectations of Italians is that they are. They expect me to talk with my hands and to laugh and cry easily. I hear them criticize others for what they accept willingly in me. On the other hand, I am often cautioned "now don't get *Italian* about this." They obviously mean don't get excited or emotional.

I have never suffered discrimination from my colleagues, but since I have been in education all my life, my experience may not be typical. Educators are generally accepting of diversity.

My own personality is to choose to have a few very close friends, but my circle of "social" friends is wide. People have told me that I am great to have at a party, "because you're Italian." I think they mean that I am gregarious and lively and have a good sense of humor.

I am also pretty much of a performer. They think these characteristics are Italian—maybe they are.

One special aspect of my social life is dining—and Italian cooking. Since my colleagues at work are not Italian, I enjoy entertaining and serving Italian food. Once in a while, when I have served other food, my friends complain. Again, their expectation is a rather stereotypical one—Italians know how to eat—and how to cook. Since I love to do both, I don't find the stereotype offensive. Besides, as a nun, I never cooked and now that I am able to entertain that way, I do.

Mary Ann

I do wish that I spoke Italian, so that I could deal with Italian community groups with more of a cultural understanding than I currently have.

In one community where I worked, a few people were condescending towards me because I had that "peculiar last name."

I was never brought up to feel that I was any different from anyone else. I have no striking ethnic features, habits or accent. My social contacts are generally with educated people who place little emphasis on a person's ethnic background.

I am seldom attracted to Italian men for a relationship. The Italian men I've known were often characterized by their volatile tempers and emotional outbursts.

I am criticized for being both too emotional and too exacting, which may or may not have any relationship to my ethnic background, but I tend to believe that it does not.

Since my mother was not Italian and her family had lived in the South and the far West from the early 19th century on, she was not conscious of ethnic characteristics. My father's relatives lived 80 miles away. When they visited us or we them, I learned of Italian foods and customs, and I watched and listened to my father, his siblings, cousins and my grandfather speak Italian to one another. These were my preschool years, but I was not aware that they were any different from anyone else's. When I was six, my best friend's family was Swedish. I realized that they spoke a different language from my relatives and had different holiday customs. The mother of this family was of English descent and she was very conscious and verbal about ethnic differences and customs.

I don't really know what the Italian traditions are that I should carry on.

Rosemarie T.

How does your ethnic background affect your social life?

I am not sure I understand the question. I don't feel that it does. My friends are a blend of Italian-Americans, Americans, Greeks, Irish-Americans and Jews. Because of a large family, I am committed to many family functions, such as weddings, baptisms, confirmations. I like cultural activities (concerts, museums, plays). I like operas. I travel a great deal. I do like cruises with an Italian crew, and I have made several trips to Italy.

Does your Italian-American background affect your professional relationships?

To some degree, yes. Sometimes I may be the butt of ethnic jokes. I am known as the "EYE"talian. Your temperament, arm and hand gestures may be labeled as "Italian" while other ethnics are not labeled as such. A "WASP," for example, may get upset over a decision or react, and the reference to his/her temperament would be their blood pressure level increased. With me and another Italian-American teacher, it would be our "Italian tempers."

Margaret Rose

I have renewed contact with "lost" Italian cousins and hope one day to make my pilgrimage, so to speak, to Sicily to learn more about our past.

As a child I was always instilled with pride in my Sicilian-American background by my father. He, himself a first-generation American, would always answer "Sicilian" or "Italian" when asked about his ethnic group or where he was from. Both my mother and my father had Sicilian-born parents and could speak the Sicilian dialect of their area and spoke English as well. English was the language my brother and I were taught. We heard the dialect when aunts and uncles came to visit, or when we kids had learned how to spell and our parents needed a "secret" adult language. Perhaps that's where my interest in languages began.

In school, my brother and I both studied Spanish and later on at the university we took Italian. Languages came "easy" to us. Although my brother went on to become a doctor, he can still remember lots of vocabulary and would be able to get by in any

Spanish- or Italian-speaking situation. He went to Italy once on vacation.

I, on the other hand, excelled in Spanish and at the university I majored in Spanish with minors in Italian and English. I also received my masters in Romance Linguistics. I have studied Portuguese, Catalan and Modern Greek. I am fluent in Spanish, Catalan and Italian. Different languages and their respective literatures and cultures have always fascinated me, but I have a special love for whatever is Southern European.

I now live in Spain and visit Italy every year. I am a trained teacher and currently teach English as a Foreign Language. I also am Head of Translations for a magazine which promotes a "Europe of the Nations" and not a Europe of the "States." This means that all ethnic and cultural minorities should be allowed to exist and flourish, not just the majority or state group. This is why many Italian dialects, among them Sicilian, are being lost.

I feel at home in Southern Europe, in Spain and Italy, and wonder why that is. My European friends kiddingly remark that I act or am "Italian," not "American," and I must admit that often that's how I feel. I am my grandparents' granddaughter, so to speak. I am the reverse immigration. I have gone back a generation, not ahead. I have returned to Europe.

Being an Italian-American has had very little effect on my career. But it is interesting to note how many Italian-surnamed Spanish teachers there are in the United States. That might make an admirable study; if Italian had been more widely offered at school, as the Spanish language is, would we have gone into Italian instead of Spanish?

In Spain, many people make jokes about my Italian heritage, especially about Sicilians, and I must admit that I make them, too. But it's all good-natured fun. I have never experienced anything but respect for my background. This is quite the contrary to what happens when I show my American passport or mention my American citizenship!

My parents always stressed the importance of an education, partially because they knew what they had missed by not being able to attend high school. My mother died when my brother and I were very young and my father always made sure that we had time to study. There were the typical sexist differences in our treatment (Italian sons and daughters are never treated the same), but at least college was offered to both of us as an option. My family has always supported my educational goals and jobs, although I find that now they wish I didn't live in Europe and consider life in the United States to be far superior.

My background does not affect professional relationships, since I work with people from all over the world. We are all treated fairly and treat each other as equals, no matter what our heritage is.

I'm not sure if my ethnic background or my career and educational preparation have influenced me more in my social life. Obviously, my friends are from school (both when I was a student and now as a teacher), and my boyfriends have always been "Latin" types. I do have friends who are non-Latin and, of course, I do not choose them on the basis of ethnic group.

My activities are often ethnically oriented. I mean: ethnic music recitals, folk dancing, movies in other languages, opera.

I do not have a spouse or mate at this time, but if I did I would expect that person to be either Italian or Latin, since we would have to share interests, culture and traditions to a certain degree. My background and personality are Latin, and I have usually gotten along with that sort of person. A former mate never considered me to be American. He always argued that I was "Italian" (He was Greek.).

My mother came from a religious family and was quite religious herself, but on marrying a divorced man, she was considered to be "living in sin." My father was ill-considered by the family because of this. All of this hurt my mother a lot and became quite important at the time of her death and burial in 1962. My parents raised us as Catholics and attended Mass with us. My father is not "too" religious, although he probably believes in the tenets of the Catholic Church. I believe in most of them, too, yet I am not a practicing Catholic. There are things that I have difficulty accepting, but being Catholic has helped to mold my life and has given me many of my moral standards. I should think it would be difficult to be Italian and not a Catholic, at least in this country; so many Italian cultural traditions and customs are directly linked to the Roman Catholic Church.

My interest in politics is mild. I vote. I keep informed in spite (or because) of living abroad, and since one often speaks about politics in Europe, I participate in such discussions. I have never actively campaigned for anybody or anything, though I have contributed small amounts of money to certain causes and politicians. I both support and am critical of United States policies and government, but I do not express my opinions about Spanish politics. Often I am called upon to defend or explain our policies, history and actions in Europe. In some cases I have been unable to, rarely from a lack of information, but rather out of a dislike for debating and arguing. I would never run for a political office.

I do not like to pigeonhole myself into any particular party or category, but I guess I would be consid-

ered a liberal Democrat (My brother feels I'm a socialist and my father thinks I'm a communist!). My father
is a staunch Democrat who has always thought that
party represented ethnic minorities as well as the
working class. I would like to think that my choice of a
politician was based on his/her ideals and ideas and
not on his/her ethnic group. I don't consider myself to
be active in politics. My father is not active in that
sense, either.

As I've said before, I've always known I am an
Italian-American, although the term took on a new
connotation after I moved to Europe in 1976.

I am researching our family roots so that I can
pass on the family tree to the rest of my relatives. I
have renewed contact with "lost" Italian cousins and
hope one day to make my pilgrimage, so to speak, to
Sicily to learn more about our past. My cousins keep
Italian culinary customs and traditions alive. Should I
ever have children, I would make sure they were
aware of the culture as well as the language of our ancestors. I intend to do this with my niece. I have made
tapes of Italian music and I have given books on Italy
and Italian things as gifts to my relatives. I intend to
improve my command of the Italian language. I am
also actively supporting the defense of the Sicilian dialect in a European forum. At the moment I am inves-
tigating the possibility of claiming Italian citizenship
through my paternal grandfather.

Caroline

Initially, my Italian-American background had an
effect on my choice of a career. Since I was the oldest
of three children and a girl, besides, I took the busi-

ness curriculum in high school, rather than pursue a college background. However, being an achiever, I became involved in school politics and was a class officer and finally a Student Council officer. Therefore, by the time I reached the early part of my senior year, I was beginning to think college. The outcome was that I was accepted by Rider College and finally transferred to Trenton State College to pursue a teaching profession.

Today I am a manager of an office for a very successful company. My being Italian-American probably affected me only in that I always felt that I had to prove that I was better and worked harder than the average person.

My parents were very proud when I decided to continue my education (particularly since I won several scholarships and awards at graduation).

My ethnic background doesn't affect my professional relationships. But in the past, it did affect my social life.

When I first came to America, I could not speak English, and I did everything in my power to learn and become like all the other children—to fit in. Since I grew up in Princeton, my peers were WASP. I did not want to be considered a "poor Italian." So I did everything possible to be accepted. My friends were "American." My boyfriends were "American." It seemed that I went out of my way to associate with the more "acceptable society."

I selected a non-Italian mate on purpose. Again, I was rebelling against what would make me different. My mate was a college graduate who became an airline pilot.

I am no longer married. After 20 years he decided that it was time to move on. Being Italian-American created both problems and benefits. Benefits in that he was exposed to a different way of life. He had an opportunity to come to Italy and meet my family there and experience the beauty and wonder of the country. Problems in that he always felt he was an outsider because he did not speak the language. He felt that there was a strong bond between my family and me that he could not break and could not belong himself.

I had no children during the marriage.

It was not until three years after I separated from my husband that I decided to return to the fold. Being Italian became important to me. I returned to Italy at least once a year. My new "friend" loved Italy and wished that he was Italian. He encouraged me to teach him what I knew and to make the dishes that he loved. Today I am happy with myself and have experienced a year with a real Italian—loving every minute of it.

Madeline

What do you think you would change?

I would get a better education.

Where were you born?

In Rossiter, Pennsylvania.

Tell me something about your family.

We had a store there. Then we moved to Trenton, New Jersey to better ourselves in 1923. I'm in my seventies now. I was born in 1910. We stayed in Rossiter about 14 years. My father worked in the mines there. I'm a second generation Italian-American. My mother and father spoke Italian in the house. Some of the children spoke Italian. There were mostly Italians in Rossiter, some Polish. But there were no problems between the Italians and the Polish in Rossiter. We didn't meet any kind of prejudice there. My parents came from Calabria. They were married in Wishaw, Pennsylvania. They came here to better themselves.

What role did each parent play in the family?

My father worked in the mines and then ran a store in Rossiter. My mother stayed home to care for her family. My father worked in a pottery for a short time in Trenton, before opening another grocery store. He preferred to be his own boss.

Why did your family move to Trenton?

A family friend told my father that there would be more work for the entire family in a city like Trenton. There was only the mines in Rossiter. The family could better itself with more work available.

Did you have any paisans in Trenton?

Just the man and his family who advised my father to come to Trenton.

Did you meet any kind of ethnic prejudice in Trenton?

No. We got along good with our neighbors.

How did being Italian-American affect you in school?

No big effect. But I only went to the fourth grade. Then I got a job at age 14. But some kids did call us wops and spaghetti benders. The usual kid stuff. No real fist fights with any of them. Just the usual name calling.

How about at work?

No problems at the Essex Rubber plant. We got along good with everybody. We had parties and picnics and went to one another's houses. We had a club and we used to meet once a month.

Did you associate with other kinds of people besides Italians?

Oh, yes. My dad had a store and we knew all kinds of people, including colored people.

How did you meet your husband?

This cousin of ours came to visit us and he met up with my husband. He had a band and he invited my husband to his house and that's how I met him.

Were you always chaperoned in his company?

No. But we still couldn't go out. We would sit in the parlor. I was too young. I was only 15 when I met my husband. We went together for about six years. I used to give my brother a dime to get him out of the room so we could kiss. And then my brother would come back and spoil our fun. We finally married in 1930. We always lived with other couples, my sisters and their husbands, to make living cheaper by sharing the rent.

But we lived with my in-laws about a month before we went out on our own. We had no problems finding a place to rent.

Children?

I had two. And they were good. But I disciplined them when necessary. My son needed more discipline than my daughter. A couple of slaps once in a while did the trick. That was enough. We got along good. We had harmony in the house. We had a close family. We had family love.

Your extended family, was it close-knit?

We all got along good. We never argued. Never any fuss. We always spoke to one another, no family bickering, nothing upsetting.

Did you have a choice about where you lived?

We always talked about that. And no matter where we lived, we always seemed to have real nice neighbors. No trouble with any of them. And any choice was made together. No one person made it. We both decided where we would live. Where the rent was cheaper was the only reason for picking the place. We didn't know if the neighbors were Italian or not.

Relationship with your husband—as to choices inside and outside the house?

We got along pretty good. We never had any problems. We worked together on disciplining the children and saving the money. I handled the family finances most of the time. I handled the purse strings and made some of the decisions where the money was going to be spent, or at least had my say about it.

Were you happy with the choices that you and your husband made on looking back?

Oh, sure. We never had any problems. We were poor, but we got along. We managed with what we had.

Would you make any changes if you could go back?

I'd marry the same man. I'd have the same children, too. I wouldn't trade them for the world.

What do you think you would change?

I would get a better education. But I was always pleased with my jobs. I had nice bosses and co-workers. Nice environment for working and making a living.

Were most of your friends of a similar background?

There was a mixture. I got along with other Italians, with the Polish and the Hungarians. Different friends of different backgrounds.

Do you think Italian-Americans have gotten a fair shake in this country?

It's hard to say. But the Italians in this country have gotten a raw deal from the media. Being honest, working hard for a living, maintaining close family ties, being happy and nice to one another, that's what family is all about.

Religious beliefs?

I believe in God, but I was never a frequent church-goer.

Did you meet any kind of prejudice?

No, not really. At least none that I noticed.

Did being Italian-American have any effect on your choices?

I took life as it came and I don't think being Italian had any big effect. What else could you do? You make the most of everything.

In your lifetime, did you see much dissension among Italian-Americans?

Italians are sometimes their own worst enemies. There's jealousy in some families, arguments that make for hurt feelings. The fighting amongst themselves helped keep them from getting ahead in this country. One kind of Italian didn't trust the other kind. Where there's no harmony, there's no getting ahead.

Angela

I don't know that I became aware of "being" Italian at any particular time of my life. I just was! I remember once saying to my grandma, when I was very young, that I would surely not get grey hair when I got old. And she asked, "Why not?" I said, "Because I don't speak Italian!" So you see, all around me were Italians; how could I *not* be aware that I was?

Italia

I think I was always quite aware of being Italian-American, probably because of my father's influence on our family in that respect. He was an attorney for the Italian Consulate office in Chicago until World War II, and he was active in Italian-American legal affairs on behalf of Italian immigrants. However, growing up in a non-Italian town such as East Chicago, Indiana, there were no Italian festivals or other Italian cultural activities with which to identify.

As I have no children, carrying on traditions is a moot point in my life. However, I think I see a disturbing fact among teenagers with Italian surnames, and that is shame and embarrassment at having an Italian name. I hope that I am incorrect in this perception.

Since many of the early immigrants are now deceased or aged, it is imperative that the immigrant experience is documented before it is lost forever. The media and the general public do not seem very interested in the immigrant story.

Unfortunately, Mafia madness has obliterated every other phase of Italian contributions to American society. An Italian surname has become synonomous with crime, thanks to the constant barrage of anti-Italian themes seen regularly on TV shows such as *Wiseguy, Crime Story* and many others too numerous to mention. Regrettably, all Italian-Americans will suffer from this unfair stigma, in my opinion.

I hold three college degrees, two of which are graduate degrees. I have worked all my life (nonstop) since the age of 17, putting myself through college without the benefit of government aid or minority scholarships. And I resent the depiction of Italian-Americans in the media as stupid, uneducated and tough-talking. I grew up in a community with very few Italians, and we had no relatives or extended family nearby. Therefore, I am largely unfamiliar with the customs and habits of Italian-Americans except as depicted in films and entertainment such as *Moonstruck* (which I sincerely hope was a false depiction of Italian-Americans).

I cannot understand why Italian-American people accept these hideous and destructive stereotypes without complaint. No other ethnic or racial groups such as Jewish people or Black people accept these negative depictions in the media, and they are very careful and vigilant that this does not happen to them. I am fearful that Italian-Americans are becoming the last victims of vicious prejudice in this country.

Mary R.

I don't know if being Italian-American has affected any of my professional relationships, as I have been mistaken by a Black man for a WASP before. Some don't associate my last name with being Italian. In my peer group, I am not sure that people are conscious of ethnic heritage enough to affect my professional life.

How does my ethnic background affect my social life? As far as my closest friends are concerned, one's parents are from Pakistan, one's are from Sweden, one's father is an American Indian, and one's father is a first generation Italian and the mother is second generation Italian. People who are exposed to me and my sisters often comment on our closeness, liveliness and argumentativeness. And I always ask friends what their ethnic background is; often they don't know, or are such a jumble that they don't remember. I am not friends with that many WASPs or Jewish people, although I did go to an Ivy League college. Two of my sisters, however, have been or are involved with men of Jewish heritage. (One is an Orthodox Jew. They have recently broken up after almost four years together.) I tend to develop friendship groups which are similar to family dynamics—less surface-oriented. We laugh, we cry, we argue. I believe it is much healthier to let most emotions out. Although I have not always allowed myself to in the past. The emoting factor of Italians seems to work in my case.

From the time I was young, I always knew I was half Italian, a quarter Irish and a quarter Swedish. This was instilled into me from childhood. While at college, I realized I was Catholic and a White ethnic. Before I had always thought that I was simply an Italian, Irish, Swedish person, with nothing meant by that beyond description. During college, I realized that certain traits and habits of mine were not common to all. After college, back in Chicago, I realized that I was basically an Italian Midwesterner, as my father was from Italy and my mother's family had been in Chicago and Iowa for a few generations. I have realized certain characteristics of being Italian (emotionalness) and Midwestern (stable, full of integrity) make up a big part of who I am. Beyond all this discipline stuff, I am a person who strives to learn, understand and experience much, in the process enjoying myself and my life. I don't know what this comes from beyond the inner core that makes me unique.

I'm not sure what traditions of past generations there are to carry on. In my family, we have created our own version of traditions. And I am sure they will continue to vary in the future. Sunday dinner, of course, was a staple of our household while we were growing up. Now that most of us are out of the house, this has lessened, although those who are within driving distance (two sisters) still come on Saturdays or Sundays for dinner. Until just recently I lived in Chicago with one of my sisters. And we always (almost) went home for the weekend or on Sunday. This might be what I will continue when I have a family. Although, I'd rather take my kids to the grandparents' house for dinner, until I learn to cook better. Beyond that, I don't know what traditions there are to continue.

Fran

As I read this question, I understood it in two different ways. I'm not sure exactly how it is intended. In one way it says to me, "When did you discover that you were different?" and in another way it says, "When did you realize with pride that you were Italian-American?"

When filling out forms as a child, and perhaps even in high school, I was always unsure of what to write in the blank marked "nationality." I was strongly aware, from my earliest recollections, that I was Italian. I also knew that I was an American citizen, so I guess even in elementary school, I knew I must be both.

Only as an adult did I consciously become aware of the term and appreciate the value of what it meant. When I was about 11 or 12 years old, I can remember a non-Italian friend, whose father had served in Italy in World War II, saying to me something like, "My father doesn't like Italians, but he thinks you're okay." I was at an impressionable age, and I can remember thinking there must be something wrong with being Italian. For some reason, my father had chosen to live in a neighborhood outside of the Italian community, so I didn't have that pride at that particular point in my life that seems to be born from the camaraderie of ethnic young people raised in the same neighborhood. It wasn't until college and when I first began teaching that the pride began to really take root and grow. Even as a child, I believe the pride was always in my heart. I just didn't know it was okay to have those feelings and to express them. Now, I am extremely proud to be Italian-American, and I deeply value my heritage.

Oh, how I wish I'd done a better job of carrying on Italian traditions. First of all, I wish I'd been better equipped to do so. As I said, I was not raised in an Italian neighborhood. I'm not sure if that was a conscious attempt on the part of my parents to "Americanize" their daughters, but that is what happened. The traditions became a bit watered-down, but whoever would have guessed how precious they would become? So, I wish I'd done a better job of learning the traditions first, and then I wish I had incorporated them a little better into our daily living. I wish I had much more of the Italian heritage for my children to carry away than just the immense pride and "pasta on Sunday."

Hopefully, my dreams will become reality this year, when I take my children to Italy this summer to meet their Italian cousins. I really want to continue to build in them an awareness and an appreciation of who they are as Italian-Americans as well.

Marilyn

My ethnic background has helped me to make many friends; most Italians are friendly, warm people.

I married an Italian, but it just happened. And we have been very good together, because our interests are so much alike. And, yes, in some small way we have considered our Italian background in some of the decisions we have made concerning our children.

I think I became most aware of being Italian-American when I started school.

To some extent I follow the traditions, but mostly I have found my own traditions.

Lois

I was told over and over that an education was not necessary for a girl, because she would just get married and have babies and be a homemaker for the rest of her life.

I find myself still trying to please men at work and acting like a mother and homemaker even in a professional atmosphere, because in our house and all my other relatives' houses men were supposed to be the boss, the king. So I find myself carrying this over into business even now.

I was not interested in politics, because my father and all my male relatives said it was for men only. They all participated in politics, but the women of my family were never invited to anything political. It was strictly a men's night out.

Catherine M.

I was different and, aside from the pre-teen bullies,
I just loved what I was.

I grew up on the east side of town . . . away from the Italian community and in an environment that recognized possibly six Italian teenagers in a high school of grades seven through 12 of approximately 2500 students. I was aware of my being Italian, not because our household was Italian, but because I believe my awareness of my heritage was inborn. I knew that I was "unique" and I loved feeling special. I could sense the uniqueness of being Italian through fragments of growing-up experiences. It was there while I accompanied my father to his old neighborhood while he shopped the small family-owned stores for home-made sausage, vermicelli, olive oil and Romano cheese. It happened when old friends would see him and the conversation was instantly Sicilian . . . rapid and dramatic, happy and loud. It was an awareness while studying history and learning of the contributions of the Italian people. It was evident when we entered family Italian restaurants and sensed the togetherness of the owners and the customers, while Italian music played in the background and the cooking aromas made my mouth water. It was also there when I would be pushed around on the school playground and called "wop" and "dago," and when I saw the graffiti on the walls of the lumber company next door to the parochial school that I attended from grades three through seven. My last name was spelled in its Italian version and written with hate of the unknown by young people who were aware of what I was from their parents and dinner tabletalk.

I was different and, aside from the pre-teen bullies, I just loved what I was. I explored every inch of a desperate need to be as Italian as possible until this year when I finally cleared the hurdle. I wrote a cookbook on the old neighborhood that I was never a part of . . . a ten-block area destroyed in 1960 by an urban renewal plan. Interspersed throughout the book is the history of the settlement that began in 1900, memories of the old residents and their children and grandchildren and photographs of the families and the buildings that disappeared. The families that I interviewed opened their doors to me, rekindled fond memories, shed tears and made me one of them. Because of the emotions that have been stirred from my compilation and their respect for me, I have finally become the Italian that I have wanted to be for 50 years.

I have, within the past five years, become specific and state that I am Sicilian, opposed to the general use of being Italian.

I am trying to establish some form of tradition through food. *Cucidati* is always made during the holidays. *Caponatina* is made throughout the summer as gardens become prolific. I constantly emphasize meals that are Italian/Sicilian, point out trivia regarding certain dishes . . . just as an awareness, I suppose . . . and even more so now due to the "new-found" healthfulness of garlic, pasta and olive oil in our everyday preparation of foods.

Louise C.

We don't have the old Italian household where the husband was the dominant character, but the wife is really the boss. We don't play that game. I wouldn't function in that situation. We function as equal adults.

Did your Italian-American background have an effect on your career choice?

I don't really think so. Except that I sort of fell into what I'm doing. I went into nursing, but my dream was always to be a physician. But there was no encouragement when I went to college. They did not prevent me from doing it, when I did go to college, but I think I would have been a physician today if somebody had encouraged me. I think at that age, most women weren't encouraged. I think the Italians do do that. Especially to the girls. They don't expect them to go on to college. They don't expect their kids, especially the girls, to do better than they did, do they? I don't think so.

Your relationship with the immigrant generation before you?

I'm the second generation. My mother came here as a child. My father came here as an adult. They didn't discourage us from being things, but they didn't encourage us, either. Because they weren't themselves. They were not professional people. But I always had the feeling when growing up that Italians as a rule did not encourage their children to venture into things that were a higher level than they had achieved themselves. I can think of one student in particular in school who came to me and said, "My father doesn't want me to go to college." Other nationalities aren't like that. She might have been third generation.

Did being an Italian-American affect your career?

I don't think there's been anything in particular. But I think I'm becoming much more aware of being an Italian now that I see other groups pushing ahead and dominating the scene and using up lots of the resources that are available. I grew up in a totally Italian neighborhood in New York, and it never occurred to me that I was different in any way. I don't think it was a handicap in any way. But as I've gotten older I realize that there is a lot more to being Italian and to being proud of it and what my heritage means.

When did you become aware of being an Italian-American?

In high school during my junior year. I switched schools and went to a Catholic high school, where I could no longer continue taking the language I was taking and I had to take Italian.

It was kind of nice understanding the language that was spoken at home. My people didn't speak it to us. And I was the only one of my sisters who ever studied Italian. I just took it for granted being Italian. I never thought about it. About being special or not being special. It was just what I was. I took all the cultural things for granted, too. As I got older I realized it, especially having gone to Italy; you see what's there.

That's what happened to my son. He always used

to say, "What's so big about being Italian-American? We're American. We don't speak Italian here, although we eat the food." And then he went to Italy and he had a totally different attitude about being Italian. And when he went to college, he took Italian.

I don't think the Italians here think enough about their heritage. That they have something to be proud of. Italians are creative people. They have contributed a great deal. We just don't do that. And other groups do do that. I think that's really a weakness. We don't support each other. And not just women. Italians don't even know who was Italian, and who isn't. I'm on a campus where groups support each other. I think it's important that we help one another out. Not at the neglect of anybody else, or being negative to anyone else. But we tend to understand each other better, when we get to know each other. We should encourage one another.

I don't have an Italian name. And I've decided not to hesitate to say that I'm Italian in my classroom. For the only reason just to be a role model. Just to encourage the Italians in my classroom that they can achieve, because here's another Italian who has. Because at the school there are loads of Italian kids. And they are the first generation to go to college, because most of their parents haven't gone to college. Most of the Italians who have gotten ahead tend to send their kids to private schools. We have to do more to encourage the young Italians, because they are being forgotten at the present time.

Was your family supportive?

They were supportive, but I don't think they even gave any thought to it that I would go to college. I remember when I went to high school in New York. You had to take the academic course to go to college, or take the commercial course to prepare to be a secretary. And when I signed up for the academic program, I remember my sister saying, "What are you doing that for?" I did my own thing. At one point I lived at home without working, even though in a sense I supported myself until I could go to college. They were supportive in that way. I didn't absolutely have to have a job. It never occurred to them to say, "You're going to college, how great!" I think they were proud when I did it, but they didn't really understand what I was doing.

Any effect on professional relationships?

It doesn't, unless I announce I'm Italian, because I don't have an Italian name. People never know what I am. Living in the Northeast, there's so many of us around, I've never notice any differences in treatment.

Any effect on your social life?

Not that I'm aware of.

Is your spouse Italian-American?

Yes, he's Italian, also. And what happened was when his grandparents came here, in the process of immigrating into the country, they changed their name. They were illiterate themselves. So the immigration people wrote their names incorrectly and it stayed that way. I'm very sorry that we don't have an Italian name, because Italian names are usually nice-sounding.

Did you consciously select an Italian for a mate?

No, I don't think so. I met him at a party. We were all professionals. It just happened, I guess. I don't even know if he knew that I was Italian, when he asked me out. I don't know if I knew that he was Italian.

Your relationship with your husband?

We don't have the old Italian household where the husband was the dominant character, but the wife is really the boss. We don't play that game. I wouldn't function in that situation. It's not his personality, either. We function as equal adults. We share the household chores.

Parenting?

I'm a health professional. I started off with nursing. I've done all kinds of nursing, health education, and now I've just gotten a degree in public health. I think in raising a child, my education had a whole lot to do with how I did it. I think I was well aware of my son's emotional needs. I was well aware of the need to encourage him intellectually. I think I was much more attentive to his needs and much more affectionate than anything I ever experienced in my house. My parents were not particularly affectionate people. I don't believe in that myth that all Italians are warm, affectionate people. Some of them are, but not all of them. A lot of it is bizarre, the kissing and all that; there's not any warmth at all, and I grew up in that. My son was not raised that way at all. He was raised with a great deal of affection and caring. I stayed home the years he was growing up.

Religion?

My father didn't go to church at all. My mother was a churchgoer, but without a sense of what it really meant. It was just ritual, going to church on Sundays and doing all those things. My husband was religious earlier in his life. I was very much involved with the Church in growing up. But quite a few years ago, we decided that my father was right all along, and so we're not involved with the Church at all now. We think it caused more problems growing up than it contributed. I have loads of experiences with the Catholic Church, since I worked with Catholic institutions. I have very negative attitudes about the Church. I live with the attitude that if there is a God making decisions, and I am a decent person, I should make out all right.

Politics?

Very interested in politics. But my being Italian-American has no effect on my political choices. I would not choose a candidate because he was an Italian. And that's what upsets me, when I see other people pushing candidates because of their race or nationality. I'm a Republican and I have worked locally. I'd like to be more active, but I'm employed and I work so far from here. My parents weren't active in politics at all.

Traditions?

I've studied Italian on and off through the years, and I'm studying it now at school with some Italian woman. I tend to like Italian food, but I don't practice traditions associated with religion, such as going to Midnight Mass and Easter Sunday Mass. We celebrate them as holidays, but not because they're religious. I have relatives in Italy that I've visited. They're on the

Island of San Pietro, which is off the west coast of Sardinia. We went the first time without them even knowing that we were coming, and we got such a wonderful reception.

Colleen

My being Italian-American has not really affected my professional relationships, unless—of course—I know someone from the "old neighborhood," in which case I support or try to help him or her.

I am still very close to people that I went to grammar school (mostly all Italian immigrant children) with. My social life holds family very dear, and I believe this is a direct result of my heritage.

I first became aware of being an Italian-American when I went to high school, and I discovered that not every name ended in a vowel!

I hope to carry on traditions of past generations and to visit Italy as often as possible. We go back every other year or so, lately.

Louise V.

When did you first become aware of being Italian-American?

I think I've always been aware of being Italian-American, but at times other exigencies in my life have suppressed the Italian side.

Do you intend to carry on the traditions of past generations?

Yes. I think it is very comforting to have a tight family unit and to participate in all the celebrations.

Antonina

As a child in a small Wisconsin city, being "Eye-talian" made me feel very different, often scorned. It was difficult being singled out, not having the right clothes or social status. I made up for it by getting better grades. After moving to California, I wasn't such an oddity. When I matured, I became very proud of my heritage and flaunted it. Friends would say affectionately that I was a "professional Sicilian."

Catherine C.

I blame my temper (I yell a lot.) on my Italian background; whereas my husband is very easygoing and less emotional and more rational with the children in disciplining them.

Dolores

When I was young and had pierced ears, I took the earrings out because I was teased so much when I moved from the Chambersburg area of Trenton to the

Greenwood Avenue section. There were many Jewish people and some Slovak and Hungarian people, but very few Italians living in the Greenwood Avenue section. The Jewish population was in the majority, and I was ashamed for a very short time to be considered the little Italian girl with the pierced ears.

As I got older and learned about the Jewish customs and some of the Slovak customs, I realized that being Italian and following our customs was something to be proud of because my Dad was very proud to be Italian and very proud to be an American.

We spoke both languages and we tried to be good American citizens. My friends enjoyed eating our favorite recipes, and I liked trying their favorite dishes and learning about their customs. All in all I feel that my background adds to my social life.

Jane

My mother, perhaps as any ethnic mother, was hesitant at first to have her daughter make such an outward display of heritage.

I direct a folk Italian song and dance group, so I think I can definitely say that indeed my background affected my career choice. When I direct and perform, I feel that this is my statement to be made. After years of not feeling comfortable in the established society, making such an elaborate statement makes me feel tremendously gratified. It's as if you've shown me yours, now here is mine and where I come from.

The effect, of course, is that I am well versed in what I do and came to the position armed with knowledge of nuances, attitudes and inter-social communication. We wrap it up with music and dance and become an appealing performance as such.

My mother, perhaps as any ethnic mother, was hesitant at first to have her daughter make such an outward display of heritage. I think they were afraid for us to make waves. The more we could "blend in" the safer it would be. But what they didn't realize was that this was an impossibility, for me anyway, for I preferred my own image, and I feel quite comfortable with my Italo-American personality. Please note that the Italo comes first for I feel more adequate with this *hat* on.

Yes, I think our backgrounds affect our professional lives, but in a positive way. I think even the uneducated Italian acquires quite young an understanding of proper etiquette and hospitality. It comes so naturally that it is not a thinking process; and thereby, it sets the mind free to maneuver easily in the business world.

My social life is limited to other Italians, which is what I prefer, for when I was young I always felt that I was not fitting in with social cliques. I had no idea at that time, of course, just what the problem was. As I matured, however, I just sensed that when I was with *my* people the challenges and the gratifications felt better.

My husband is an Italian immigrant. And, yes, I consciously selected an Italian; however, the attraction was always for Italian men. We understand each other's values and expectations perfectly. We know how to fulfill for each other and with our respective families.

My ethnic background does affect my parenting. And my daughter is presently a folk song expert and has performed extensively with my group. We go out as a family to present Italian folklore. My son turned his back for a period on our heritage, insisting that we are a melting pot and that we should merge. But, suddenly, since he is married and now has a son of his own, he has become more Italian than I am. He also performs with my group and the family.

Carmella

Traditions add stability to life.

The effects of my ethnic background, in retrospect, are most interesting. I remember, as a little girl, hiding behind the curtain (substitute for a door) and watching my accordion-playing father having a grand time with his friends and their families. And when I was a teenager (I now realize), I was always trying to "not be an Italian." I sought friends of Polish, Hungarian, German and American heritage. Anything but Italian. Upon maturing, I now seek out friends of Italian heritage. At present, I am the president of the New Jersey (Italian-American) Professional Women, Incorporated, a 51-year-old organization. This is my third consecutive year as president. This summer I was awarded a fellowship by the Arts Foundation of New Jersey to the World of Leonardo Da Vinci Teacher Institute, and in September, I had the director of the entire program, Joyce Milton Maso, address my group at a luncheon.

I first became aware of being an Italian-American as a little girl of about ten, when I was made to feel shame for having that heritage.

After examining my family and Italian religious traditions, I do most strongly intend to continue to observe those traditions for a number of reasons.

Tradition adds stability to life. It also provides expectancy and adds pleasure and joy. Tradition assists in keeping family unity strong. And it helps parents teach their children about the responsibility of parenting. Foods are another marvelous way to teach the children to love and to respect their bodies and to show love and respect to others.

Maria M.

I preferred selecting an Italian mate, but was very careful not to select a spouse who had the old-fashioned Italian ideas.

As a child in school, I can still remember the discrimination against the Italians. It seemed that I was always in competition with my fellow students. They used to wait with bated breath to see what my marks were. This made me determined to do the best I could in school, and later, when I was in the job market. Since having an office job was considered a "white-collar job" and "professional," at that time (most of my neighbors and friends worked in factories) I aspired to do office work.

After some years, the discrimination subsided when the Italian-Americans kept proving to the community that they could and did contribute effectively. By working hard, I was able to progress. In retrospect, my first job interview after graduation from 12th grade was most discouraging. He was a lawyer of Italian-American background who was condescending and patronizing. He kept reminding me that he was being very generous in selecting a person with my Italian-American background and insisted on my having my hair done once a week. Needless to say, I did

not accept the position. I felt that he was too prejudiced against his own kind.

My mother, who came to America when she was
six years old and attended school here understood and
encouraged me, but she had to submit to my father's
wishes and demands. My father, even though he could
well afford to send me to college, would not allow me
to accept one of the four scholarships offered to me. I
had graduated 35th out of my class of 985. He said
that boys only should continue on to college. That I
would end up getting married and wouldn't need, or
use, a college education. I had to go to work. And since
it was depression time, I had a difficult time getting
a job. There just weren't any jobs. Finally, I did get a
position, but didn't stay too long because I had taken
a Civil Service exam and accepted a position as soon
as I was called. A Civil Service job was a plum at that
time. It was secure.

Years later, when I visited my father's place of
birth, I came to realize why he was driven and set in
his thinking. He was born in humble surroundings
and had worked very hard to make his way in the new
world. Now, since I have retired, I am attending Mercer County Community College, and I am thrilled to
be attending college, at last, even at this late date. I
was inducted into the Foreign Language Honor Society
for attaining straight A's and feel such a sense of
accomplishment.

I feel very comfortable with my professional relationships. I have always been able to contribute to any
job.

I do not feel my ethnic background affects my social life—past or present. I have always joined the
groups I was interested in and have many friends from
all ethnic backgrounds and, for the most part, feel
very comfortable with them. I have traveled extensively and feel I can contribute to any conversation. I

will say that once in a while I do come up against
some person who still has prejudices and this is reflected in his or her relationship, but I try to overlook
it and ignore it, and try harder to prove myself.

My husband was an Italian-American.

I preferred selecting an Italian mate, but was
very careful not to select a spouse who had the old-
fashioned Italian ideas. As it was, I never dreamed of
the controversy I would encounter in marrying an Italian who had parents from a different part of Italy as
my parents. My father wanted me to marry a person
whose parents had originated from the same part of
Italy as he had, but I was very adamant in my choice
in spite of his objections. My father gave me a very bad
time.

My husband always encouraged me to think for
myself and to make my own decisions—right or wrong.
He was not the typical Italian-American husband,
thank God!

I can still remember the prejudices at school
against the Italians, and so I insisted that my children
always remember that they are as good as anyone—
not better—but as good as. I can still remember how
many of my Italian-American friends were reluctant to
admit they were of Italian parentage in school and
never spoke of it. I, on the other hand, went around
saying how proud I was to be from Italian parents.
They were very annoyed with me.

Truthfully, my religion has been more meaningful
to me than it was to my parents. I would always make
it a point to attend Mass every Sunday with my
friend, even though my parents did not attend. In
later years, my mother did start attending regularly. I
realized when I went to Italy for the first time why
this was so—the people in Italy are not churchgoers
as a rule. On going for religious instructions, we were

taught that we had to attend Mass on penalty of Mortal Sin. I don't believe that fear was ever instilled in the residents of Italy.

I am mildly interested in politics. I get very disillusioned by all the corruption. But we always voted and we were very proud to be American citizens. My parents never even wanted to visit Italy.

Growing up, I thought that all Italians were of the same political party, but I was very mistaken.

Mary B.

My family says that when I was in my teens, I said I would not marry an Italian but a German at age 28. I married a German at age 29.

I'm not sure that being Italian-American had anything to do with whether or not I chose to have a career; however, we were not well-off, or even comfortable by any means, and I knew that I didn't want to remain at that station in life. So I made sure that what I took at school would help me reach my goal. I became a secretary. From there I went on to college, a master's program, and now I am a professional supervisor. I was the seventh child in the family (and the last), a first generation Italian-American, but by the time I was in my teens we were pretty "Americanized," and my father died. I was left to make many choices on my own, which I did.

If there was an *effect,* it was that being the youngest I learned to survive; and growing up in a large city (St. Louis), I was streetwise. Even as a youngster, I thought that lots of the Italian-American ways were hard for me to accept. It is important to note that at three months of age, I was placed into an Italian orphan home run by nuns and "Americanized" by them. At age 9½ I returned home to a very Italian family living in a totally Italian neighborhood.

The reason for my removal from home and family was that my mother was incapacitated. All but two of the children were in the same home, but we were not raised as siblings normally would be. When I came home, it was like looking at, and living in, a foreign atmosphere (perhaps alien world is a better term). My two oldest brothers, who remained home, were totally "Italianized" and so as I grew and matured, I went in a different direction from the rest of the family.

My family was neither supportive nor nonsupportive. They went to public schools, I went to Catholic schools. They were married by the time I got out of high school, and I was left on my own. I made my own decisions.

My educational preparation was to insure my secretarial abilities.

And, yes, I believe that my ethnic background has affected my professional relationships. I learned to be a survivor. I'm not the typical working female. I'm assertive. I know what is best for me. I'm more the Geraldine Ferraro type, and I have been kidded about that.

I think Italians are a fun-loving culture. We know how to have social savoir faire. I use it all the time, and I love doing it. I learned early on how to make situations work best for me and to accept some things. I can also make hard decisions, but I am not ruthless. When I first started my career, I had an attitude which said sort of "me first," although it was in a fun sort of way. I would not rationalize too well, if I thought I was being mistreated. Since then I have learned to stop, think and calculate. I think growing up poor and being number seven in the family caused a lot of the first; the background of the orphange developed the latter; and growing up with a cultural background that enjoyed life was helpful in both instances. As a teenager and young adult, I was called Mary Happy Go Lucky. As an adult, I have lots of friends who say they enjoy being around me. Being Italian-American, I think, made me sensitive to emotions; raised by nuns gave me a religious background, which is tremendously important in the overall person.

My family says that when I was in my teens, I said I would not marry an Italian but a German at age 28. I married a German at 29.

He was very conservative. He didn't take many risks. He was programmed to keep things inside of himself. My culture and ways changed a lot of that in him, and his quietness helped me to be more rational and calculating. So we have changed each other. He is more vocal and fun now. He enjoys my family and a lot about being Italian.

I have no children.

Religion is much more meaningful to me than it was to my parents.

My interest in politics is somewhere between mildly and very. I assisted in a political campaign and enjoyed it, but I don't seem to keep up as well with the issues as someone who is *very* interested. My personality is to be always busy, and as a result, I do not have many singular priorities.

My family was Democratic and I was always more favorable to the Republican viewpoint. The entire Italian neighborhood was Democrat. I wasn't in rebellion; I simply thought the Republicans were more in line with my thinking, which—I admit—was probably different because I was not raised at home. When I even thought about politics, it was without the family's orientation.

When I came home at 9½ from the orphanage was when I became aware of being Italian-American. And I guess I have become more aware and more proud as I have matured, and really when I had an Italian exchange student from Milan living in my home for one year. This was quite an interesting experience because my descent is Sicilian and he was Lombard. I learned that Sicilians are called *torone* by the Lombards and how negatively they thought of them. He had a hard time at first classifying me with "them" (over there) because of my Americanization, and yet I was so proudly Italian that I didn't think in terms of being Sicilian. But that's a whole different story.

I am not so familiar with what Italian traditions were, but I like the ones I know; if I knew more, I would incorporate them as much as is feasible into my life.

Carol Bonomo Ahearn

When I taught in a private prep school, I felt at odds in this milieu of children from very well-off families (and mainly old money) after having taught, by choice, in the South Bronx. I chose that area because I believed in the traditional route for immigrants of upward mobility through education. The basic difference between the two groups was that the "old monied" children knew that the world would adjust to them rather than they would have to adjust to it. They had high expectations for themselves, and they viewed others as vehicles for supplying and fulfilling their needs. Needless to say, my Puerto Rican students expected little and were grateful for the basics of life, when and if they had them.

BOOK TWO

FAMILY

Since I was the oldest of the girls, there was no education for me. I got as far as the ninth grade, and then I had to go to work.

Lily

... it's very significant that I went into psychology and my brother went into medicine. I attribute that to the Italianness of my parents. The capacity for empathy.

Diana

I like being Italian-American, the security and the closeness of family.

Maria F.

I didn't want to live away from home. It's part of my Italian background. The pull that keeps me close to home.

Donna

I think it made it easier to have both spouses Italian-American. We both knew where the other was coming from.... we were less scornful of the other's family.

Teresa

One of my aunts thought it was a disgrace that I lived away from home.

Angelina

REMARKS BY JANICE A. PICCININI
TO THE AMERICAN COMMITTEE ON
ITALIAN MIGRATION
NOVEMBER 8, 1986

MEMBERS OF THE AMERICAN COMMITTEE ON ITALIAN MIGRATION, MEMBERS AND FRIENDS OF MY ETHNIC FAMILY:

I AM DEEPLY HONORED TO BE THIS YEAR'S RECIPIENT OF THE ACIM LADY LIBERTY AWARD. WITH THE EXCEPTION OF THE AMERICAN FLAG, THERE IS NO SYMBOL MORE TREASURED IN OUR COUNTRY THAN THE STATUE OF LIBERTY. FOR THE MILLIONS OF IMMIGRANTS WHO PASSED BENEATH HER GREAT SHADOW, SHE REPRESENTED FREEDOM, OPPORTUNITY AND A NEW BEGINNING. MORE THAN FIVE MILLION OF THOSE IMMIGRANTS CAME FROM ITALY, THAT DISTANT LAND THAT WE STILL THINK OF AS OUR CULTURAL HOME. MY GRANDPARENTS AND MY FATHER WERE AMONG THOSE EARLY IMMIGRANTS.

AS A FIRST-GENERATION AMERICAN, I AM GRATEFUL TO HAVE BEEN RAISED WITH A KNOWLEDGE OF, AN APPRECIATION FOR, THE CONTRIBUTIONS AND THE STRUGGLES OF ITALIANS IN AMERICA. IT HAS GIVEN ME A SENSE OF PRIDE, A SENSE OF PURPOSE AND A SENSE OF WHOLENESS TO KNOW THAT THE OPPORTUNITIES AFFORDED ME ARE THE FULFILLMENT OF THE DREAMS OF SO MANY WHO PASSED THROUGH ELLIS ISLAND.

WHAT GREATER GIFT CAN BE PASSED ON FROM ONE GENERATION TO THE NEXT THAN THE GIFT OF A FUTURE UNLIMITED BY ETHNIC AND CULTURAL BARRIERS, A FUTURE UNRESTRICTED IN FREEDOM OF CHOICE AND ACTION.

NO IDEA IS MORE POWERFUL THAN FREEDOM—THE FREEDOM TO DREAM AND THE OPPORTUNITY TO BRING THEM INTO REALITY. BUT FOR MANY OF THE EARLY IMMIGRANTS, THE OPPORTUNITY WAS MORE A PROMISE THAN A REALITY.

WOMEN OF MY GRANDMOTHER'S GENERATION SELDOM ATTENDED SUCH GALA OCCASIONS AS WE HAVE BEEN INVITED TO THIS EVENING. THEY WERE NOT SEEN AT PUBLIC FORUMS. THEY DID NOT ENGAGE IN PUBLIC DEBATES NOR WERE THEIR CONTRIBUTIONS PUBLICLY ACKNOWLEDGED, MUCH LESS HONORED.

MY GRANDMOTHER'S NAME WAS ROSA. SHE WAS A GENTLE, SELFLESS WOMAN WHO RARELY VENTURED FAR FROM HER FAMILY AND HOME. SHE NEVER MASTERED THE ENGLISH LANGUAGE, NOR DID SHE HAVE THE BENEFIT OF A FORMAL EDUCATION. BUT SHE WAS SO PROUD OF MY GRANDFATHER, AND SHE HELD SO MUCH HOPE FOR HER CHILDREN AND GRANDCHILDREN THAT HER LIFE TOOK ON A SPECIAL MEANING AND PURPOSE. SHE SHOWED LOVE AND ENCOURAGEMENT IN WAYS THAT ONLY THOSE WHO WERE THERE COULD APPRECIATE, AND IN WAYS THAT ARE DIFFICULT TO MEASURE BY TODAY'S STANDARDS.

MY GRANDMOTHER ALWAYS ATE LAST. SHE DIDN'T SIT AT THE DINNER TABLE WITH HER

FAMILY. SHE COOKED THE DINNER AND SHE SERVED THE FAMILY—FIRST MY GRANDFATHER IN THE DINING ROOM AND THEN THE CHILDREN. BUT MY GRANDMOTHER ALWAYS ATE LAST. HERS WAS NOT AN APPEALING ROLE, NOR WAS IT ONE THAT SHE WISHED FOR HER DAUGHTERS, BUT SHE CARRIED IT OUT WITH ENORMOUS DIGNITY AND PRIDE.

SHE WAS TYPICAL OF WOMEN OF HER GENERATION, WHOSE ROLE AS PIONEERS HAS SELDOM BEEN RECOGNIZED. THEY, TOO, WERE DREAMERS, BUT THEIR VISION OF THE FUTURE WAS SEEN THROUGH THE LIVES OF THEIR CHILDREN. THESE WOMEN DEVOTED THEMSELVES TO ESTABLISHING A FAMILIAR AND STABLE HOME FOR THEIR HUSBANDS AND CHILDREN WHO WOULD HAVE TO DEAL WITH NEW WAYS IN A NEW LAND WITH A NEW LANGUAGE. AND THEY INSTILLED IN THEIR CHILDREN THE VALUES OF THE OLD COUNTRY WHICH WOULD SERVE THEM WELL IN THE NEW. THEY PASSED ON A PROFOUND LOVE FOR OUR CULTURAL HERITAGE, A DEEP COMMITMENT TO FAMILY UNITY, A THIRST FOR EDUCATION, AND A RESPECT FOR THE DIGNITY OF WORK. *THAT* WAS THE ITALIAN WOMAN'S GIFT TO AMERICA'S FUTURE. THAT WAS MY GRANDMOTHER ROSA'S GIFT TO ME.

I ACCEPT THIS HONOR TONIGHT ON BEHALF OF ALL THE ROSAS WHO TOUCHED OUR LIVES, BUT WHO SOUGHT NO SUCH HONORS FOR THEMSELVES. THEY LIVED SIMPLY SO THAT WE MIGHT LIVE BETTER. THEY LIVED HUMBLY SO THAT THEIR DAUGHTERS AND GRANDDAUGHTERS MIGHT LEAD MORE FULFILLING LIVES. HOW PROUD THEY WOULD BE

TO KNOW THAT IN THIS YEAR, 1986, WHILE ONE ITALIAN-AMERICAN SON, ANTONIN SCALIA, ASSUMED AN HONORED SEAT ON THE BENCH OF THE SUPREME COURT OF THE UNITED STATES—AN ITALIAN-AMERICAN DAUGHTER, RITA LEVI-MONTALCINI, WILL LEAVE AN HONORED SEAT AT A HEAD TABLE IN A ROOM IN OSLO, NORWAY TO ACCEPT THE NOBEL PRIZE.

A CHALLENGE REMAINS FOR ALL OF US TO REMEMBER THAT WHAT WAS WON BY ONE GENERATION AT GREAT PERSONAL PRICE CAN BE EASILY LOST BY THE NEXT GENERATION. THE STATUE OF LIBERTY HERSELF REMINDS US THAT "THE PRICE OF LIBERTY IS ETERNAL VIGILANCE." AS ITALIAN-AMERICANS WE WILL CONTINUE TO PROSPER IN THIS GREAT COUNTRY—BUT NOT AT THE COST OF FORGETTING OUR PAST OR THE PRICE PAID FOR "OPPORTUNITY" AS WE KNOW IT TODAY.

I AM PROUD TO BE AN ITALIAN-AMERICAN WOMAN, AND I AM PROUD TO BE THE GRANDDAUGHTER OF A ROSA, WHO WOULD WANT ME TO ACKNOWLEDGE MY MOTHER, A GRACIOUS AND LOVING LADY, WHO CHOSE TO MAKE MY ITALIAN HERITAGE A LINK BETWEEN MY PAST AND MY FUTURE.

* * * *

Lois

My social life is still very much involved with family life, the same as it was when I was growing up. Sundays are for family dinners and we have numerous parties for family weddings, graduations, birthdays.

Almost all my weekends are taken up by obligations. Sometimes I resent this because I can never make other plans to do things with friends. Weeknights and especially Fridays are the only times I can make plans with my friends.

I am now divorced. My ex-husband was of German descent. I deliberately picked a non-Italian because I thought he would be different from the Italian boys I grew up with, and that I would get away from being subservient. It turned out that he was brought up in the same type of European household as I was, where the father was boss and the mother subservient. This caused a lot conflict, because I did not want to perpetuate this way of life.

We had a very stormy marriage with each partner always trying to have the dominant role. It caused a lot of tension and arguing and wound up in divorce.

I did not want my children to grow up the way I did and, therefore, I bent over backward to try to have them become independent, free-thinking individuals. I taught my daughter and both sons how to clean, cook, wash; so that there would be no "women's work" or "men's work" in our house. This has worked very well; and when my children went away to college, they knew how to take care of themselves. This was very much unlike my boy cousins and friends who act completely helpless and must always have a women taking care of them. Also, my daughter, who is now married, has a 50–50 marriage. She and her husband share the house chores and the shopping.

Carol Bonomo Ahearn

My ex-spouse was not Italian-American. The Italian-American boys I met were mainly studying to be engineers and, frankly, I found them dull and with what I described as having an "Italian" mentality towards women. What I meant by that in those days, I'm not sure any longer. Perhaps that women should cook and clean and know their place as inferior to a man.

I have regrets that I didn't marry an Italian-American, since the marriage ended in divorce—unthinkable for an Italian-American—because there would have been a greater similarity of values if I could have found an Italian-American man interested in the arts and without an Italian mentality towards women, whatever that was. Actually, I did meet one Italian-American like that, but he wasn't interested in me. For my generation, they were few and far between. Or at least I never met many.

I think it's easier—through no guarantee of success—marrying someone of your own ethnic background in that you start out with the same basic assumptions about life and share the same "history" of a people; the images are the same. Hopefully, by extension the values are the same.

In theory, this commonality should help a couple to communicate effectively—something so important in marriage. But Italians who marry Italians also divorce, so that it seems there are too many variables to predict that commonality alone guarantees a successful marriage.

My ethnic background affects my parenting in that now that my children are grown, I have expectations that they will remain close, or rather, closely connected to me and to the extended family. Not geographically close, as one lives 50 miles away, the other 200; and not emotionally dependent, but connected.

I enjoy the connections of the extended family as my nieces and nephews marry and have children, and spending time when possible (I live 200 miles away from my family of origin.) with my mother, aunt and my godmother, brother and his family.

Up until my children were about ten years old or so, we used to spend the summer at my parents' summer house on Long Island to be close to them and to my brother and his family of five children.

Lily

Tell me something about your background.

I came to America with my mother when I was four years old. My father was here first. He came here in 1912. We came in 1913. My mother, my brother and I. We didn't speak a word of English. We had to learn to speak English. We went to grammar school in Bayonne. My brother started grammar school when he was seven and graduated high school when he was 17. I went to the ninth grade.

Any problems in school besides the language barrier?

No. My only problem was that while in America my mother had a new baby every two years. And I had to stay home to help take care of the babies, so that my mother could scrub clothes by hand. I missed a lot of school. And I had a lot of trouble learning. Missing two or three days a week of school, I couldn't catch up with the work. In those days, they didn't believe a girl needed an education, because she got married and became a mother and a housewife. All my brothers got an education and so did my two younger sisters. They graduated from high school. Those days high school was enough. They didn't have to further their education. They all got good jobs, being high school graduates.

What kind of work did you do?

I went to work as a seamstress when I was 14 to help educate my brothers and sisters. I worked in a factory from when I was 14 until I was 22, when I got married. The burden of helping the family fell on my shoulders because I was the oldest. My brother went to the University of Maryland and became a dentist. Since I was the oldest of the girls, there was no education for me. I got as far as the ninth grade and then I had to go to work.

Did you have any choice in picking a husband?

I was matched up. My husband was in Trenton and I was in Bayonne. I came to Trenton to visit my aunt and I met my husband. I was in Trenton for two weeks. After two weeks, my aunt called me and said my husband wanted to go with me. We kept company three months. He came to my house. He wanted to be introduced. It was approved by my family. After three months we got married and I moved to Trenton. I was a housewife for 23 years. After that I went to work to help educate my children and send them to private school and to college. I did commercial sewing. I learned how to sew at home first. My mother taught me.

Did being Italian affect where you chose to live?

We started out in an apartment in Chambersburg's Italian section. We lived there four and a half years, then we moved to East Trenton. I opened a little business, a grocery store, while my husband did painting and wallpapering. We had the business about five years. After my second child was born, it became too much for me. We moved back into the "Burg" and I sent all three girls to Catholic school. We moved back there because the home was close to the school and close to the church. Sending my children to Catholic school was very important to us.

What type of relationship did you have with other Italians in the Burg?

I didn't have much contact with other Italians. I was too busy. I had the housework. I sewed all my children's clothing. I canned vegetables. I didn't have time to socialize.

Your relationship with your husband—did it include sharing of household tasks?

My husband helped me a lot. Whenever he was home and he wasn't working on a job and had a day off, he would do the windows and all the heavy work. He loved to cook. When he was home on a Saturday or a Sunday, he did the cooking.

How about the raising of the children?

My husband was a very strict man. I was a little less strict. But I didn't have the opportunity to be less strict. Besides, my husband, there were three girls, and he would say to me that if any of those girls did anything wrong, you better not be around, you both better be out. I knew he wouldn't have done it, but that was the way he used to put it to me. And so I was always to be the bad guy. He never said anything to my daughters. He never spoke to them directly about what they were to do, but he was in the background, *my background*. The girls thought he was the good guy and that I was the bad guy. If they wanted to go to a dance, I would say to them, "Go ask your father." And he would say, "Go ask your mother." Then he would say to me, "She better not go." I was the mean one because I told them they couldn't go to the dance. Until this day, they still think that I was the mean one. But my husband loved his children very much. They meant too much to him to see them get hurt by anybody.

Religion was important to the family?

Very much so. Religion was important to us, keeping the family close. They were taught to honor their father and mother, and to respect their elders. They learned the Italian language a little bit. In those days, the Catholic school in Chambersburg used to teach the Italian language one day a week. And with the nuns, they were kept strict, to my way of thinking.

Children should have respect for their elders, their teachers, and if they came home and they said the teacher said something to them, I would want to know why the teacher said something to them. I would tell my children, "You had to do something for the teacher to scold you." Then I would talk to the teacher and find out why they were scolded.

How about choices as a woman?

I helped make the family decisions. We talked everything over. No matter whether it was a business problem or a household problem like decorating the home, we talked things over; and whatever was decid-ed,that's what we did.

Satisfied with your choices?

Yes, I'm satisfied. The choices I made or helped to make were always right. My husband was a business man, and he knew what was right and what was wrong. He was very conservative. He always provided and he always prepared for the days to come when we would be older. Thank God that he worked hard and provided for us, and I don't have to bother my children for anything. He worried about our life, and he worried about leaving me alone. We sacrificed. We didn't waste our money. We canned food from our garden that my husband cultivated. We didn't need for anything. For recreation, we only went to the shore for a week in the summer. We didn't go to the movies. We enjoyed ourselves visiting with our relatives, because we had a close-knit family, a typical, close Italian family.

Rosemarie W.

My family was supportive of my goals, but they were extremely critical.

My mate is not an Italian-American, but my deceased husband was. I did not seek any nationality because we lived in a non-Italian neighborhood. Although my husband is not Italian, he loves Italian food and feels as much Italian as I do. Here in Chicago, many Italians have married into Polish families.

Parenting my children as an Italian-American has not been noticeable, but they do appreciate the culture and the heritage.

Antonina

I feel that my Sicilian-American background had nothing to do with my *choice* of a career. My parents were so proud and pleased to have us in a university that they wouldn't have dreamed of interfering. I was encouraged to pursue any career that I wanted. (As it was, I studied English literature, and eventually taught.)

I married early, had an Anglo-Saxon married name, so that my being "Sicilian" was not obvious. In California it is considered ultra chic, anyway, to come from a rather exotic background.

My immigrant parents valued education above all. It was taken for granted that the five of us would all go on to a university. We were expected to get scholarships and to work our own way through, and to achieve good grades as well.

My spouse is English and I consciously selected a non-Italian. As a girl, I deliberately avoided dating any Italians, because most Italian boys in our neighborhood treated us as second-class citizens. They seemed always to aspire to marry an "American." It was a step up the social ladder. Also, subconsciously, I felt that I'd have a better chance at equality in marriage if I married a non-Italian.

My husband's of Puritan English background, which is so different from mine that it has often stunned us. I tend to be more relaxed, social, family oriented, which I think is the Italian tradition. The differences make for an exciting, but often troubled marriage.

As a mother, I tended to be as strict a disciplinarian as I had seen my parents be. I expected a great deal from my children.

My four children consider themselves "Sicilian." They were always made aware that they had different backgrounds than their peers. They learned Sicilian words for our food (always different), household objects. They knew their *nonna* and *nonni* spoke differently, thus they are always tolerant, never frightened of anyone who is different or foreign. They keep the strong family ties intact and feel very proud to be Sicilian.

Teresa

As Italian-Americans, my children, as were we, were exposed at home to the opera, the arts, another language—Italian—excellent food and its accoutrements, and the ability to create beauty. Very Italian!

With the exception of my best friend, who was male, Irish-American, my teenage friends were Italian-Americans and Jewish. My early married life was spent in a mixed neighborhood, where my neighbors and friends and relatives were Italian. When I moved to the suburbs, my friends were predominently Jewish and Italian.

My husband of 34 years is Italian-American, third generation. I did not consciously select him based on his ethnic background, but at age 17 when we were engaged, my realm of dating choices was mainly Italian-American. My sister, who was 3½ years older than I, was practically engaged to a Jewish young man who had spent World War II fleeing the Nazis in Europe.

All four sisters in my family married Italian-

Americans. I think it made it easier to have both spouses Italian-American. We both knew where the other was coming from. There were differences, however, in that his parents were born in the United States and mine were immigrants. In some ways my parents were more progressive than his. What I'm trying to say is that we didn't fight each other on whose tribe was better or who said better prayers (in our case, neither of us is religious). It also helps to be able to celebrate the same holidays, with the same traditions. Coming from the same background, we were less scornful of the other's family.

I have two children. A daughter born when I was 20, a son born when I was 25. My husband and I and the children always shared a two-family home with my parents and an aunt. This is very positive when raising children. My family was unique in that, although the grandparents and great aunt played a large part in their lives, they did not interfere in the actual decision making on the upbringing of these children. There was love and guidance, but no butting in. I wouldn't allow that. Both children were encouraged to move to their own apartments at 18 years old and were subsidized by me for years. As Italian-Americans my children, as were we, were exposed at home to the opera, the arts, another language—Italian—excellent food and its accoutrements, and the ability to create beauty. Very Italian!

My parents were very progressive in many ways, nonjudgmental, and never used racist or religious slurs around the children or anyone, for that matter. The grandparents, being *artiginati,* taught my children to create beautiful things, which has stood them in good stead in their careers. As an Italian-American, I have continued the traditional and cultural facets of my background, but have never imposed strict religious, or what I consider to be outdated, strictures on my children.

My parents were believers. My mother and aunt are still living in the same house with me. We have never been considered churchgoers, although we received the sacraments. Religion played a larger part in the lives of my parents while they lived in Italy, but that changed when they came to the United States. I am an agnostic. My husband is a nonpracticing Catholic. My children are also nonpracticing Catholics, but both expressed a wish that when they have children, those children also be exposed to a religious education.

Katherine

My Italian-American background may have affected my parenting, since my upbringing was fairly strict, and I am fairly strict with my children as well.

Rosemarie B.

Does your Italian-American background affect your relationship with your husband?

I give him the love and respect that my parents gave each other.

Does it affect your parenting?

Yes, I'm an Italian-American from the old school, combining this with the progress of the eighties.

Alba

My husband is Polish. And there was nothing selective about the choice from an ethnic standpoint. I married whom I loved. We have fun with jokes and we respect each other's background. And my children love being Polish and Italian.

Angelina

Thank God my family was very supportive of my career choice. My father, age 61 when I graduated high school, was very supportive. It was his idea that I live on campus (30 miles away), because he sympathized that I had to take a train daily (I did so for eight weeks.). He cried like a baby when I left the homestead.

One of my aunts thought it was a disgrace that I lived away from home.

My relationship with my husband is affected by my Italian-American background in that his background is not a demonstrative one regarding displays of affection. He found it hard to respond to mine.

My children were raised to respect relatives and kissing was a part of this respect.

Diana

My parents taught us the culture. My mother told me about the Roman Empire and its expansion, long before I ever learned about it in Latin classes.

Did your ethnic background affect your career choice?

Probably it had an effect. When I was choosing a career, it was limited to the helping professions: teaching, medicine and, ultimately, psychology. So I see the relationship of what my parents taught me as role models about the value of people and empathy for those in need. I can remember people who were illiterate coming to my mother's house. She was always writing letters for them to their relatives in Italy. People who needed a birth certificate, a passport. My mother was a social worker, so to speak. My parents had lived in New York City and knew their way and would always help them.

My father was a businessman. He had a pharmacy in a small city upstate, Middletown. And he was the consumate social worker, too. He had to sell his business after five or six years, because he couldn't deny credit to people who couldn't afford to buy prescriptions for cash. They were just very kind and caring people. These were the post-depression years in the late thirties. Our milkman had three diabetic children and a diabetic wife and no other pharmacist in town would sell him insulin on credit except my father, because he couldn't deny it to him. So it's very significant that I went into psychology and my brother went into medicine. And I attribute that to the Italianness of my parents. The capacity for empathy. The value of reaching out and doing for others. You didn't have to be rich, you could give your services.

After World War I, my mother wanted to do something for the children orphaned by the war. She knew there were children all over the Mediterranean basin who had been affected. She had nothing she could give of value except three handmade bedspreads knitted by my grandmother for her trousseau. She didn't need all three, so she wanted to donate one and was looking around to see who could raise the most money. She took it to the Catholic church first. They thought they could raise fifty dollars by holding a raffle. The thread alone was worth more than that. It was a magnificent piece. She mentioned it to a Jewish friend of hers who told her the Hadassah could probably raise at least a thousand dollars. So she gave it to the Hadassah and in fact they raised three thousand. And they planted ten trees in Israel in my mother's honor. They would always invite her to their annual dinner and she was very thrilled. She specified that the money go only to help children who had been orphaned.

Effect on your career at present?

I continue with those characteristics. I think I am a very conscientious person in my field. This is one of the other things that my parents pushed. Whether this was characteristic of their whole culture, how can I know, I have not lived in that culture. I have known other descendants of that culture, or representatives of it. A lot of them seem to be caring people, altruistic, who reach out to others. But there was the value that my parents admired of always seeking to improve yourself through intellectual and cultural growth. And here I am, probably a few years from retirement, still going to conferences to learn the latest about my field. That's very much a value that was built into me by my parents. Always seek to know the most and do the best—whatever it is you're doing.

Was your family supportive?

Absolutely. I always knew that I would go to college. I always knew they would support me. They would have walked on nails and eaten stones if they had to. I had only one brother, and he was supportive of me. We were in college at the same time.

Any effect on your professional relationships?

The characteristics that drew me to my profession are evident. I often go the extra mile in my casework. Other people do. I'm not chauvinistic about my Italianness. I think the culture that is most like Italian is the Jewish culture. I work with quite a few Jewish colleagues, and they are very compassionate and caring. I wouldn't attribute those traits to all Mediterranean cultures. I have seen some examples of extreme self-centeredness. Even today, although I would like to see Paris as one of the seats of culture and beauty, I am angry at the French government and do not want to leave a cent of my money in their country, therefore I won't go there, not until they change their posture toward the United States.

Does your background have any effect on your social life?

In the past, it did not affect my social life very much. I always felt that people should be judged as people. I sought out my friends where I went to school, where I worked, where I lived, and if I liked them and their characteristics, it didn't matter what their ethnic background was. It just happened that a number of them were Italian. Actually, my Italian background has had more of an effect in recent years. My husband and I have joined local organizations of Italian-Americans. I like their programs. And I've met some very nice people. I think it's lovely. It's a way of keeping my Italian current. I also get a chance to live vicariously my trips to Europe when I see these slide presentations that they have. My Italian background came full circle. Twenty years ago I would never have considered joining an Italian-American organization. I had never been to Italy. My parents taught us about the culture. My mother told me about the Roman Empire and its expansion, long before I ever learned about it in Latin classes. But when you see it, you appreciate it at a totally different level. Seeing it made it all come alive. Nobody's ever been able to describe it and do it justice. We are passionately in love with Italy, to the point that my husband and I might spend part of each year in Italy once we retire. The problem is going to be deciding where to stay. There are so many places in Italy that are so lovely.

Is your spouse Italian-American?

Yes.

Did you consciously select an Italian for a husband?

No, I don't think so. I met my husband in college when we were freshmen. I went to a Catholic university where a lot of the people were Italian and Irish. There was a good mixing of the ethnic groups. I was in a sorority with all kinds of people. I was comfortable with people of all sorts. I met my husband in class. We happened to sit next to each other in a biology class, and he tried to sell me a ticket to a basketball game in Madison Square Garden. I wouldn't buy it. "Well, okay, I'll take you," he said.

Does your background affect your relationship with your husband?

For one thing we're pretty open about our feelings. We're both Italian and we're both psychologists, so there's no hang ups about talking about our feelings. If I'm angry about something, I certainly let my anger show and we talk about it. I am more typically Italian than he is. He's more reserved. I have more emotional ups and downs, and I can lose my cool more so than he does. I'm more of a hothead than he is. There's no dominance thing going on. It might be a departure from many marriages where one mate tries to dominate the other. The husband is the titular head; however, the wife rules the roost. The important decisions we make together. The less important ones my husband doesn't care if I make them. If it's something I want him to like, I'll consult him, such as buying furniture. I want him to be happy with it and pick out something that both of us would like. He's very agreeable at most times.

Did your background have an effect on raising your children?

I modeled my home after my mother's, with some departures. I was less strict than my mother, but I was more strict than our contemporary culture, especially with girls. I was probably more strict with my daughters than my sons. That's the way it was done in my family, that's the way it's done culturally. Girls traditionally have to be above reproach. That's a far cry from today's culture here where they don't know what above reproach even means. Once they hit eighteen, it's pretty hard to maintain control over children. You do it more by persuasion than by force. We tried to teach them respect, typical Italian values; church, home, family, achievement. My cultural background had an effect on the way I raised my children. I think everybody's cultural background has an effect on the way they bring up their children. It's what shaped you. And in this country, many of us are dual-cultured. I consider myself as being very American as well as having a lot of Italianness in me. I'm not totally like the Italians in Italy, and I'm not totally like most Americans here. We have a diversity. No question about it—we are hyphenated Americans. There's much less women's lib in Italy. One of my cousins is in his forties and his wife is in her early thirties, and he can decide that she will not learn how to drive. He's not mean about it, or tyrannical, but he very strongly discourages her. He uses persuasion against her learning to drive. When I asked her about it, whether she wanted to learn to drive or not, she said that she wanted to but didn't because her husband didn't want her to. If my husband were to tell me here that he didn't want me to drive, I'd say, "Well, I'm going to learn how to drive, unless you can give me a damn good reason why I shouldn't, not just a preference." I suspect it's control. These cousins of mine are not from the provinces, they're from a more metropolitan area, a suburb near Naples. And Naples, despite the negative things you hear about it, has cultural centers and is a very modern and beautiful city.

My children were willing to buy into some of my values, but not others. They, too, are the products of their culture. Certainly, I didn't raise them in a vacuum where Italianness prevailed and that's all. They went to school every day and were with children of other ethnic backgrounds, so were subject to all the forces that prevail here. The permissiveness of the late sixties and the early seventies certainly affected my children. I tried to protect them from it, but how could I? There was no way. Fortunately, they all turned out nicely, but they caused me worries that my parents never had to dream about. There were no drugs when I was in high school, but there certainly were when my children were in high school. And being in the field, I know that no parents, no matter how good or how hard they try, could rest assured that their children would be immune from drugs.

Is religion as meaningful to you as it was to your parents?

It's probably more meaningful for me than is was for my parents. I think our values are the same, except for observance of the rituals. My mother grew up with a prelate in the family, and there was a chapel in her house. She didn't have to leave her home to go to Mass. It was said right there on Sundays. My father had uncles who were priests, and yet when they came to this country, neither of them went to church regularly. Yet I considered them to be very moral and ethical people, very honest, very caring. I raised my children Catholic and I went to Sunday school on my own when I was eight. I saw some of my friends in the neighborhood go, and I wanted to go, too. My parents had no objections, so I went. But they never pushed me toward it. My father suggested a Catholic university. I loved it there. My brother went there the following year. It was St. John's, right in Brooklyn, one of the biggest cities in the world, very metropolitan. There were students of all creeds, although they were mostly Catholic. It strengthened me, no doubt about that. When I learned the philosophical basis for Catholicism, it strengthened my faith, and my husband's, too. So we have gone regularly to Mass, and for the first time, I'm even active in a church group. My husband and I have found a lot of solace in our religion, since three years ago when our 26-year-old daughter died.

Ann S.

Family members were supportive of my becoming a registered nurse, and they were equally supportive when I took my bachelor and master degrees.

My spouse was not Italian and my selection of a mate, regarding nationality, was not deliberate. But my background had profound untoward effects on my marriage.

I have only one child and she is very pro-Italian. My nationality made my parenting a warm relationship.

Olympia

My husband is fifty percent Italian-American as I am. So—I suppose my ethnic background has affected my close-knit family ties with my family and my husband's family.

Fran

My parents were definitely supportive of professional goals, though I had uncles who thought it foolish for girls to go to college. I thought they were foolish and narrow-minded for believing so. Neither of my parents was educated. I was told that my father went only to the first grade in the old country. My mother had only a fourth grade education in this country, as she was forced to drop out of school to help care for her younger brothers and sisters. She was always embarrassed by this, so she never told anyone.

She would be very embarrassed if she knew I were sharing this information. However, I am extremely proud of my parents' accomplishments in spite of their lack of education.

As a result of their lack of education, they placed a great deal of importance on education itself. I can remember my mother saying countless times while I was growing up, "It's something that no one can ever take away from you." They placed a tremendous value on education and were very proud of my sister and me when we graduated from high school. College was not an option. I knew they *expected* me to go. I can remember wishing I could drop out of college after my sophomore year, but I knew that my parents would be devastated. I couldn't disappoint them and shatter their dreams, so I never said a word about it and continued until graduation.

My Italian-American background has affected my parenting as well. Because I was overprotected in many ways myself and not allowed as much freedom as my non-Italian friends, I try to be reasonable in my child rearing—not too strict, not too permissive. Here again, my husband has provided a balance. When I think the children are too young to do something, he reminds me of how old they are and assures me that they are capable of handling the situation. I am more compassionate and sympathetic and empathetic in dealing with the children than my husband is because of my background. He would call it "soft-hearted." I am also an affectionate mother who is family oriented. I've always tried to impress upon our four children that no one will care about them more than their own family, and that they will probably always be there for one another when there is a need. The importance and value of family to me is a direct result of how I've been raised.

My spouse is Irish-American and I did not consciously choose a non-Italian mate. My parents never put any pressure on me to marry an Italian. In fact, when my sister and I expressed an interest in an Italian boy, my father might comment that he didn't care for the family. In high school, I think my parents had a general fear of our dating, period; so perhaps this was one way of discouraging a steady relationship. There was a young man I dated for three years while I was in college. They liked him very much. He was Italian. But it was most important to them that I marry a man who could provide for me, and who would treat me with kindness and respect. My mother's words were: "As long as he's good to you, that's all that matters."

I believe my background has definitely affected my relationship with my husband. As an Italian-American, I am more affectionate than he is. I feel emotional stirrings in response to most of life's situations and in relationships with others that I know he does not experience . . . or at least not as frequently. We see things through different eyes because of our different backgrounds. Although my husband is a sensitive, caring and extremely thoughtful person, I am more open to others. I think I tend to feel a warm acceptance of others that he can't always relate to. Over the years, I've been the one ready to always jump in with both feet and get involved in things and with other people at every opportunity, while he is the one to pull the reins on my enthusiasm with a realistic assessment of what time and job and family responsibilities will allow. We've managed to achieve a balance!

Although my father's family remained in Italy and most of my mother's family lived out of town, I still grew up with a strong sense of extended family. My parents' friends and the family of an in-law were like our own family and many holidays were celebrated with them. My husband's family, on the other hand (with the exception of one sister who lives out of town), is very private. Over the 21 years we've been married, we've gathered with his family for the holidays since my only sister and I have lived miles apart for most of those years, and because we live in my husband's hometown miles from my own. Somehow, I always felt that getting together was an obligation for them rather than a warm, enjoyable family gathering. There's not a great deal of affection expressed in his family. I'm a "hugger" which I believe comes from being raised in an Italian environment where friends are like family and affection was expressed.

Our relationship has also been affected by the differing views we brought to the marriage regarding child rearing, and again, affection is one small part of that.

Angela

Looking back, perhaps subconsciously, I looked for an Italian-American to marry; but then again, our family was surrounded by Italian-Americans back East.

My husband and I are very strong in our heritage and traditions. We share common interests in music, opera, art. We explore the backgrounds of our parents, and we have done much research on their lives.

With our three children, we have tried to let them understand and keep up our traditions. However, they are grown and married, each to non-Italians. The complete Italian-American families are slowly fading, and becoming a melting pot of many nationalities. There are not the "neighborhoods" of the past, and so, much as we try to keep the traditions, I fear they will be lost before long. I am being a realist, though I sometimes dream the reverse could be true.

Toni

Living in Princeton, I didn't know what the heck I was.

Let's talk about your marriage to an Irish husband.

I was accepted by his family and he was accepted by my family. There were no problems socially, except that my husband came from an Irish community up there in Scranton, Pennsylvania, where just about everybody is Catholic, and he couldn't understand the prejudice against Catholics in Princeton. You have to live there to believe it. And as a result of that, I never wanted to raise my family in Princeton. So we moved to Pennington. We're only seven miles from Princeton and can take advantage of its cultural aspects, but no way on God's earth was I going to raise my children in that town!

On raising your children, did being Italian-American have an effect?

I have two sons. I don't think my background had any real effect. My father was born in Italy and came here when he was 11. My mother was born here of Italian background. But I didn't really enjoy being an Italian until five years ago, when I went to Italy for the first time. I don't know what the Italian family syndrome is, except for being the one and only daughter of a strict Italian father. I didn't have a large immediate family. We didn't have have an extended family, either. It was just my father and my mother and I, with no aunts or uncles and cousins, no relatives constantly visiting on Sundays and holidays for macaroni dinner. My father's Italian customers and friends would come during Christmas and Easter with their pastries and give them to us. My mother didn't make them. She didn't know how, I guess. These were the customs, and there again, I think that we didn't have any customs. To this day I don't have any customs. I'm really an oddball Italian. But I got my Italianism back when I went to Italy. I loved it there. After I came back, I studied Italian and I was so proud of being an Italian. I went with my college alumnae group to Rome, Pompei, Salerno and Sorrento, then north to Florence and Venice. But a distant relative contacted my father's family in Italy (Campania), and when we were in Sorrento, I got a phone call from this unknown relative. It turned out that they were in the lobby of the hotel, when I had expected *just* a distant phone call. I burst into tears when I found out that these people came out of their way to meet me. I didn't know what to expect. But Florie was a beautiful Italian woman, beautiful features, dark hair, petite, vivacious. Her brother and two brothers-in-law were there, also. We greeted one another, hugged and so forth. We were cousins. When we went out to the parking lot, was I surprised; they had a Mercedes. Her husband was a pediatrician and she was a teacher. When we got to their apartment in Naples, they had all the family waiting—five or six brothers, an attorney or two, a journalist, these were professional people. I found out when I went back to

Laviano with them, that my father's family owned the only hotel in the town, which had been destroyed in the earthquake with the rest of the town. That's why they were never out in the fields working like the others. He never soiled his hands. He was never part of the peasants. These cousins of mine (This was my father's brother's family.) were all educated. As far as genes and heredity go, when I looked at this younger Florie, I was astounded. I had never met her before, but I was amazed at how similar we were. At the time of the earthquake, she made daily trips from Naples to Laviano, which was maybe 70 miles each way, with food and medical supplies. Since her husband was a doctor, she had access to medical supplies, and she became the Florence Nightingale of the village. The people had to be housed, clothed, cared for—and she did a solo number. She was like the Red Cross herself. I thought that she was doing probably what I would have done in the same case, maybe not in the same manner, but the same type of social work. When we were visiting the town together, several years after the earthquake, she would go in and out of the houses to see how the people were doing in the rebuilt section lower on the mountain. The original town higher up was totally destroyed and is uninhabitable, as though it had been bombed, completely devastated. I never dreamed I would have that experience, and as a result of that reality, I came back to the United States feeling very Italian. I guess you have to get back to your roots. It was the first time ever that I was proud to be an Italian, knowing that I had a proud heritage. Up until then it was like not being committed to being Italian. I was a misfit. I was neither fish nor fowl. Living in Princeton, I didn't know what the heck I was.

Philosophy of life?

I don't know if my philosophy of life came from my Italian heritage, except that my father was extremely patriotic. He came here when he was young and never went back to Italy, and never had any desire to go back. He felt that this country gave him his livelihood and he was 100 percent American, even though he loved his Italian heritage. He was patriotic to the nth degree. During the early thirties (I hate to use the word Mafia), when they were trying to get the shop-keepers to make kickbacks to get protection, he was approached by these hoodlums; he absolutely refused and told them he would turn them in to the authori-ties, if they made further advances. A lot of people knuckled under. He didn't. He did have the courage of his convictions. One day, when I didn't come home from school—we were off eating cherries up in a cherry tree—my mother told my father and he thought that I had been kidnapped, so he called the police. Then they found out that I was right around the corner and that I was all right. But I think there was one of those death wreaths laid on our porch at home to scare us. As far as philosophy goes, I took on a lot of my father's traits that I admired. He was a man of integrity, a man of convictions, which I have tried to pass on to my children. He was honest to a fault. He never owed a cent to anyone. Always held his head up high. He valued a good reputation. That was why he wanted his daughter to walk the straight and nar-row and not be found up in some student's room in a Princeton dormitory like lots of the girls were doing back then. They had their raids then, too. There was hashish. They had a prince of Asian royalty there. A lot of the girls got caught up in that. My mother, who had a lot of input in my philosophy, said that you could be and do anything you wanted to *be* and *do*. She was a very independent person. She was a smart business

woman. She would have been college material had she
had the opportunity back in her time. Even 20 years
later when I went back for my master's, I said, "Gee, I
don't know if I can do it." And she said there was no
reason why I couldn't do it. No qualms on her part.
And I did it—as she said I could. I wanted to add this
before, when I was talking about growing up; my father spoke beautiful pure Italian, and where he got it,
I don't know. Many of his customers would come into
the shop who had traveled to Italy, and they would
love to converse with him in Italian. He did not speak
dialect. As far as speaking Italian in the home, the
only time it was used was when my parents wanted to
talk about scandal or money. Otherwise, we spoke
English. I never picked it up. Never wanted to learn it,
until I went to college. And didn't I take German the
first year and Italian the second year. I can still see
my father looking at me, as if saying, "You wouldn't let
me teach you here, and you have to go take it in college?" I didn't learn that much in college. Mostly
grammar for reading, not speaking.

Religion?

My mother was very religious. My father wasn't as
much. In those days, they thought that if the woman
went to Mass, the man didn't have to go. But he saw to
it that I went and made all the sacraments. He contributed to the Church. He belonged to the Knights of
Columbus. He was one of the early members. Religion
was very much a part of our lives. My mother was very
active in the Mount Carmel Guild in Princeton. No, I
was not equal to them as far as religion goes. I'm almost nondenominational. I just feel that in my own
philosophies you find God on your own. I don't care for
organized religion. I believe in God, but I don't care for

the ritual. Now they run up and down the aisles shaking hands and hugging you. I don't care for it. It turned my husband off, too. All this back slapping. At one time in Catholicism, the lay people would observe and regurgitate it, and you were not supposed to process it in your head. You were not supposed to be a thinking person. That turned me off since I was 16. I went to Catholic school, I had the whole spiel. I hated to say the rosary from the fifth grade. It used to put me to sleep. It was hypnotic to me.

Politics?

My father was very political. He was a Democrat. He was the Democratic leader of the Italian community. I am political now. But the first time I voted, I disappointed my father by voting Republican. It broke his heart. I really didn't care about the parties back then. I wasn't that committed. I had taken a stand. I voted for Wendell Wilkie. I knew Roosevelt would win. Today, I'm a Democrat and much more liberal-minded. My older son was politically oriented. If my father had lived, he would have adored my older son, who was involved in politics and was on the constitutional committee for New Jersey, the new charter. He wanted to pursue politics. But the young lady he married, it was not her style. Consequently, he's not pursuing it. But he still has a very active interest in politics. His wife is an Anglo-Saxon. But I'm beginning to see a change. He's starting to do what he wants to.

Mary R.

My Italian grandmother believes I shouldn't think so much as it will hurt my brain.

Family members were quite supportive of my professional and educational preparation, as long as it was going to be worthwhile to me in the long term. My dad still feels that I could have worked in the business world for a few years after college to earn more money and then to quit eventually and pursue my own goals. I, however, needed to break out of the white-collar, middle- and upper-middle-class career path. And so I did. He has accepted it. In my first year out of college, I wrote the first draft of a novel, and my parents supported me. So I would say that I have been quite lucky to have such open parents. I don't know how much this has to do with being Italian-American, since my Italian grandmother, who lives with us, believes I shouldn't think so much as it will hurt my brain. Her mother sent her to school only until the fourth grade, but allowed her brothers to continue. My grandma tells us this with resentment, I believe. But then in her next statement, she says how awful it is for you to think so much. So she was socialized in the southern Italian peasant mentality. My father, as a rebellion perhaps, has sent three daughters to college (one to medical school). One son's in college and one daughter will begin next year. My parents, I think, believe it is important to stretch the mind. I know I believe it.

Jennie

I was unable to pursue my chosen career due to the death of my mother when I was a junior in high school. The following year I assumed my mother's duties at home. We were six children ranging in ages from 1½ to 20.

My parents were supportive of my professional goals. Although my mother was illiterate (She had been taught the domestic arts as young girl.), she was very much interested in our education and was most encouraging, as was my father, who was educated in Italy. With the help of his children, he read our report cards with great care and interest, asking us many questions. We were all good students and he was proud of our accomplishments. I remember him saying he wanted us all to have a good education.

As a child and a very young girl, I was ashamed of my Italian name, of my beautiful custom-made, hand-knitted woolen dresses, of the delicious sandwiches my mother made with the Italian bread, and of the oil-stained bag holding my lunch. I was also embarrassed because my parents could not speak English.

At some point later in my life I realized how fortunate I was to be Italian. I developed a great pride in my heritage.

Although my husband is an Italian-American, I did not consciously select an Italian mate. The qualities I was looking for in a husband just happened to be found in this man. But the fact that we are both Italian, I'm sure, has helped us both understand each other better. We share a common interest in our love of the Italian culture, its literature, music, art, drama, traditions, food.

Yes, my ethnic background had an effect on my parenting. I think that perhaps as parents, we were more protective of our children—stricter—more caring. Our family ties have always been close.

Religion is as meaningful to me as it was to my parents.

At this point in my life I feel that I am very much interested in politics. I have more time to read and to think about how our governmental actions and operations affect us. I have never been active in partisan politics, but I never fail to vote. My father's independent thinking on political matters may have influenced me.

JoAnn

Did your Italian-American background affect your choice of a career?

Yes, it did. I chose the career of laboratory technician, because when I went to school in the fifties, women either became teachers, nurses, secretaries, or lab technicians, jobs you had until you got married. That was expected of you at that time. I went to Rider College, instead of going to lab school only, because the hospital's (St. Francis) lab school was affiliated with Rider; and if I wanted to get into lab school, I had to take Rider's four-year program. That was fine, and if I wanted to become a lab technician, then I was allowed to go to college. When I got to college, I realized that my heart was more into law or political science, but that was not what a woman of my background did at that time.

Did you get the support of your family members?

Yes. My mother wanted me to go to school. That was very important to her. I at one time had wanted to quit when I got over to St. Francis Hospital the last year. I really didn't like it. And she would not let me quit. It was important to her that I finish school. I didn't have to cook or clean or do any other housework, as long as I studied. That was what she wanted for me. My uncle paid my tuition. My schooling was expensive at the time, and I don't know what I would have done. My uncle offered to pay for my schooling. He had no children; he was unmarried. We were really his second family.

Any effect on your professional relationships?

Sometimes. I know that I am very touchy when people make remarks, and I am always on the defensive. I've noticed that. This has happened as I've gotten older. I am much more sensitive about my background. I really don't like it when people tell Italian jokes. Another example: when Mario Cuomo decided not to run for president, and we were at work, having coffee at break time, someone said that the *Italiano* is not running. I got very upset. I thought it was derogatory and it really bothered me. When I was going to school, I was going to join a sorority, and my father was upset with me. He said that they were elitist and left people out, not just for racial reasons, but for ethnic and religious backgrounds. "You're going to be part of something like that?" he said to me. I figured that if you don't join a sorority, you don't have any social life at Rider. He just thought that was weird. He always told me about the Ku Klux Klan; that it's not only blacks they're against, they're against Jews, Catholics, Italians and others. I found that interesting.

Does your ethnic background affect your social life?

I can say that it does. When I was younger, I took courses in Italian, and I have friends who are Italian. Their people come from the same part of Italy as my parents, so we enjoy the same foods. I have friends of different ethnic backgrounds, yet I enjoy being in the company of people of my own ethnic background. It's very difficult to go out to eat with people who don't enjoy the same foods. At work some of the people think you're nuts when you mention different foods that you like to eat. And in school, I was always embarrassed by my name. They used to call me JoAnn Macaroni. At one time I wanted to change my name, and I couldn't understand why my father got upset with me, but now I can. That's why my mother was right in not naming me Angelina. She said she couldn't do that to me when I was born. It really bothers you when the other kids make fun of you. But I really noticed the differences between them and us when I went to Trenton High. In Junior Four we were all ethnics from working-class backgrounds, but at Trenton High we met kids whose parents were professionals, and they looked down their noses at us. The better clubs there were dominated by the kids from Junior Three, and they didn't want us in them. That was a totally different world for me. In Junior Four it didn't show that you were Italian or came from a working-class background, we were all from the working class. There were very few professional Italians in those days. In seventh grade one of my Italian-American teachers told us that one of her professors told her that she was going to have a hard time making it through school with her Italian name. I didn't really understand the impact of what she had said back then, but I do now. You're new in the school and you don't know and you try to join a club and you don't know why you get rejected. I ended up joining the Italian Club and got myself involved in other things. But I was never part of that other Junior Three crowd, they wouldn't let you be. We had to do our own thing.

Religion?

I didn't come from a religious family. No one went to church. I went and I belonged to the church organizations at that time, but as I got older, I drifted away, too. I didn't go to Catholic schools, I went to public schools. I have been in groups of people where I was the only one who didn't go to Catholic school, and I found that interesting. And they weren't all Italian. I did go to catechism classes and I did make my sacraments, but I didn't come from a family that *had* to go to church and pray to the saints. While I was growing up, I went through an indoctrination at religious school, and I went to Mass every day. I was embarrassed one day when the nun asked how many went to Mass, and I didn't raise my hand, and she told me to tell my parents to roll out of bed and to take me to church.

Any interest in politics?

Very much interested in politics. My brother is a Mercer County Republican Party official, and I grew up an avid Democrat. My father was so strong a Democrat that he wouldn't even watch a television show if a Republican was on it. Yet it's interesting that my brother and I are from the same household and we are so far apart politically. I'm very strong in my opinions, and I follow all the primaries and all the elections. My father was like that and I think that's how you pick up a lot of your ideas. He was really into politics. He did have a strong influence on me in my choice of party. As I grew older and I learned, I got more involved in the political system, and I am still inclined to agree with him. He felt that he was a working person and a working person didn't belong anywhere but in the Democratic Party. And I still feel that, and I can still remember him arguing with my brother one day when

Jimmy Carter was running for president against Jerry Ford. My brother asked my father, "You are going to vote for Jimmy Carter?" And my father replied, "Yes, I am. I am a working man, and the Republican Party did nothing for me." My niece was in the first grade then, and she came home one day after a mock election in school and told her mother that she didn't vote for Jerry Ford. She said that she had heard Pop and had listened to what he had said and voted for Jimmy Carter. And look at my brother, he's the total opposite. When I look around me, I feel that is where I fit in. I feel you can never escape your background. I don't care how much money you have, or if you change your name, you're still an Italian-American. I feel strongly about that. I'm as interested in politics as my parents were, but I'm not actively working in politics. I went to the Democratic Party Convention in 1980. I went to the Democratic Party fund raiser and had my picture taken with Mario Cuomo. After hearing his keynote speech at the convention, I felt that I identified with him. And for an Italian-American to make it in the higher levels of politics, in this country today, he has to be squeaky clean, because he will get undue investigative scrutiny from the media as to any connection to organized crime. *Any* kind of a connection would hurt him politically. An example of that recently was the husband of Geraldine Ferraro getting into trouble and causing problems for his wife's campaign. She should have been aware of what he was doing and how it would affect her political aspirations. That really bothered me. People do really feel that if you're Italian, you're in the Mafia. It really bothers me, because I feel that people are quick to connect anything to us. The recent drug arrests are an example. People said, "What do you expect, they're from Chambersburg." Nobody remembers the prominent people from here. People think the worst about us in

Chambersburg when something bad gets front page headlines. We have a lot of people in this neighborhood who went to prestigious colleges and did well for themselves. They don't get noticed by the newspapers, but the drug busts do. It's the few greedy ones in the drug business who make the headlines and give a bad name to the rest of us. And they do ridiculous things with all the money they make from drugs. I heard one of them had his teeth pearled at $700 a tooth. That's ridiculous.

Do you consciously seek out friends of Italian descent?

I don't, but I do have friends who are. As far as dating, it's very difficult to find men of my age group who are not married and who are also professional. I shouldn't limit myself, but as you get older, you get choosier. I don't know if I would be satisfied with someone from a working-class background now, not that I'm so high up there. Men of my age group might be more male chauvinistic and not appreciate a woman who works professionally and owns her own home, an educated, independent woman. I had a Jewish sixth grade teacher who thought it was wonderful that I had an uncle who was an artist and who would take me to bookstores and art museums. We met her in Traver's Bookstore one day. And she said that they didn't think people from Chambersburg did that. My uncle had a big influence on me. He used to lecture on paintings to us in the Metropolitan Museum in New York City during the times he took us there to see all the great art. My uncle introduced us to literature, also. And my father always had his classical records so he could listen to good music. He was a factory worker, too. My father, my uncle, my mother in her own way, they did have an influence. We did aspire to better things and a better education, and others did, too, in this neighborhood.

And I had a father who let me do things. He also got me interested in sports, and I used to watch baseball games with him on television. There were always discussions with him about politics and sports. I didn't have to clean up after a meal while the men would sit around and talk. But yet I know people who did. But I do admit that I identify with people from the same background. You can grow out of this neighborhood, but I think it's always in you. I don't think you can ever leave it. When you go into somebody's house, you see how differently they live, how they eat, what they eat. It's totally different—back then, and even now.

Stephanie

When I married, I did not consciously select my spouse based on his being non-Italian or Italian. However, at the present time, being single, I would most likely choose to marry someone of Italian heritage. When I was married to a non-Italian, I was teased a lot, but wrote it off as fun—it gets hard to live with after a while.

If in the future I do decide to have children, I will always teach them about their heritage, so they may pass this on to their children. It is a great sense of security to know who you are and how you came about.

Mary R.

I don't think that my background will affect how I raise my children beyond the fact that I believe in a strong family—but one that allows space and freedom in closeness.

Lenore

My husband was born in Italy, but he is American because of his father's American citizenship. Our similar interests were a strong motivating force for us to marry. We have common ground for a meeting of the minds. And, I suppose, my parenting was affected by the values instilled in me and have "rubbed off" on my children.

Rosemarie T.

A "woman" was not supposed to know "men's" business. To say it was frustrating, is an understatement.

My family, especially my sisters, was most supportive of my professional goals and educational preparation. They were proud that I had chosen a career that served me well. Remember, I was the only one in the family who did attend and complete college. My parents were supportive. However, my father really did not feel that he should continue to send me to school for *graduate work*. I completed two years using my own resources while I continued to work. (I did my graduate work evenings and summers.)

In some ways, I was a threat to my brothers, because I had the education. I can't recall any encouragement or praise from either of them for my accomplishments. My sisters-in-law did not have college educations.

I was not asked by my brothers for any input relating to the family business. My father had difficulty with me when it came to business matters; however, in his retirement years, he did accept my opinions and help in running his personal business. But it didn't happen without some resistance or question. A "woman" was not supposed to know "men's" business. To say it was frustrating, is an understatement.

Oddly enough, whenever I could help as a notary public, it was viewed as simply "assisting" to expedite a document. The women in the family came to rely upon my background in business and civil law and often asked for advice in legal matters. They were quick to point out that I should have been a lawyer.

My ex-husband was not Italian-American, but he spoke the Italian language fluently. His first wife was an Italian and they lived in Milan, her native hometown. He was part Greek.

I consciously selected a non-Italian. I was determined not to marry an Italian-American. I did not like the way Italian-American men behaved toward women, nor did I like the way they were doted upon by their mothers. The fact that he was married to a native Italian and knew the language and the customs, probably influenced me.

During my marriage, my background influenced the way I treated my husband. I carried the load in the relationship; the chores, the finances and the social obligations. I was more inclined to let him relax, but then I would resent his not helping me. We both worked, but he did not help with the household chores. Having been married to a wealthy Italian woman, he was accustomed to being "waited" on. He never cooked a meal, helped with the laundry or shopped for groceries. I was "conditioned" to do those things in a marriage. I subconsciously allowed him more of the creature comforts than I did myself. He had more leisure time to pursue his golf, tennis and other recreational activities. Yet—I allowed it; but deep inside, I resented it. Eventually, the relationship deteriorated and the marriage failed.

Louise V.

My mother drove me to the extra science classes and to the science fairs. My parents paid for my college and made sure I was set up at school. They didn't single out science specifically. Since they weren't from a scientific background, I didn't get particular guidance in making my way in such a field. They imbued me with curiosity and I pursued it as best I could, getting help from various advisors along the way. I paid my own expenses for my second bachelor's degree and for my master's degree. It was an Italian-American professor at Columbia who introduced me to the school.

It took a *definite* break from the family and a *physical* move 800 miles away from my home in Chicago to the East Coast in order to proceed with my career. The pressure to conform to the family way was strong and persistent; to marry and have kids. The issue now is to integrate the past traditions with my independent, scientific background. Progress is being made in stages. I am going to be the godmother of my nephew, and I've joined an Italian-American club.

Karen

I have a certain passion in everything that I do.

Effect of ethnic background on career choices?

I honestly don't think it affected it. After I decided that I wanted to paint, I got very excited about the creating and the selling of my work. And when I went to college, that's what I intended to do. But I think now that you just can't stay home and paint. I am doing something else. Meanwhile, I am still an artist and that may be ultimately what I'll do. While I was in school, I got very excited about Italian art history and about being Italian. And as I learned more about the subject, the fact that I was an Italian-American became special. So being Italian didn't affect my choice in the beginning. I don't think anything affected my choice of a career. When I was very little, I remember telling my mother, and saying to just about everybody, that I wanted to be a brain surgeon. Then I wanted to be a professional tap dancer. The next day I wanted to be a nun. But that passed very quickly. It depended on what I read at the time. Actually, I never felt that I *couldn't* do something. I always felt that I could do anything. And I think a lot had to do with my mother, who is not a burn-your-bra women's libber obnoxious personality. But all my life I was aware of who Gloria Steinem was and what she was doing, and about women's rights. I was always aware of that even as a child. I'm sure I was up on the newsreels and TV and everything else. As a little kid, I always said that I would never be held back because I was a female. Never. So if anything had held me back, being Italian-American would have. But being a woman came first. I could do anything I wanted to and nationality made no difference, either. My mother was a role model. She always let me know that if there was something I wanted to do, I could attain it—if I really wanted it.

Was your sister a role model, also?

We didn't get along as children. She's four years older than I am. I was the younger pain-in-the-neck. When she was a teenager, I was still a little kid. I don't feel that we really grew up together. We had different interests. She'd be out with her friends, and I'd be with my mother a lot. I don't think she was a role model. Although, there was a part of her life that I liked. She was independent at 17 when I was 13. Beyond that, she was not a role model, as far as her goals.

Effect of ethnic background on your career at present?

I don't think it has affected my career. I enjoy being an Italian-American. And where I work now there are a lot of Italian-Americans. It's very playful, with a lot of camaraderie. We've grown up with the same foods. We talk about food and the non-Italians think we're weird. We go on and on about food. There's a bond among us of similar cultural experiences. It makes you closer. So being Italian-American hasn't held me back in my work career. The only problem I have is my frizzy, curly hair. But nowadays curly-style minority hairdos are chic.

Did your family support your goals?

My mother always was supportive of my goals. My mother minored in fine arts in college for her bachelor degree. I think I always knew when I entered high school that I wanted to be a professional painter. No, I didn't know then that I wanted to be a painter, but I knew I wanted to go to art school. But, thinking in practical terms, I decided on set design. I had no idea that people actually studied painting and drawing in college. That I learned when I got there. After the first couple of months, that's what I knew I had to do, as opposed to being a set designer, which was something I picked because it was the most creative, I thought, and expressive for commercial and graphic art work, rather than sitting at a desk and trying to do what someone else tells you to do. Set designing was more free and I could express creativity and it was large, nine feet square on the average. Then I realized that NO, I can't do that. My father didn't deter me, but he couldn't anyway, since my desire was so strong. And when I chose fine arts as a major, he was burdened by what I was going to do. How I was going to make a living? Set design was less risky to him. My mother, all along, was supportive.

Let's get back to your hair and your interesting comment about it.

I have felt self-conscious about my hair all my life. Even as a child, I knew people were turning around and looking at me because of my curly hair. I don't remember what nationalities they were, but I remember getting looks at my hair, people wondering who I was. Who was this minority child among us? I don't know what would have bothered these people more, whether I was Italian or Spanish. I can *imagine* what would have bothered them more! My frizzy hair always bothered me. And now that I have an office job, my hair is impossible to keep well groomed.

Was your family supportive of your educational preparation?

I didn't really need help. But my father always had to get me up for school. I pretty much did my school work on my own. I was always independent. Nobody could tell me I couldn't do something, especially as a child and in my teens. I'd be damned if anybody said I couldn't do something; I was going to do it. My husband, when I was looking for a job and when I would get a job, would always be supportive; but after I had the job a couple of weeks, he would say I'm only making so much money and that I could be making more. Then I'd get another job and make a little more money, and he'd tell me that I was only making so much money and that I could be making more. I wasn't working up to my potential. I would wonder, how does he know what I'm supposed to do. *I* don't even know how I'm supposed to fit into this world. How is an artist supposed to fit into this world and make a paycheck? I was thinking that if I could be a secretary I could be making more. Then he would say, "Who would want a lousy secretary? You can't type, you can't do this, you can't do that." Now, in the company I work for, there are two vice presidents who want me to be their executive secretary. I can type now just as much as I could then when I had a certain person telling me what a lousy secretary I would be. I don't even want to be a secretary. But the irony is, that now, he would probably say that I'm living up to my potential, but I got the job after we were separated. I did it all by myself—on my own. The irony is that two vice presidents, without me even soliciting them, want me for their secretary.

Does your Italian-American background affect your professional relationships?

If anything, it may make them more casual. As I said before, when we talk about food among us Italians. With non-Italians, I don't think it has any effect at all. If it does, I'm oblivious to it. From my perspective, there is no problem. If others have a problem with my background, it's their problem, not mine. If Italians make remarks to one another, they think nothing of it, but if non-Italians make derogatory remarks, that's something else.

Any effect on your social life?

I never felt inferior or incapable because of my background. My mother made me realize early on that we're all alike, nothing different from you or me or them. I can make friends with Italians or non-Italians.

Husband?

There was no conscious selection of a husband because of his background. I didn't consciously end up with him, either. I never consciously chose a person. I never thought I'd get married. I never thought I'd be in a partnership. Just knowing my personality, independent as I was, I just always thought I'd live alone and have a couple cats, my friends and probably a more Bohemian lifestyle than I'm having now. He came into my life at a time when I certainly needed someone. I was in a low period. I was not myself. I was very dependent at the time. And it was awful, because I didn't feel like myself. I used to go to bed at night and know how independent I had been and think it was all over. It was terrible. I can't tell you how good I feel now. Not that he was responsible for my dependency. I didn't go looking for a husband. If anything, I avoided it. And I didn't go looking for a certain kind of husband.

Effect on relationship?

All along, except for the very beginning, whenever we

were at a family function, he would give me a look like, "Let's get going." I wanted to hang around. I was having fun. I wanted to talk and scream and yell and eat sitting around the family table. He could take the family stuff only to a point; you eat, you visit and then you leave. He couldn't stand two hours of dessert and coffee and hanging around the table getting sugar on your elbows. It just drove him mad. He had to get out. He always said that my family was crazy. He didn't understand the feelings, the openness, the honesty of emotions that occurred in my family. His family was very tight-lipped. They would get mad at one another and wouldn't talk. He saw my family as everybody being a hothead and so emotional. As good a person as he is, I love him, and I always will love him, and he would probably die if he heard this, that when I was really at a bad point, an emotional point, high or low, he really wasn't there for me, because he really couldn't tune in to what was going on. If I were very upset about something, or very emotional, he just couldn't connect to that. He was distant from me. He was too stiff-upper-lipped. Not flexible. I think my Italian-American background had an effect on my marriage. I have a certain passion in everything that I do, the way I live my life, even the way I wake up in the morning. I didn't think my passion for life would be so annoying to him. That was me, whether getting something out of the refrigerator, or reading. I'm very ritualistic. He was very critical. Ritual was part of my passion. I think you can spot the passionate people in the world; they're easy to talk to, and I'm easy to talk to. I'm at a reception desk and people come in and they start talking to me, and they're not always Italian, either. People who have certain passions in life are easy talkers and are warm.

Religion?

Religion was probably as meaningful to me as it was to my parents, because it was pretty much nonexistent. I made my communion and I was confirmed and I went to religious classes. But we didn't live religion at home. In that way, I really had a choice. I was always exposed and I chose what I believed and didn't believe. I didn't believe there's a chalkboard to keep score of sins, even as a child. If people told me that and scolded me, I just rejected it. And I rejected them, because I thought, why are you lying to me? I remember when I was in high school and I had an argument with a nun. She was saying something and I questioned her, and she had no answer to my question. They never had answers to my questions. They saw that I was challenging them. It infuriated them. I became a pain-in-the-neck to them.

Politics?

I'm not interested at all. I'm not sure whether I'm registered or not. My sister is into politics and I'm not. So now you know why we were never close and she wasn't a role model. One of my goals, after I get all my possessions straightened out and organized and in the same location, is to get more politically active. I believe in the other functions of politics like Walk America.

Anything else you want to add?

In the middle of my separation and my marriage, I signed up for an Italian class, because I wanted to learn how to speak Italian so that the next time I go back to Italy I'll be able to speak the language to the natives there. My going to Italian class on Tuesday night made more problems in my marriage. Taking the Italian course with my mother helped me to get closer to her, since we studied the language phrases together, but it took time away from my husband. So the Italian class was the turning point in the disintegration of my marriage. It kind of got me in tune to *me* again. And the fact that I was independent again. So Italian class was, for me, tied up with a lot of terrible times.

Celia

. . . A lot of my heritage was lost for "convenience" sake.

I guess you would define my "career" as wife and mother, although I do hold a full-time job as a collector in the financial department of an insurance company (CIGNA).

Since I was the wife of an Air Force man for over 20 years, I really did not have many choices to make as far as a career went.

For the first ten years of marriage, my family was the most important thing in my life, almost to the exclusion of everything else. My Italian-American background had a pervasive effect on parenting. To me, the father's word was final and I brought my children up the same way. Catholic education and the Church were most important as a family activity.

My mother was very verbal and I think I am the same way. I always expected certain things from everyone in the family as far as loyalty to one another. My husband is not Italian, but he "acts" Italian. I always thought I'd marry a strong man, but never thought of nationalities. I did date several Italian-American males in Rochester, New York (my hometown), but never thought of it that way.

My father had a college degree, the only one in his family. My mother grew up in a small town where there was a lot of prejudice against the only Italian family living in it. So I think a lot of my heritage was lost for "convenience" sake.

Now that my children are grown and my husband has retired from the military, I feel I can explore my own choices more freely. He is quite secure in his job and he gives me a lot of support. I still would not compete with him to be head of the household.

Being in the military, we learned not to be too interested in politics. I was fiercely patriotic during the Vietnam War, and I never doubted the government's position or decisions. But now that I am older, I can see that blind trust isn't always the right thing.

Presently, I would say that I am mildly interested in politics.

Doris

My Italian-American background had no effect on my choice of a career, and it has no effect in the present. And my family was not supportive, since money was scarce. I had to argue to be allowed to attend a two-year college, but they were proud when I received my diploma.

I married a man of English descent, whose ancestors have been in America since the 1800s. And very few of our friends or acquaintances are Italian.

Since my parents' marriage was not a happy one (they divorced), my mother, being of Danish descent, suggested that I not date or marry an Italian.

Catherine M.

If you wonder why there was little "Italianism" in our household, it was due to three things. First, my mother was from Hungary of Hungarian-German parents. Her cooking was that of her mother. Although she did learn how to make excellent sauce and meatballs and a wonderful Sicilian omelet, most of our meals were non-Italian. Second, my father's father was murdered in his driveway by fellow Sicilians in 1915 when my father was twelve years of age. He witnessed the shooting and was threatened never to say who was responsible or they would murder him, too. He hated "his people" for what they did to his father and, subsequently, the hardship that was placed on his mother, who was very dear to him, and to his little brother, age two. He wanted people to like him and he wanted to make something of himself—to be proud and to be American. So he severed himself from the community as much as he could. He Americanized his last name and lived for high school graduation so that he could leave the old neighborhood to pursue being an American. He was a fine athlete and played football for a southern college. When he returned, he found employment on the east side of town, married an east-sider and established himself as a respected citizen. He was and still is respected by the Italian/Sicilians from his neighborhood who knew him well and understood his trauma, but is still criticized by a small element of those who are ten years younger than he is. Third, although there was a certain amount of revisiting the old neighborhood for their festivals, shopping markets and dining at restaurants, there was no other need to visit the community. His mother died in her fifties of a heart problem and our grandmother was probably the link necessary for my sister and me to establish ourselves with the neighborhood and its culture.

There is a mystique involved here and part of it might be one of the reasons for my obsession. It is the unknown. My father, the inspiration in my life, refuses to discuss what happened that evening in 1915. I have learned about it through microfilm at the library. My grandmother died five days before I was born. She wanted desperately to see me. I was named after her. She was loved and respected by the entire neighborhood. I believe that I am very much a part of her. I hope all of this makes some sense.

Frani

I came from a family that didn't have a lot of material things, but we could give the little things—like love.

Your age?

I'm 19.

Importance of education in your family?

A lot. My background is unique. My mother is an educated woman. She went to college. She didn't get married until she was 28. She's a teacher. Education was very important to her. To be obedient and to do our schoolwork came first. Our schoolwork had to be done before we could go out to play. She always praised us when we did a good job and encouraged us to do a better job when we didn't. We all turned out differently. I'm the youngest of seven kids. I really took to it. I realized that she was stressing education as important. I picked that up, and I feel it's important, too. My dad died when I was young, and she raised us all by herself. She said that if she hadn't been educated, she could never have raised us by herself and kept us together. We would have been separated. She feels that she learned enough in her life that she was able to keep us all together. She used that to judge how important education really was.

Education of grandparents?

Both finished high school. My grandfather came from Italy and my grandmother was born here. My great-grandparents came here from Italy.

Your mother?

My mother finished college and has credits for a master's degree, but she doesn't actually have the degree. She got married and started to have a family and never went back to finish getting her master's. She's just a few credits away. She was a teacher and went part time.

Your father?

My father was a college graduate and went to graduate school. He was a professor. And he ran a construction business.

How was education supported?

My father died when I was seven. I remember the good things. We went to museums and places like that.

Your educational background?

Public grammar school to eighth grade and Catholic high school.

Did you have a role model?

My mother. She had to be a strong influence.

Your motivation for going to college?

Basically to be self-supporting, self-sufficient. I want a certain degree of independence.

Why did you choose to attend Holy Family College?

I went to a Catholic academy. It's a high school and it's run by the same nuns who run the college here. But I went to Temple for my first semester of college. I thought I'd like the experience of different people and the atmosphere was a lot freer down there with a lot of people to talk to and bigger classes. You were pretty much on your own, which I thought was pretty nice, and I could gain a lot of independence. But I decided it wasn't for me. I came from the academy and we were really close. I loved the attention I had. So I decided to come here. I like the smaller classes and the personal attention.

Your major?

Mathematics. I've always had a fascination with numbers. My mom was a science teacher. I guess I got interested in math and science from her. My dad was always very good in science and logic. I kind of drifted that way.

Future plans?

To find a job in a big corporation. If I wanted to, I could advance. I intend to get married and I want a family, but I won't know until I'm out in the work force whether I want to climb the corporate ladder. I think maybe I will.

Has your ethnic background been a hindrance, or not, in terms of education?

I don't think it has been either way.

Do you feel Italian-American?

I don't really think about it too much. I don't think I'm too much different from any other background. I am a little bit in some of the ways, I think. I was never treated any differently because I was Italian. No one thought I was more or less intelligent because I was Italian.

Socially?

I was always brought up where you put the men on a pedestal, and I get enjoyment out of doing things for other people that make them happy. Little things, like cooking for somebody. It goes with my personality. My mom was like that and my grandmother waited on my grandfather hand and foot. It made him happy and it made her happy. I guess I would like to make the man in my life happy. I came from a family that didn't have a lot of material things, but we could give the little things—like love.

Choice of friends?

I do have Italian friends and we do feel a bond because we are Italian. We come from the same background and we think alike. I had a friend who was German and the two of us totally clashed. She was very headstrong and always thought that she was right. Never compromised. Living with six brothers and sisters, I have learned how to compromise—I had to. I feel comfortable with my Italian friends. We get along real good.

Activities?

No real effect. I don't go to Italian dances or Italian operas. I don't think my Italian-American background has anything to do with my activities.

Personal freedom?

It would help more than it would hinder, but I'm not quite sure how it would help.

Choices?

A lot. The way I was brought up. But I don't stop to think that I made a decision because I'm Italian. It's become such a part of me that maybe I don't even consciously think about why I make a decision. I don't think that if I were a different nationality, I would make a different choice.

Religion?

It's important to me, but I see the way that my parents were very strict about religion and always followed the Church and everything the Church said. They followed it no questions asked. I know that what the Church says is right, but sometimes I feel that I don't agree with what the Church says is right or what it says is wrong. I don't know if it's from being in the eighties. My religion is important to me, but it's not like it's written in stone.

Your mother and father, grandparents, were they interested in politics?

It was not part of my grandparents' background. My parents kept aware of what was going on in society, but they were never active in politics. I'm not interested in politics myself.

Any preference in regard to political candidates?

If a candidate were Italian, it might influence me. But it would depend on what he stood for, but it couldn't be for less than what I stand for. But if the other candidate, who wasn't an Italian-American, stood for the same principles I stand for and the Italian-American candidate didn't, I would vote for the non-Italian.

What about future goals requiring that you move from the area?

There would be a definite effect. I wouldn't want to be

away from my family. That's why I didn't go away to college. There are only two of us left in the house of the seven children, and we are still as close as we've ever been. We visit. Sundays are still a big day for family visiting, and we usually get together for Sunday dinner. Visiting my grandmother on Sundays—I wouldn't want to give that up. I'm not saying that it would end if I moved away; I'd still keep in close contact. We've been through the rough times, and we celebrate the good times.

Why are you taking Italian?

I had it in high school and I wanted to be able to speak it to my grandparents. I wanted to learn a little bit more of the culture.

Carmella

My spouse is an Italian-American, but he is a Baptist, not a Catholic, as I am. I think, subconsciously, I selected an Italian-American because I felt more comfortable with a person of a similar background. The Italianness of my mate made it easier to understand each other's families; however, the religious differences caused a considerable degree of unhappiness—even to this day—especially rearing the children in religion.

I have two children: a son, 34, a daughter, 33. I reared them as "Americans," consciously omitting Italian expressions from my daily life. Only in the past 15 or so years have I tried to reverse the trend and make them proud of their Italian heritage.

My mother was a true, nonchurch-attending Catholic (She never had the leisure to attend church.); my father professed not to believe in God, but observed every St. Joseph's day by not going to work. The true "brotherhood of man" and Christianity were very, very important to him.

Dolores

My husband is of Italian and Polish background. And, no, I did not consciously select a non-Italian or Italian mate. But with some Italian blood on his side, he likes many things I like; and yet he feels that sometimes we are not willing to take chances, because we are afraid. I don't always agree. I do feel that even though I think I am doing as I please, sometimes I tend to let him overrule me, because my mother allowed my dad to decide most financial ventures.

Yes, my background has affected my parenting. Without a doubt, I would die for my children. I do for them and give to them first. Fortunately, my husband does not feel that he is second, because he is Number One as my spouse and can never be Number One as my children are.

Maria F.

I was thinking about going down south . . . even thinking about living away. My mother didn't want me to leave the house . . . to let her baby go.

This is your second year at Holy Family College?

Yes.

Importance of education in your family?

I'm the first one to go to college in my family. It's important for me. My brother's not going to college. My family, especially my grandmom, place a lot of emphasis on my marks and the fact that I'm in college. It's hard for me, because I have to live up to their expectations.

Education of parents?

My father finished tenth grade in high school. My mother finished high school and took one college course. This year she went back and she works full time. She takes courses at a community college.

Did they stress education?

Yes, all through my childhood. I was a B student in grade school. In high school, I was a high B. I'm doing better in college—about an A. My parents and my grandmom saw to it that I got better in college. They keep pushing me. My mother pays for my courses.

Do they support education?

I guess a little. Not as much as other families would. It was mostly family things rather than educational things. I went to parochial school. It just seemed that I would go to parochial school. And that I would go on to college.

Who is your role model?

My mother mostly. She always wanted to go back to school. She would say how lucky I was being in college. Now that she's back in school, she knows what I'm going through. Finals and everything. When I complained, she wouldn't understand; now she's on the same level. It's a good relationship. We're like best friends.

College choice?

I was thinking about going down south. I was even thinking about living away. My mother didn't want me to leave the house. She didn't want to let her baby go. She didn't want me to be too far away. I go home every night.

Your major?

Special education. I had a younger brother and he died a few years ago. He was mentally retarded. I used to do volunteer work at the different schools that he was in. I became interested in it. A personal situation led me into my major.

Your background—is it a help or a hindrance?

I wouldn't have picked the Italian course, if I weren't Italian. A lot of my friends are Spanish, French or something else. Even in high school I took Italian. It does help. I hear it with my grandmom. I can understand what she's saying. It helps. My family has a lot to do with my getting an education. We have a lot of tradition with Christmas and the other holidays. I can appreciate getting an education. My mother's paying for it.

Social life?

I dated a lot of Irish earlier. But now I'm starting to go for Italians. It just seemed to happen that way.

Choice of friends?

Most of my friends are Irish. People I went to high school with and that I met in college.

Does your background affect your activities?

No, I don't think it would matter.

Are your choices affected by your background?

It has a lot to do with my family. Italian families are different from other kinds of families. A lot of my choices are because of my family. We have a really strong relationship.

Examples?

Just the fact that my mom had her baby and she was older, and she and my father were having trouble; and my grandfather died right around then, and my grandmother moved in. Some families would have broken up because of that. But my grandmother is really strict with tradition and with being Italian. My mom was born in Italy. So it's a really strong positive thing. I don't think anything could break us up.

Future plans?

To start teaching right away and then go back for a

doctorate. I do want to get married, but not until I have a good career established.

Any restrictions as to moving away?

Not right now—I wouldn't do it. My mother wouldn't say I can't go. I just wouldn't want to move too far away from my home and family.

Religion?

My mother doesn't push religion on me as such—as much as my grandmother did with her. My mother was adopted by my grandmother, who was strict with her. I go to church every Sunday. It's just what I learned. I just do it.

Politics?

I have no real interest. I'm not active in politics. I don't belong to any political party.

Anything to add?

I think being Italian-American is being different from everyone else—the other nationalities. The family is really strong. I guess it's because we have more freedom in America than we would someplace else. I wouldn't choose to be anything else. I like being Italian-American, the security and the closeness of family. I guess because I was brought up with it, and I don't know how to do without it. Some of my Irish friends live away from their families. They couldn't care less and couldn't wait to get away to school. They thought I was crazy for not wanting to get away from home. Once they turned 18, they wanted to get out. I'm different that way.

Catherine M.

My non-Italian husband grew up in a predominantly Italian neighborhood in Warren, Ohio vowing to never marry one. We chuckle about it now because the only reasons he felt like that was due to "garlic breath" in study halls and all the arguing he remembers between driveways of residences and with other Italians in the neighborhood.

We have been married 26 years. He *loves* my being Italian, loves the food, the country, the music and caters to me when I express an interest in visiting Italian restaurants in town. He understands my need to be fed with all of this culture, and he enjoys it just as much as I do. His English and Scotch heritage is seldom mentioned and, although we have visited his countries, it is never the topic of conversation that our trip to Rome was or our trip to Sicily in two weeks will be.

Because my father "became" an American and lived away from the community, our upbringing was very *American,* also. Because of that, my parenting is also American.

Marie

I consciously selected an Italian to try to please my mother.

My choice of a career was that of wife and mother at the age of 17. This is the reason why. I was born to middle-aged parents in 1946. My mother was 40, my father was 49. When I was seven, my parents divorced, and my mother was left to care for me and my 17-year-old brother.

My mother expected to raise an American-born teenage girl in the 1960s as she had been raised in Sicily some 45 years earlier. It was a constant battle to be like my peers. Dating boys, riding in a car with a boy; my mother knew nothing of these customs. I was rebellious. The fights between my mother and me became unbearable and so I married. That resulted in my mother and I not speaking to each other for ten years. She never saw her only grandchildren until they were nine and five years old. This is how my Italian background had an effect on my choice of a "career."

My mother would have wanted me to go to college.

As a child I grew up in a Jewish neighborhood and ultimately was ignored and made to feel different. As an adult I have had no similar problems.

My husband is also Italian-American. I consciously selected an Italian to try to please my mother.

My 24-year marriage has deteriorated to the point of serious discussions of divorce. My husband was raised with the Italian male attitudes of generations ago. A wife is submissive, does not work and basically has no rights. His word is law. Twelve years ago I begged to be able to work part time. He reluctantly agreed as long as I didn't let my job interfere with my wifely duties. I received absolutely no help from my husband with household chores, or in the raising of our two sons.

My background affects my parenting in the sense of making my sons proud of their heritage. My 23-year-old son is very interested in his background. He has been to Italy four times and is fluent in the language.

Donna

Importance of education in your family?

Very important because my parents didn't go to college. They didn't have the opportunities presented to them. So they placed a lot of emphasis on education. I was always encouraged to do well and to try to do my best.

Education of parents?

My father went to high school, but he didn't go to college. My mother went to vocational school. She didn't go to a regular high school. And she didn't go to college.

Then they went into regular employment?

My mother worked up until about nine years ago and then she quit. And my father is a pension clerk in town.

Did they stress education?

Yes, they did stress education for me.

Did they support education?

My mother always tried to get involved in what I did. If I had a question, she always tried to answer it and tried to help me. Even if she really couldn't answer it, because her education was kind of minimal.

Did your father participate?

Not as much. He was not that much involved. The push for education comes more from my mother.

Your educational background?

I went to Catholic school in Philadelphia. Twelve years. Eight years of grammar school and four years of high school. This is my first year in college at Holy Family.

Your major in high school?

We didn't have a major. But I did take the academic course. I knew I wanted to further my education. I didn't have any interest in the business course.

Role model in school?

My sister was my role model. She was the one who really taught me how to read. And how to write, when I was little. She taught me a lot. My older sister taught me when I was two or three. By the time I got to kindergarten, I already knew how to write. All throughout grade school, my sister helped me a lot with math. She was a math major. I sort of got to like it, you know. Even when I was in high school, she continued to be my role model, all the time, rather than a teacher or a nun.

College choice and major?

I'm majoring in psychology. I liked this college because of its location and because it was Catholic and I wanted to commute. I didn't want to live away from home. I preferred it because I have a good home. It's part of my Italian background. The pull that keeps me closer to home. If I went away, I would miss it, the home cooking, the support of my family. Also, the college is located in a safe neighborhood.

What made you choose psychology as a major?

I took a psychology course during the summer (General Psychology), and I really liked it. And besides that, when I was in high school, I had health; and I always thought a lot about the brain and behavior, even though it was only a minor course in high school. I really enjoyed it.

What do your parents think about your major?

I haven't discussed my major with my parents in any great depth. It was my decision and they are backing it up. They have not pushed me to take something more practical. I want to go on to graduate school. At least to get a master's degree. From what I hear, you can't go very far with just a bachelor's degree. I'm not sure what I'll major in when I'm in graduate school. Probably in the same area of study.

Future plans?

Just graduate school for now, but I'm not sure on my major, at this time, as I said before.

Is your ethnic background a help or a hindrance, as to education?

It didn't hinder me in any way. I think it was a help. Support of my family and my whole upbringing; my parents, you know, always encouraging me to do well.

Socially?

My parents are strict. In a way there's a problem. I was brought up real sheltered; and I'm shy, because that's the way my parents were. It's very hard for me to socialize with people, especially with males.

Choice of friends?

It doesn't matter to me if they're Italian-Americans or not.

Activities?

If I were more outward, I would be more involved in activities. I'm not involved in any school activities.

Does your Italian-American background have an effect while you're in school?

I don't believe it has any effect at all.

On your personal freedom?

It did have an adverse effect. My parents were overprotective and it had an effect on my dating. When I talked to other girls, they didn't have a curfew—and I have.

On your choices?

It depends on what the choice is about. If it has to do with a moral choice, with another human being, I always try to make the choice as to what's best for the other person.

Is your interest in religion the same as your parents?

I would say no. My parents are more religious. My mother, especially. They go to church every Sunday, and I do, too. But they are more into ritual. They're from the old Catholic religion. They don't eat meat on Fridays, light candles in church, go to confession, even though they don't go to confession that much, while I don't go at all. So I'm less religious from a ritual and practicing standpoint. I think I'm more liberal in my religious outlook, and they're more structured; the catechism kind of thing, cut and dried, black and white.

Politics?

I have no interest in politics at all. And I don't even know what party my parents belong to. I don't talk to them about politics. They vote. But I don't have any interest in politics or the coming presidential elections. But they're not active, either.

Dating?—Boyfriends?

I didn't look specifically for an Italian-American. I date a non-Italian. And in a way, I'd rather he not be an Italian. I'd be afraid that he'd be too spoiled. Italian mothers have a tendency to spoil their sons. They might be stuck up, and I don't like that. Italian men have a tendency to be conceited.

Any pet peeves?

I have no problems with derogatory Italian references. The only regret I have is having been brought up being very sheltered. And when I hear other people talk about the things they do, like skiing, or whatever, it kind of makes me feel inferior that I haven't done all those things, also. Besides being shy, I'm timid, too. I hold myself back.

Colleen

I consciously selected a non-Italian, because my mother always told us never to marry an Italian.

My whole family of four children graduated from college, and we were all very supportive of each other. My mother pushed hard for us to get degrees and has been supportive since.

My husband wasn't Italian (we're divorced). I consciously selected a non-Italian male, because my mother always told us never to marry an Italian man. My father mistreated my mother, and she deeply resented it. She believed it was because of the way Italian men were traditionally raised; women in the home, men do whatever they please.

My husband thought I screamed too much and blamed it on my background. (Maybe it's true? Maybe not.)

I feel that I have a good attitude with my daughter because of my heritage. I had her when I was 30, and I wanted a child badly. Children are a very important part of my life, and without them, family life wouldn't be complete. I hope I can give her all that my mother has given to me. I am strict with her, but very loving, as I was raised.

Catherine C.

. . . unlike my mother, I do not treat my husband like a "king."

No, my husband is not an Italian-American. And

did I consciously select a non-Italian? Yes and no. My older sister married a fellow who was here on vacation from Italy. My parents knew him and his family. They were all from the same little town in southern Italy. My sister was young (I'm five years younger), and I was very surprised when my parents announced that she was marrying. This Italian visitor was here only a short time before marriage plans became a reality. Everything was rushed so he wouldn't have to return to Italy after his vacation visa expired. In a way, I suppose the marriage was an "arranged one." My sister eventually "fell in love" with her spouse, and they remain married to this day (21 years later). With this in mind, I suppose I could have deliberately not dated "Italian boys." Somehow, I did not want my parents to have that much control over my life, or I resented what they had been part of with my sister's marriage. However, with every boy I dated in college, the same questions were asked by my parents, especially my father: "Is he Italian? Are his parents Italian? Is he Catholic?" If he proved to be Polish or Jewish, etc., I knew they disapproved. They were prejudiced against other nationalities.

I married an Irish-German Protestant man who, at first, my parents did not like. After 1½ years of dating and my insistence to my parents that I loved him, we married. There were difficulties in the beginning because of our families. However, my parents soon realized that I was happy and that my husband was a good person regardless of his nationality. Today, they think the world of him.

My relationship with my husband is very good. I am not sure if my ethnic background affects this relationship. My Italian background definitely affects my idea that marriage is important, to be faithful and loyal to your partner, and to make a marriage work! Unlike my mother, I do not treat my husband like a "king." Instead, we share responsibility, and we are very considerate of each other. I cut the lawn if it is needed, and he vacuums if it is needed. There are no clear-cut "women's work" areas that are present in my parents' house. My father does not wash dishes, clean or cook. My mother does many subservient chores for my father, always has, always will. He is helpless in many ways and needs to rely on her.

I am strict with my children and cautious of their activities, as my parents were with me. However, unlike my childhood, my children have done so much more (economics being a factor). I grew up one of five children, so funds were limited. My dad worked two jobs. My two children have so much more than I ever had. In a way I'm grateful. In other ways I would love to be able to teach them the humility of coming from an ordinary family where love and sticking together is everything, where simpler pleasures are enjoyed.

Perhaps my mother's presence at home and, still to this day, influenced my choice to remain at home with my children. I have had part-time jobs off and on the past nine years since I stopped teaching. But my family has always remained my first priority when I have looked into part-time employment; can I be home in the summer? Can I be home by 3:30 for the children?

Also, my brothers and sister are so important to me. I miss them tremendously since my husband's job has taken us outside of driving range. My brothers and sister still live in the same town as my parents do. I'm the black sheep who has moved away. I wish I were closer, because I miss everyone and I love our family get-togethers at holidays. I want my sons to be around their aunts and uncles and grandparents, to witness strong family unity and develop strong family ties. My family is the most important thing to me; first my immediate family (husband and sons), and my extended family. I want my home to develop a loyalty and closeness that will stay with them through life, whether they're oceans apart or minutes away. My husband is not close to his brother as I am with mine, at least I don't witness the closeness, or see it revealed as often.

Also, as a daughter of Italian parents, I have been made to feel a lot of guilt for having moved away from the family. My mother still cries when we talk, and she lets me know that she wants all her children to be around her. Even though she left her parents in Italy in the fifties to come to the United States, she wants us to be living near her.

Rosina Raggio

Though my parents were not educated beyond elementary school, they were cultured people who had a great appreciation for education. My mother, in particular, wanted me to be a good student, and though I had a long list of tasks to do at home, she never let them interfere with studying. I never worked after school or on Saturdays because my parents thought I should spend my time being a good student. I was also allowed to be very active in school—the school paper, drama club, Catholic Action groups.

My father was a barber and he always wanted me and my brother and sister to be better educated than he. And although he had a very successful business in downtown Chicago, he refused to let my brother even think of taking it over. To be a professional person was very important to him. This may have come from the fact that my father's brothers in Italy were doctors and lawyers. If he had not come to America, he may have gone on to a profession. I think he wanted us to have what he never had—a profession, a position, a title.

My parents were proud that I was the first college graduate in the family, but my father would have preferred that I didn't have to be that educated person in the convent.

My early social life, that is before I went to the convent, was almost completely an extended family life. Though I had friends at school, as a family we socialized mostly with my mother's brothers and sisters. My father had only one nephew in the United States, and he was also included in this extended family.

Usually, my aunts and uncles and cousins came over to our house on Saturday evenings. They played cards or sat on the front porch while we played in the street or the vacant lot on the corner. Then my mother and my aunts would fix something to eat, and we would sit around eating for a while. People went home about ten or later, but they were all back again sometime on Sunday afternoon, when my mother held a kind of informal "open house." Her relatives would drop in and whoever was there when it was time to eat, ate with us.

We had a very matriarchal home. My mother was in charge, though my father was the titular head of the house. She made all the day-to-day decisions. He made all the big ones. My sister had to ask him if she could get married; I had to ask him if I could go to the convent; my brother had to ask him if he could volunteer for the Air Force in World War II.

My mother, the oldest of 12 children, was also a kind of matriarch to her brothers and sisters. She was the focus of their lives, too. As my mother's sisters and their families moved away, our family opened a little to nonfamily members. But my mother's best friends were always her sisters—and her expectations were that we would find our best friends among our cousins. I think my mother was a little disappointed that we didn't.

My parents were good, observant Roman Catholics. I think religion was a matter of habit, a matter of expectation. They didn't make much fuss about it. You were Catholic; you went to Mass; you obeyed the laws of the Church.

My mother's personal piety was tinged, in my opinion, with superstition and fear. "What will happen to us, if I don't go to Mass, or don't say the Rosary?" But she was sincere and devoted.

I left home at 16, a product of Catholic schools and began a formal study of theology when I entered college at 17. In my own way, I am religious, though not nearly as "observant" as my parents. This may have more to do with being a nun than with being Italian.

My parents were not active in party politics. My father was active in UNICO and the Order of the Sons of Italy and the Knights of Columbus. My mother was active in the Ladies of Isabella and parish and school activities.

In later years my parents voted for General Eisenhower because he was a hero of World War II. They liked Kennedy because he was a Catholic. And if they were still living, they would probably vote for Dukakis because his parents were immigrants. They weren't very sophisticated politically—but pretty consistent.

Denise D.

. . . my mother definitely steered me toward teaching. If you're a secretary, it's not that professional. A teacher is much nicer. It was that kind of thing.

Did your Italian-American background have an effect on your choice of a career?

No, but my mother had more or less to do with my choice of a career, she being an Italian-American. She was a seamstress and worked as a member of the International Ladies Garment Workers. She just retired after working 40 years. While I was growing up, she said to me, "You don't want to do this all your life. Break your back on a machine. You have a chance to get an education." At that time, teachers were respected. She thought it would be a wonderful job. I could be home at three o'clock, and if I got married and had children, I could still have the career. I could be off summers with them. She was giving me the whole thing; I could have a family and a career. I could do it all. She had stopped working when I was a little baby, then she went back when I was older, only now she worked in the neighborhood and could be home at four o'clock to prepare dinner. She didn't work in Manhattan anymore, because she didn't want to get home that late. It was sort of a part-time thing. Once in high school, and since I liked English, I decided to go into high school teaching. My mother had preferred elementary school. She pictured the little children. Teaching high school English instead, became my own choice. But my mother definitely steered me toward teaching. If you're a secretary, it's not that professional. If she had a daughter in 1988, she would not advise her to be a teacher, because she sees what has happened to the system. The abuse a teacher has to take, and now there are other fields open that are nicer for women. When I was going to school, there were only three choices, teacher, nurse, secretary. You could be a beautician, or any other kind of clerical or service worker, but that would be on another level, not professional. If you wanted to get some sort of education, you had business, but it had to be secretarial, you were not going to be a CPA. Times make the change. I wouldn't advise my child, male or female, to teach. If they wanted to, I would probably be so negative about it, they'd change their minds. My mother was negative toward the sewing field; no, that's backbreaking, a factory, horrible sweatshops. So I moved up to the next step—professional. But the teaching profession is not looked up to with the regard it used to have. So now I'm in a Ph.D. program. I got a fellowship scholarship. I might want a little better level than teaching. Maybe move into supervision. Once you have a Ph.D., you can manipulate a lot more. I've outgrown high school teaching after 16 years. Status quo is all right for some people who want that, but I feel that I'm still young, and to have to do the same thing, it's like rote now, nothing. I need to make the transition. So looking back, my mother did have some influence on my career choice.

Effect of your background on your career to the present?

I taught in a Catholic parochial school first. When I got out of college, there wasn't an abundance of teaching positions available because of Vietnam. It was a Dominican school and the nuns were mostly Irish-American. I didn't have any problems with them ethnically. They were having their own rivalries. Some had their own apartments, some didn't; who wanted you to watch for the kids' uniforms, some didn't care. It was traditional versus liberal rather than ethnic. In the public schools, in Lafayette High School in the Bensonhurst section of Brooklyn, which was more of an Italian area, the principal thought I related better to the students because I had an Italian last name. But some of the students didn't even realize that I was

Italian even though my name ended in a vowel. Some students would ask, "Are you Italian?" "How can you not think so with a vowel at the end of my name?" I'd reply. "You have a vowel at the end of your name." They thought that maybe I had married an Italian. Because all their teachers were Jewish. So I must've been Jewish even though my name ended in a vowel. Somehow, I was Jewish to them. So when they found out I was Italian, they tried to get me to pass them because we were both Italian. "You're Italian. I'm Italian. Give me a good mark. You're from Bensonhurst, too." That sort of thing. But they would tell me things. They were closer to me than to their other teachers, because they felt that ethnic bond. And I felt that I was a role model. Most of the students came from homes of blue-collar workers. Most of the girls, even though it was the seventies, still didn't aspire to higher goals. Very few went on to college. They became secretaries. They set lower goals for themselves. So with my being a role model, my ethnic background definitely entered into that. Later, I went on to teach at Madison. That school still has predominately Jewish teachers. From the principal on down, 90 percent of the staff is Jewish. Italians are a real minority in the New York City Board of Education. I found that the Christian teachers, whether Italian or Irish or other groups, do not complain as much as their Jewish colleagues. We do a lot more without getting a freebie thrown in. The typical New York Jewish teacher will say to an administrator that I'm not going to do *that* unless I get *this*. I felt that I was called upon to do some jobs because they knew that I wouldn't ask for anything special in return. I feel I did my job and what was asked of me because I was brought up that way. In Catholic school, you were taught not to question, just do it. My consciousness has been raised a lot more since I've been a teacher in public school situations. Now I say I'm not going to do *that*. I was too goody-goody in the beginning.

Another point about the effect on my career: When I told my principal that I was going on sabbatical for my dissertation, he wanted to know my topic. I told him it was the Italian Festa History in New York City from 1880 to the present. Then when I had to submit my application to the sabbatical committee, one of the people on the committee called me and said that she would be very interested in reading it. And my principal wanted to know why she called me. I told him that she wanted to know the exact date when I was going to finish my dissertation, so that she could read it. And he said, "Why would she want to read it, she's not Italian?" I couldn't believe that this was a principal speaking. How narrow can you get? I said to him, "You have to be Jewish to eat rye bread?" It was just a couple of months ago that that remark was made to me. I was so incensed. How could this man in the eighties say this to me? As if anyone who would want to look at this information would only be Italian. It boggles the mind. And he was named Principal of the Year by the Jewish League. So there has been an effect on my career, my being Italian.

Family support of professional goals?

My family was very supportive. The fact that I'm on sabbatical now, they came over yesterday and they were saying we won't be long, you should be working on your paper. My grandfather clock arrived yesterday, so they came to see it. They were always concerned about my work and my career, always encouraging. My mother would excuse me from doing any household

chores to study. "Go upstairs and study, you don't have
to help with the dishes." She wouldn't play any music,
so I could study. I was an only child. They didn't have
the problem of keeping the other children quiet, but
I'm sure if they did, they would have encouraged the
other children to study, also. It would have been a
quiet house, with everyone in his individual room
studying. But I was not the type that they had to push
to study. I was always worrying about failing this or
that. My father didn't have to point out a low grade
and say, "How dare you!" Never anything like that. Or
that I'd cut class. Never anything like that. But they
didn't say hurry up and get married. Never. It was the
opposite. My mother would say, "You got plenty of time
to get married, to cook, to clean, to shop. Study,
travel." My mother wasn't pushy in that area at all.
She got married relatively old, because my father was
in World War II. So they had to wait. She met him just
before he went in, and then they wrote. When he came
back after the war in the mid-forties, they had to save
money. And the thing that was traditional, there was
the fact that my father's mother died while they were
engaged; the family wouldn't let them get married for
a year. They had to observe a year of mourning. She
didn't get married until 1947. She knew my father at
least six years. She said, "We didn't have parents to
say, "Here's money for the wedding and the furniture."
So they needed time. He was in the army maybe three
years in Panama. My mother thought the year of
mourning was very old-fashioned, even ridiculous, because she was born here. My father was born in Italy.
He came here at age 12. But he was basically American. Still his relatives said, "No, you can't get married
for a year." My mother couldn't do anything about it.
They were both in their late twenties. My mother was
28, which could be considered old, especially back

then. But she had my father committed. She was secure in knowing they would be married someday. Today, there wouldn't be that kind of commitment. She
had known my father a month before he left for the
service. They wrote to each other every day. My
mother still has the piles of love letters.

My mother's sister didn't do that. Her sister also had a
boyfriend who was drafted, but she didn't want to
wait. She eloped. My grandmother was disgraced and
wouldn't talk to her. When she came back and had a
baby, my grandmother relented and accepted her back
into the family. The day my mother's sister eloped, my
grandmother went to her room and wouldn't talk
to anybody, because her daughter had slapped her in
the face.

My mother was not that kind. She was more respectful
toward her mother's needs and feelings. She would
never have eloped with my father. She thought her sister's eloping was wrong. She brought it up to me about
what her sister had done. After you raise a daughter,
to get such disrespect from her is wrong.

She also thinks that when a woman has lived with a
man, to wear a white gown at the wedding is ridiculous. But even though I think so, too, if she wants to
get dressed up as a bride, okay, every girl has her day.
I don't see this living together thing myself. I didn't
date my husband for years on end. We met, dated and
got engaged within eight months. We were older already. If you're in your early twenties and still going
to college, or trying to save money, it holds up the
works. But if you're older and you know what you
want, that's it, there's no living together.

I wanted to get my own apartment when I was 30.
I was still at home. My parents felt it was ridiculous
for me to move out and gave me a hard time about
it. My mother made me feel really guilty, and I was
not strong enough to say, "Look, I'm doing it." They
would've been so devastated if I had left. I couldn't
have taken the grief that they would've given me. The
emotional turmoil would've been too much. Since I was
the only one, it made it worse. If I had a brother or a
sister, it would've been easier for me to make the
break. So, finally, in my parents' two-family house, I
got to move to the other place. That's as liberated as I
got: I moved downstairs. I had my own separate entrance and my own apartment. My parents felt comfortable with that, even though they thought it was
silly. Okay, she's 30, unmarried, she wants her own
space. Now I didn't have to bring in my dates to meet
my parents every time I went out. Who needs that?
Sometimes you go out with the guy only once. While I
was living with my parents the last year, I would meet
most of my dates someplace else, at a restaurant or
something. If it went beyond that, I'd have them pick
me up at the house. I didn't want to go through the
formal introductions to my parents with every Joe
Shmoe that I dated. Finally, when I had my own
apartment, it was different. I could relax. But the
irony of it was that within six months of having my
own apartment, I met my husband. He turned out to
be Mr. Right. I had the apartment furnished since my
father sold furniture, and I could buy better things at
cost. My husband was impressed with my furnished
place. Most young girls on their own have any old slop
together. So it was a positive thing for him to see that
I knew how to keep a place. After we married, we lived
in my apartment. And after that, we lived in a two-

family house owned by my husband's people, before coming to New Jersey because of my husband's job and buying this house. Then my parents sold their house in Brooklyn and moved to New Jersey to one of those adult communities in the Whiting area. My father even changed his job to New Jersey, but now he's retired. They followed me to be closer. It was a good excuse, since my father wanted out of Brooklyn. I led them to New Jersey. My father's sister lives next door to them on their cul-de-sac in Crestwood Village. She did the same thing. Two of her children live in New Jersey; so she sold and moved here. Brooklyn people are moving to Staten Island, and Staten Island people are moving to New Jersey.

Does your Italian-American background affect your professional relationships?

At New York University, going for this doctorate, the topic was proposed by my advisor, who is non-Italian. He suggested that I do the Italian-American festa in Manhattan. He said, "You're Italian. Why don't you do that? You taught in Catholic school. You'll be able to get through all the ins and outs necessary to interview the people you have to, like the church people, and go to the festa." He thought I'd have a very easy time. They were into this ethnic and racial thing at NYU. Somebody was doing the Yiddish theatre and somebody was doing the Black theatre, and because I was Italian, that topic was suggested. It might be kind of fun. Little did I know that it was very complicated and extremely difficult. I've had problems getting information. A lot of the church people don't want to give it, or they threw it all out long ago. Italians are very secretive and suspicious. It happened with the festa club on Mulberry Street. They did not allow me to interview them just because I was a female. They didn't want any women in there: from the president on down. I went there and they told me that I couldn't go in. "What is this for? What do you want? We're not going to show you any financial transactions." I think they were afraid I was going to uncover something *funny.* "No," I said, "it's historical. I just want to know about the festa, nothing about the money." They replied, "We don't have anything. We threw the old records out. Go to the church, if you want information about the festa. Our Lady of Pompeii and Precious Blood." They were like the mafiosa types. I went to the churches and they didn't have anything. They never save records. The priest said, "Go to the New York Public Library." I didn't need him to tell me that. "Go to the New York Times." I had looked through the Times already. The New York Times is not what I needed; I needed hands-on things from their archives. He said, "We don't have any archives." I told my advisor about my difficulties getting information from the Italians in Little Italy. That they are not nice and wholesome and cooperative as you think they are, and not receptive to women. So what did I have to do to get access to the festa club? Two men had to go with me. My father was working at that time for a furniture store down there, and the store would donate to the festa club, ads in the booklet, pledges; and my father's boss knew the president. So they had the manager of the store call up the president of the festa club and say there's a girl who would like to interview you about the festa. They agreed only because of that. But when I went there, I had to go with two godfathers—the manager and my father. And they warned me beforehand that they wouldn't talk about money. I told them that I didn't intend to ask them about financial matters. But they had very little to tell me. They were not historians, by any means. I knew more about the feast already than they actually did. They gave me a couple of brochures from recent years. I really didn't get anything valuable from them. So I've had to switch gears and do less on the Manhattan-based festa and do more on the festa styles, about all the other things, such as the bands and other festas.

Effect of your background on your social life?

The strong sense of family has an effect. I wound up marrying an Italian. I met him at a party at my place where everybody invited was supposed to bring one male friend. We wanted more single men there. And it turned out that he was a last-minute invitation, since he met my girl friend's boyfriend on Wall Street. They had gone to college together and hadn't seen each other for a while. My girl friend suggested to her boyfriend to call and invite him to the party. Actually, I didn't talk to him that much because of the large, successful turnout. I just said a few words to him. He went to St. Francis and I went to St. Joseph's. They were brother and sister schools. We just talked about mutual friends and about my dissertation. And when he asked me what I was going to do with it, I replied, "Not much." He liked the answer. That I didn't give him a long spiel about being liberated and was casual about the whole thing. Then one thing led to another, and as they say, the rest is history.

Your background and friends?

Not all my friends were Italian. I had Jewish friends, Irish friends. I branched out socially. I was engaged to a Jewish man when I was 25. My family liked him, but my mother said to make sure you get married in the

Church and raise the kids Catholic. After we got engaged, he started saying that he didn't want anything
Catholic. There was pressure on my side and on his
side and we ended the engagement. He really wasn't
religious. He could've gone either way. He got cold feet
when it came to getting married. A few years later, he
wrote to me and said he wanted to go back with me
and was sorry he made a negative decision. But no
way for me. After that I just refused to go out with
anybody who was not Catholic. I didn't want to put up
with that again. It was the late seventies and people
said you could work it out, but when it came down to
the wire, it didn't work for me and it didn't work for
him. Now that I'm married, I realize it would not have
worked out. My husband and I are Italian-Americans
raised similarly. He's one of three children. We went to
Catholic schools and colleges, yet there are still differences. Personality differences. So if we had all the
other differences, it would lead to only more problems.
I wanted to keep my name. I do use it professionally
on occasion. I was not even going to use his. But he
said, "No way!" He's from a long-time Italian-American
family. His parents were born here, his grandparents
were born here; you'd think he'd be a little more ad-
vanced, a little more liberated. But no. He said, "There
will be no wedding unless you take my name." I
thought it was stupid. But all right, I can bend, so I
took it. When it's professional, I hyphenate my name;
but when I get my degree, I want my diploma to have
both names.

*Did you consciously select an Italian-American for a
mate?*

I don't think I did, but since that bad experience, I
limited my choices, vowing to never go out with anyone

who was Jewish. I would have gone out with Irish-Catholics or German-Catholics, maybe even a Protestant. But I wanted to go for the closest to my own. Things just worked out for me. I had never married, he wasn't divorced. It helped a lot. A lot of people are divorced by age 30. They don't want to get married again, or they don't want kids. You have to listen to a lot of sob stories, the whole saga of their lives. I was getting ready to do my dissertation, so I joined Italian-American cultural organizations and a political club to meet more Italian-American professional men. That was the problem. Here I am well-educated and a lot of Italian men were not. They were blue collar. It was difficult in New York to meet an Italian-American man who was 30, professional and not married. I didn't have anything in common with the Joe Blows from Brooklyn who could hardly speak English. But all the nice men in those clubs were married. So I guess meeting my husband was my destiny. He wasn't seeing anybody at the time of my party. He was educated. He was single. He was Italian-American. He was made to order.

How does your background affect your relationship with your husband?

I think he thinks I should be a better cook. Being Italian, I should really slave over the stove. "Your mother makes it. Learn from her." He likes a good meal. His mother served him and he likes to be served. After his mother died, his sister served him. That catering kind of thing. The other day I had to go out. I left him to take care of himself. I told him there were stuffed shells in the freezer and to stick them in the microwave oven. There's sauce there. You can do the whole thing. "Write it out," he said. He's helpless. I got home that night tired after doing interviews, and he had it all prepared and he did serve me. A step forward. There's hope for him that he's supportive. This male thing could be Italian, or it could be European in general. When we first moved to this residential complex, there was a block party. The people living here are mixed nationalities, religions, including Italians. And one lady, who was Jewish from Long Island, I thought she'd be above it. When she met me and heard my Italian name said, "Oh, are you related to the Mafia?" I thought, what kind of nonsense is this? I said to her, "Well, that's ridiculous. In this day and age, just because my name ends in a vowel, I would automatically be involved in the Mafia?" I was annoyed. I couldn't believe her. I got on a committee in this development to find out what's going on. We meet in different homes, and you can see the differences in how people live. The house where they were obviously more Americanized, the wife was aloof and didn't serve or cater to us, the husband took care of what was available and we served ourselves. The other house where the name was not American but European, the wife served us in the dining room. She wasn't on the committee. The husband had her there to be maid service, while in the other home the wife was Miss Glamorpuss and didn't bother with us. The different ethnic socialization was pointed out to me by one of my neighbors when we left. I didn't even think of it myself. My neighbor said her husband would serve, but she'd probably prepare everything. My husband would have probably have said, "I'll serve the people, but you prepare everything." You know, get the dishes out, as if he never lived here. Where's this, where's that?

Children?

I would like to have children, but I've had two miscarriages. My husband said that he can't take it. One more miscarriage and that's it. I'm not going through that again. He says he can't deal with it, watching me like that. Me, I'm still saying let's give it another shot.

Your religious beliefs in comparison to your parents?

We're still practicing Catholics. My parents believe in a more naive way, since they were never schooled in the Scriptures. My husband and I had all the theology courses in Catholic schools and colleges, while my parents went to public schools. That kind of thing gives us different pictures of religion. We ended up getting more than they did as far as religion was concerned. A different foundation from that of our parents.

Politics?

My interest is in between mildly and very. I was in a political organization: The Democratic Club. I worked in a few campaigns, going around getting petitions signed, basic political legwork. I worked for Cuomo when he was running for mayor of New York. If he ever ran for President of the United States, I would want to help. I would work for a non-Italian candidate, if I thought it worthwhile. I don't have a definite party at present. I have worked for other Italian candidates besides Cuomo.

Did your background affect your choice of political party?

My parents were Democrats, but my father is more independent now. He'll go with the candidate he likes. He doesn't vote for just the Democratic candidate. And besides being Democrats, Italians had the union mentality. But it was for their own protection. Even the social clubs were for their protection as well as their social lives when they came here from Italy. The feasts were really supported through the social clubs, not the churches. The churches got a kickback. That's why that festa club in Manhattan didn't want to devulge any information to me about their financial activities.

Nicole

I understand that you have a special story to tell about your birth.

Every February eighth (my birthday), my mother told me the story of her arrival to this country and that of my birth. It became a ritual that the story be told.

My father had been a married man with three children. He, for profit and/or adventure, traveled across the ocean to America very often. He'd come to America, work for some time, then return to his hometown, Pescara. When my father's wife died, he needed a new wife to help raise his three children. And so it was that my father, through some intermediary, learned about a woman in her forties who never married. She lived in the next town.

When the intermediary approached my mother's father to ask him if she'd like to marry a man with three children, my mother "jumped in" and said, "Yes, *IF* he promises to take me to America." Naturally, my father promised.

After the nuptials were arranged, my mother gathered

her *biancheria* [handmade bed linens and pillowcases], and they were married.

Soon after the marriage was consummated, my father, for reasons which were never totally explained, said to my mother: "Why do we want to go to that cold country? Why take chances? We have a piece of land here. Let's stay here, work the land, and live comfortably." My father obviously did not know the extent of my mother's desire to come to America. She was furious. She must have ranted and raged. She refused to listen to any explanations. She said that he had reneged on his promise. It must have been quite a scene. Being pregnant with me, she said, "I want my child to be born in America. That's that!" She must have nagged him until he "caved in," or she must have pushed him to the shipping office. But whatever, she got her way. And so my parents came to America: he for the sixth or seventh time; she for the first time; and both of them for the last time, for my mother vowed never to return to Italy.

They arrived in America two months before I was born. Although my mother never mentioned it, the crossing must have been horrible for her, since she was in the seventh month of her maternity.

When they arrived in this area, they lived in a shack-like hut on some friend's property in West Trenton. The conditions were not fit for human habitation. There was no heat. A metal box for firewood, which was placed in the middle of the floor, served as the heating unit.

The shack had a flimsy roof. On the night of my birth, a severe blizzard raged outside and inside, for a part of the roof gave way, creating a hole. Snow poured into the shack as my mother, aided by a midwife, brought her American baby into the world as she had dreamed.

In telling the story of how I was born under adverse conditions, my mother wanted to remind me of my own strength. In retrospect, the story reveals my *mother's* strength: a woman, uneducated and approaching menopause, who came to America so that her children would be born here.

BOOK THREE

SELF

My father discouraged my interest in law by saying that it was no place for a woman, associating with criminals as I would have to do as a lawyer, so I became a teacher.

Carol Bonomo
Ahearn

I was encouraged to leave school upon high school graduation.

Sofia

With my daughter, I want her to try everything. I want her to be exposed to everything. I want a more expanded world for her.

Kelly

As an Italian-American woman I had to work harder than most to prove that I could achieve my goals and objectives.

Piccolina

There is a positive image to being an Italian female, since Italian fashion, sports cars and actresses such as Sophia Loren present such a positive image in the world today.

Dale

I have never appreciated the role I perceive the female to play who lives with an Italian male.

Elia

DEDICATION TO ITALIAN WOMEN IMMIGRANTS
SPEECH BY JANICE A. PICCININI TO
THE AMERICAN COMMITTEE ON
ITALIAN MIGRATION
NOVEMBER 5, 1988

THIS EVENING IS DEDICATED TO THE ITAL-
IAN WOMEN IMMIGRANTS WHOSE STRENGTH,
DEDICATION AND LOYALTY BUILT THE FOUNDA-
TION AND FRAMEWORK OF THE ITALIAN-
AMERICAN CULTURE.

THEIRS IS NOT ONE STORY BUT MILLIONS
OF STORIES FILTERED THROUGH INDIVIDUAL
FAMILY HISTORIES AND MEMORIES, DEPICTING
THE PROFOUND DETERMINATION OF ITALIAN
WOMEN TO PRESERVE THE SANCTITY AND DU-
RABILITY OF THE FAMILY AS A UNIT. THE INEV-
ITABILITY OF CHANGE THRUST UPON THESE
GENTLE AND SELFLESS WOMEN WAS ELO-
QUENTLY CAPTURED IN THE WORDS OF AN
ITALIAN MOTHER WHO WHISPERED TO HER
SON WHILE WORKING IN THE FIELDS OF
ABRUZZI:

"YOUR FATHER HAS DECIDED TO GO TO
AMERICA. . . . I CANNOT BLAME HIM. HE WORKS
SO HARD. AND WE NEVER SEEM TO GET ANY
BETTER. I MUST BEND MYSELF TO WHAT HAS
TO BE."

THUS BEGAN THE EXPERIENCE OF IMMI-
GRATION FOR THE ITALIAN WOMAN. FRIGHT-
ENING, OFTEN PAINFUL. IT IS A SERIES OF
STORIES: OF HUSBANDS LEAVING THEIR WIVES
AND CHILDREN, OFTEN TO RETURN TO BRING

THEM BACK TO AMERICA; OF YOUNG ITALIAN MEN LEAVING THEIR NATIVE LAND, ONLY TO GO BACK TO MARRY A TRUE DAUGHTER OF ITALY AND THEN RETURN WITH HER TO START AN AMERICAN FAMILY; OF MARRIED ITALIAN WOMEN, WHO IN THEIR OWN COUNTRY WOULD NOT GO UNCHAPERONED TO THE NEXT VILLAGE, CROSSING THE ATLANTIC, NEGOTIATING THE IMMIGRATION SYSTEM, TRAVELING ALONE WITH HUNGRY, FRIGHTENED CHILDREN WITH ONE GOAL IN MIND—TO REUNITE THE FAMILY.

TO SOME SHE WAS UNKNOWN EXCEPT AS A NAME ON A STEERAGE LIST. BUT TO MANY IN THIS ROOM, SHE WAS KNOWN AS *"MAMA."* TO OTHERS SHE WAS *"NONA."* TONIGHT WE REFLECT ON HER AS THE MOTHER OF ALL ITALIAN-AMERICANS.

YOU REMEMBER HER. . . .

SHE CAME TO THESE SHORES BECAUSE THE FAMILY WAS THE FIXED CENTER OF HER LIFE AND SHE RELINQUISHED HER OWN DESIRES TO HER FAMILY'S NEEDS. SHE DID NOT COME WITH IDEAS OF SELF-TRANSFORMATION; RATHER, SHE CHERISHED HER ROLE AS THE GUARDIAN OF A CLASSIC CULTURE IN THIS NEW WORLD, AS THE SOURCE OF STABILITY AND FAMILIARITY FOR HER FAMILY, AND AS THE PROVIDER OF NOURISHMENT AND NUTURING THAT ONLY A MOTHER CAN GIVE.

SHE WAS ENORMOUSLY RESILIENT, THIS DAUGHTER OF ITALY. WITHOUT BENEFIT OF AN EXTENDED FAMILY OR UNDERSTANDING OF THIS COUNTRY, ITS PEOPLE OR ITS LANGUAGE, SHE WAS DOGGEDLY DETERMINE TO CREATE A HOME AS IF THE CLUTTERED STREET ON WHICH SHE LIVED WERE HER NATIVE VILLAGE.

SHAPED TO RESEMBLE HER VALUES AND LIFE-STYLE, HER HOME WAS A SANCTUARY, AN INSULAR ETHNIC SUPPORT SYSTEM FOR THOSE WHO MUST "AMERICANIZE" BEYOND ITS BOUNDARIES. IT REFLECTED THE SILENT ELOQUENCE OF HER ENDLESS WORK TO ASSURE THAT RELIGIOUS AND CULTURAL TRADITIONS WOULD ALWAYS REMAIN CONSTANT. IT WAS HERE THAT SHE COMFORTED, ENCOURAGED, DRIED THE MANY TEARS AND SHARED THE FEARS OF HER HUSBAND AND CHILDREN. AND IT WAS FROM THE SECURITY OF THIS HOME THAT SHE WITNESSED AN EMERGING GENERATION OF ETHNIC AMERICANS COMMITTED TO SPEAKING ENGLISH, VYING FOR SUCCESS IN MAINSTREAM AMERICAN SOCIETY.

SHE WAS ACCUSTOMED TO POVERTY IN BOTH WORLDS BUT VIEWED "WORK" AS THE VITAL EXPRESSION OF HOPE FOR THE FUTURE IN AMERICA. THE FUTURE WAS FOR HER CHILDREN; OPPORTUNITY WAS FOR HER CHILDREN; FINANCIAL SUCCESS WAS FOR HER CHILDREN—BUT NOT WITHOUT WORK. THOUGH SHE SELDOM VENTURED FAR FROM HER HOME, IT WAS NOT UNCOMMON FOR THESE WOMEN TO WORK IN THE GARMENT FACTORIES OR TAKE IN PIECE WORK, STITCHING BUTTONS AND LININGS LONG INTO THE NIGHT, OFTEN PLACING A CHAIR UPON THE KITCHEN TABLE TO BE CLOSER TO THE LIGHT. TO HER, SELF-SACRIFICE WAS PART OF RAISING A FAMILY, BUT WORK WAS THE HYMN OF LIFE.

PERHAPS HER MOST EFFECTIVE MEANS OF COMMUNICATING WITH THE OUTSIDE WORLD WAS THROUGH HER COOKING. THE AROMA FROM HER KITCHEN ENABLED HER TO SHARE

HER ITALIAN HERITAGE BETTER THAN ANY
LANGUAGE. SHE ALWAYS USED IMPORTED OL-
IVE OIL REGARDLESS OF FINANCIAL RE-
STRAINTS. BUT THEN, SHE ALWAYS DID
MANAGE TO MAKE ENDS MEET NO MATTER
HOW DIFFICULT THE TIMES. REMEMBER HOW
SHE MADE HOMEMADE SAUCE AND SOUP FROM
SCRATCH *EVERY DAY*! AND HOMEMADE NOO-
DLES WERE A HOUSEHOLD STAPLE, NOT TO
MENTION THE PROSCIUTTO AND CHEESE SENT
OVER BY RELATIVES FROM THE HOMELAND.
CHILDREN FROM THE NEIGHBORHOOD GATH-
ERED IN HER KITCHEN AS THOUGH THE WORD
"FOREIGN" DIDN'T EXIST. AS TIME PASSED,
ITALIAN FOOD BECAME A COMMON PART OF
AMERICAN LIFE AND OTHER ITALIAN INFLU-
ENCES FOLLOWED. ALL OF THIS, FROM A
WOMAN COOKING FOR HER FAMILY.

RETURNING TO HER HOMELAND FOR A
VISIT WAS ONE OF THE FEW DREAMS SHE AL-
LOWED FOR HERSELF, AND SHE SPOKE OF IT
OFTEN. YEARS LATER, WHEN SHE DID RETURN,
SHE SENSED A CHANGE. TO BE SURE, ALL
SEEMED LESS GRAND THAN HER CHILDHOOD
MEMORIES, BUT THE DIFFERENCE THAT
ELUDED HER WAS CLEAR TO HER ITALIAN FAM-
ILY AND FRIENDS. IT WAS *SHE* WHO HAD
CHANGED. SHE SEEMED MORE INDEPENDENT,
SELF-ASSURED, MORE IN COMMAND—AS IF SHE
HAD MASTERED SOME GREAT TEST. YES, ITALY
WOULD ALWAYS BE HER BELOVED HOMELAND,
BUT SHE WAS ANXIOUS TO RETURN HOME.

SHE HAD STARTED ON A JOURNEY THAT
WOULD TRANSFORM AMERICA, AND IN THE
PROCESS, SHE HAD TRANSFORMED HERSELF.
SHE WAS, INDEED, AN ITALIAN WHO BECAME

AN AMERICAN—ONE EQUALLY PROUD OF THE CULTURE SHE HAD BROUGHT WITH HER AND THE NEW ONE SHE HAD HELPED CREATE. I DON'T KNOW WHEN SHE STOPPED BEING AN ITALIAN AND STARTED BEING AN AMERICAN. MAYBE IT WAS THE MINUTE SHE SET FOOT ON ELLIS ISLAND. OR MAYBE SHE NEVER DID. MAYBE THE MIRACLE OF AMERICA IS THAT SHE DID NOT HAVE TO STOP BEING ONE TO BECOME THE OTHER.*

FOR HER MANY CONTRIBUTIONS TO THIS COUNTRY, THE ITALIAN IMMIGRANT WOMAN RECEIVED MOSTLY SILENCE IN OUR HISTORY BOOKS. TO BE SURE, SHE DID NOT FEEL SUFFICIENTLY SELF-IMPORTANT TO LEAVE A WRITTEN RECORD OF HERSELF, ALTHOUGH OTHERS MIGHT HAVE. STILL, SHE GAVE SO MUCH MORE THAN SHE TOOK FROM LIFE, AS IF AT SOME FUTURE DATE WE MIGHT UNWRAP A GIFT OF THOUGHT FROM HER. HER LEGACY TO US WAS THE DETERMINATION TO MEET THE NEW WORLD ON ITS OWN TERMS AND TO GIVE TOMORROW TO HER CHILDREN.

WE ARE HER CHILDREN. WE ARE HER LEGACY. WE ARE LIVING A LIFE SHE TOOK FOR DREAMS.

YES, WE REMEMBER HER. . . .

LIKE HER CULTURE, SHE PERSONIFIED VALUES THAT TRANSCEND TIME AND PLACE.

LIKE HER LIFE, HER FACE WAS DIGNIFIED BY A GRACE OF ITS OWN NATURE.

SHE DESERVES TO BE REMEMBERED.

*Adapted from comments by Lee Iacocca included in his Epilogue in the book *The Italian Americans* by Allon Schoener; Macmillan Publishing Company, 1987.

SHE HAD THE COURAGE TO MAKE HOPE
COME TRUE IN OUR LIVES.

TO US SHE WAS, AND TO THE FUTURE SHE
WILL BE, AS BEAUTIFUL A SPECIMEN OF MOTH-
ERHOOD AS GOD COULD PRODUCE.

* * * *

Italia

I obtained my Bachelor's Degree in Education in
1954 when it was the norm for all women to enter into
the teaching or nursing fields.

I do not feel that being an Italian-American has
had any effect on my career because of the nature of
the community in which I worked. The entire community was composed of sons and daughters of immigrants from Eastern Europe, mainly Polish. There
were virtually no Italians in the community and minimal prejudice against anyone from a different background. I do not feel that the prejudice, which is being
lashed out against Italian-Americans today, began until the media barrage started in Hollywood in the
1970s. Apparently, the entertainment industry has an
extreme interest in bashing one ethnic group. Their
lack of creativity can find no other theme for scripts
except Mafia madness, in my opinion, because we permit them to do so.

My family was extremely supportive of my professional goals. My father, who emmigrated to the USA in
1912 at age 12, became an attorney in 1929 and prac-
ticed law for almost 50 years. My brother, who passed
away in 1980, was also an attorney.

Because of the fact that the school system in
which I work has now become largely Black and Lat-

ino, the entire system has become extremely politicized. However, as there are approximately only four teachers of Italian extraction in the entire school system, we have no power, and I do not feel that my heritage has much bearing on anything.

I do not feel that my ethnic background has affected my social life because of the ethnic diversity of the community. However, I am sure that this is not true in other less diverse areas of the country.

I have never married.

I feel that my religion is as meaningful to me as it was to my parents.

I am extremely interested in politics, probably because my parents were highly interested in the subject. The main topic around the dinner table was usually politics, and thus we children became interested. I find it endlessly fascinating.

I don't feel that my Italian-American background has had any effect on my choice of a political party as I am an Independent. However, I was happy to see Geraldine Ferraro become active on the national level. I felt that the press was extremely unfair to her and that she paid a heavy price because of her Italian background. In my opinion, the hatred of the media toward anything Italian was never more obvious than in their biased reports on her campaign.

Antonina

I feel that being Sicilian-American had no effect on my professional life. It simply never was relevant.

As for my religion, it is not as meaningful to me as it was to my parents.

I am extremely interested in politics. My parents

came from a town in Sicily that was instrumental in turning the tide for Garibaldi's *Reggimento,* so I grew up hearing of that and other political subjects. Because this village is considered radical, my politics have been liberal, following this tradition.

I am more active politically than my parents. They always voted and studied issues, but because of the language barrier and prejudice, stayed in the background. I work in campaigns and contribute money.

Terri

My mother would help us in the beginning when we were in school, up until high school. She went only to the third grade in Italy. She wanted us girls to do better, to get out of the rut.

My mother always thought that I ought to be a teacher. She liked that very much. I sort of went along with her. Every child wants to be a teacher in first grade. So I carried it through. My mother thought it would be nice. My father thought it was fine. Anything else he wouldn't go for. My sisters had battles with him. One wanted to be a nurse. What?! One wanted to be a secretary. He knew what went on in the office. My younger sister went into buying for stores and things like that. All my father could think of was bed pans, when it came to nursing, for my one sister. My other sister went to business school for a while and then she got a state job and that pleased my father, because she wouldn't be one-on-one with a man in an office. She was in a big office with a lot of girls. That was a different office situation. My father's Italian male fear of other males was alleviated.

One teacher at the Trenton Normal School didn't want anybody to know he was Italian, since he had an Anglicized name. He came from a real good family from North Jersey. His brother sang in the opera, a couple of sisters were at Montclair College. How he got relegated down here, I'll never know. But he was strange that way. In fact he's the one who told us that if we wanted to get jobs, to remove the vowel at the end of our names. Of course, it was depression time, and they were strict on whom they were picking up. That's what he told us. And he never let us know that he was Italian. Everybody around there knew him. Students were coming from North Jersey, too, and they knew the family. He taught us the math class. And it was the little things, like when he came in to tell us our test results, and he looked right at me and said: "And you had to have a perfect paper." It was the way he said it. My friend in class asked me why didn't he want me to have a perfect paper. He resented me, the Italian, doing better than the non-Italians in the class. He didn't want to give his own kind credit. We didn't like him and feared him, but we would never stand up to him or anything like that. Everything depended on getting through school, on getting a job. But very few of us got jobs. We had to go out on our own and get substituting jobs. The school never really helped us get them. The girls who had contacts, at wherever they came from, used those people who had the influence to put them in a teaching position. But those of us who didn't have any connections, we had to fend for ourselves.

I never pushed my nationality. And I never found any resentment toward me and my background. But I was considered to be a "crackerjack" sub. In fact they used to send me to the hard classes. I needed the money so bad that I would go into a class with a lot of boys, the manual training classes where they sawed and hammered wood all day long. Other girls would refuse to take those classes. I got along well with everybody, my supervisors and the other teachers.

My mother would help us in the beginning when we were in school, up until high school. She couldn't help us with algebra or other subjects. She went only to the third grade in Italy. She could help us with long division. She wanted us girls to do better, to get out of the rut. She had foresight. She was bright and had the gumption to want more for her family. When things got tough, she went to work in the "Doll" factory. A lot of women in that area worked there. Worked and maintained their homes. The day had passed for some of them to just stay home and do only housework. They would help each other in the neighborhood. There was a coat factory on Carroll Street that farmed out coat work. Somebody told them that some lady had girls, but that she wouldn't let them come up to the factory. And the bosses said that they had work that could be taken to their home. So every night about six this man would come to our house with bundles of coats and my mother would make buttonholes, while I would stitch the lining under the collar and my sisters would stitch the lining in the sleeves. It all had to be done by hand. My mother got two cents apiece for those buttonholes. I learned how she did it, giving each buttonhole that beaded look on better garments. So we learned from her while she was earning money for us.

There were other Italian-Americans in various schools in the Trenton system. I was in Harrison, and I was the only one of Italian extraction, until one other Italian came to the school. In my school we had a nice group. And I never had any problems with the other teachers about being Italian. There were cliques in other schools by the floors, but I was never bothered with that kind of thing.

During the war we used to go to the Old Barracks on Willow Street to help roll bandages. In those days during the Second World War you could walk on State Street and Willow Street without getting clobbered. And we'd work there from seven to nine, my sister and I. Things like that. We'd come home together. We used to visit with some Italian girls, because they had a brother who was a priest. We knew most of the professionals. We had to, how could you miss? And we attended different affairs to support different groups. But our social life did revolve more around our family at that time. Families were important in those days. They're not as important now as they were then. My sister likes to keep the family together. That's why she spends so much time shopping for family members and mailing the things to them. Family members lived closer to one another those days. You didn't need a car to get around to see them. And we walked. On Sundays we would go to somebody's house; somebody who knew how to tell our fortunes with cards, something like that. We'd laugh and talk, it was fun. We were comfortable with one another. We didn't always receive acceptance from other kinds of people. We got our acceptance from within our own family, and from our own kind. Families were pretty big, and by the time you visited this one and that one, it took up all your free time.

As for a spouse, I didn't select my husband because he was an Italian. It was an accident. And in our relationship, there's nothing going on that's really ethnic; not after 40 years. I do the masculine things. I handle the money. He doesn't want to be bothered. We never had any differences like that.

My mother was more religious than my father, especially from a ritual standpoint. I try to do the holidays and things like that and I donate to the church. But oldtimers were more religious, going to Mass every morning. Even my father went to church every Sunday, the last Mass, but he went.

I was more active in politics when I was younger, but I'm still interested. We helped to organize the Young Republicans in Mercer County. We had meetings and picnics and tried to organize the Italians, but we didn't stand a chance with them. We became Republicans after my father had a run-in with some Democrat. He used to do a lot of work for the Democrats for nothing. Other men from different nationality groups made sure they got paid for any work they did. My father always figured that someday the party would help us when we needed it. But it didn't turn out that way. So he got mad and switched parties. The Young Republicans did get the younger Italians to go Republican and some seniors to go with them, also, after they got the young ones. My father went to the meetings, but my mother just went to the polls to vote. We told her how to vote. She could read the names. We got my sister a job on the polls during one election, and didn't we have trouble with one of our own kind about my sister being underage. We needed that money for the family. We had to get some politician to help her stay on the job. My mother got so mad that she went to that woman's bar and told her off about what she had tried to do against my sister. We children were more active in politics in general than our parents were, but we aren't as active now; although we still belong and still donate to the party.

Lois

All my growing-up years I was told that women

should be teachers or secretaries. They did not need an education, because they would get married early and have babies. I was 21 when I married and was almost the last one of my friends to get married. My family kept saying that I would never have babies; I was getting too old. I had three children by the time I was 27.

Because I had no education other than high school (secretarial training), I am still doing secretarial work. I quit my job when I had babies and only did part-time work that was convenient to my family members' schedules until I went back to work when my last child was in junior high school. I have progressed somewhat in the secretarial field in the last eight years, and I am now an Ad Executive Secretary/ Administrative Assistant. Basically, though, this is still secretarial work and not much different from the work I did in 1958 right out of high school.

I stopped going to church a long time ago when it became too much of a struggle to get three children dressed and ready to go. It wore me to a frazzle every Sunday morning. Also, I feel that the Church is another stronghold of male dominance, and I do not care to be a part of prolonging this male-controlled domain.

Denise F.

I really never thought of a career, just thought of working. I feel that Italian-American families believe that education and careers make the children grow up and leave home—something they do not seem to like. Otherwise, I would have been more serious about a career and my future.

My parents were supportive. However, they didn't give much direction. They felt it was my choice.

I feel that associates and superiors find Italian-Americans hard-working and loyal—not too ambitious or serious about work—more serious about family and life.

I find my social life to be more family-oriented as I get older. When I was younger, it was friend-oriented. Also, as I get older, it is more business-oriented.

Having married twice, I selected people I thought I wanted to share my life with. My first marriage was affected by different cultural values and priorities, at times too overwhelming for the other party. With my second marriage, life is simpler. Values and priorities are similar, giving us a common denominator.

Religion gives me strength, faith and a positive life attitude. I find my parents belief in religion has fear and superstition in it, giving them a negative view of the world.

Presently, I am mildly interested in politics. However, I would like to be more interested in the future. I just find it very time-consuming. I'm probably not ready to make a commitment yet. My parents are Democrats and I am a Republican. I am not, nor are my parents, active in politics.

Angelina

I selected teaching because in my senior year of high school I was notified by my counselor that I was going to be valedictorian. She felt that, as a result, I should go on to college. If this had not occurred, I probably would have followed my sister into the secretarial field.

I am now a department head/supervisor for business and computers at a high school. I still teach some classes. I respect my career in education, since my parents and family always respected teachers. Their word was final!

Rosalie

Did being Italian-American restrict your goals as far as education was concerned?

Yes. I can still remember my mother saying that education is wasted on a girl. She gets married and has children and any education she has is left unused, since she becomes a housewife. I was a good student and received good grades and was on the Honor Society. But I was encouraged only to finish high school and not to go to college. I remember her saying, "High school is good enough for a girl, educate the boys."

Did your father feel that way, too?

I don't remember him saying very much. Money was tight. It was best used for the boys. I'm glad my brothers have an education. They're smart boys. I'm proud of them. But I feel cheated; still feel resentment. That's why I go to night school—to fill a need. I read a lot. I did take some tests recently for Mercer County and the woman told me that I'm college level, and I felt very good about that—I haven't regressed to being a dumbbell.

Did you meet any kind of prejudice in school?

One teacher. A French teacher. I could sense it and feel it. In Trenton High you could request a change—and I did. I got transferred to another French teacher. He was great. And it's funny, but my brother after me had the same French teacher and felt the same way, although he didn't request a transfer. Many years later, after we were both out of school, we got to talking about this same teacher. It wasn't personal. It was just that this French teacher didn't like Italians. Neither my brother nor I was comfortable in his class.

How about your non-Italian classmates?

No direct kind of prejudice. But I noticed the group from the western part of Trenton didn't bother with us Italians or other ethnics. They stayed with their own West Trenton group. I had friends of other ethnic groups. The West Trenton gang always thought that they were better than we were—and they dressed beautifully. I could even sit with them in class and they wouldn't become my friends. I felt like the poor relative.

Was your ethnicity a detriment to social mobility?

I was never invited to any parties or dances with outsiders. We just stayed socially with our own kind; our cousins and other relatives. Sunday nights we spent at my aunt's house and she'd make the pizza pie. We'd listen to Jack Benny on the radio on Sunday evenings, the two families. And we'd walk home afterwards. That was our social life. I don't remember going anywhere as a kid other than to relatives' houses. An aunt and uncle's house on my mother's side and an aunt and uncle's on my father's side, both in the Chambersburg section of Trenton. That was our social life. And to the pines in the summertime where we had our small bungalow in Pine Lake Park near Lakehurst. We still stayed in our own group there. We met some people who lived in a log cabin at the other end of the summer vacation development who were Italian. And I remember my mother and my aunt exchanging garlic and basil leaves with the lady. I drive by that log cabin just to see if those people are still there. I don't remember their names. Despite the distance—you couldn't walk between the bungalows—we Italians found each other.

Your relations with other ethnics?

We had friendly relations with other kinds of ethnic people. My mother used to exchange recipes with them. She taught them how to make ravioli and they taught her how to make poppyseed bread or cake, egg-ball and other dishes. Things like that.

Did you look for an Italian-American for a mate?

I didn't personally. I just wanted a good, stable man. But I do remember my mother saying that he had to be a Catholic. She didn't want me getting mixed up with anybody who wasn't Catholic. My parents didn't push the Italian thing, but in my mother's generation they stressed marrying your own kind. My generation—it seemed to be religion. This generation—you don't stress anything. You just hope your daughter marries someone who is stable and a good provider, a steady worker; same as what I looked for, and one who doesn't drink or gamble. I can still remember my mother saying that about not marrying a man who drank or gambled. So it wasn't a question of Italian or non-Italian in finding a mate for me.

Friends?

My friends were from the neighborhood, but they didn't have to be Italian. They were ethnics, but not necessarily Italian. Ethnics tend to be more family-oriented, so I was more comfortable with them in addition to being with my family members. I always remember my father saying that blood is thicker than water. He wanted us to stick together as a family.

How about work?

Not getting the college education that I wanted, I had to settle for something less in life. I didn't strive for higher goals. I had a bit of a complex, feeling that I wasn't as good. But now, later in life, I have become more extroverted. I settled for a mediocre job in the old American Ferment plant in the parcel post room when I could have done much better. But it gave me a good background, and I met lots of different people. Now I do temp work and go from job to job and meet lots of interesting people. I even dance alone on the floor at the senior citizens dinner and call out to the older ladies to join me on the dance floor. I would never do that 20 years ago. I'm coming out of my shell in my old age. I also feel that my mother held me back. She'd always say to stay with one job. Don't change jobs. Look for security. Italians look for security. That's why they came to America in the first place. But people today don't follow the security pattern with their work. They stay a few years and go on to another job that pays better or has possibilities for advancement, not just steady work or security. You don't find employees who are dedicated workers anymore. I used to work Saturdays when the boss asked me to, when it was only the janitor and I in the whole plant. You just don't find that anymore in workers. I was 26 years with A&P and 13 years with American Ferment. I left American Ferment to have my daughter. The boss promised to let me have my job back, but when I asked for it, he said he couldn't do it. And he had promised me. Now the girls today wouldn't allow that to happen. I lost my pension and seniority and everything.

Your relationship with your husband?

My husband isn't Italian, but I cook Italian meals for him and wait on him hand and foot and he likes it. My mother did it for my father. And when I was left home with my brothers, when my mother had to leave the house, she'd give me instructions to take care of the boys. Feed them, do the dishes. Being the oldest and the girl, I seemed to follow in my mother's footsteps. But I don't resent that. I lay out my husband's clothes, prepare something for him for breakfast, and then go on to work. It's just automatic with me.

Who's in charge of the purse strings in the family?

I am. My husband likes it that way. He gets his spending money, and he doesn't have to worry about the checkbook. He never resented handing me his check and letting me run the household expenses. It's bad in a way; God forbid if I go first. I tell my daughter that she'll have to help her father manage, and she tells me that she didn't spoil him—that I did.

Your relationship with your daughter?

I'm glad I had her. Being Italian had an effect on the way I raised her. Whenever I corrected her, I'd tell her that was the way my mother and father taught me, and that's what I'm teaching you. She didn't always agree with me and would question the discipline. But I felt it was the right way. I find myself repeating the things that my mother and father used to say to us, or thinking along the lines of what my parents said to us about life. I feel they gave us a good background. A stable home. My father had his barbershop in the house. He was always there in the house, if my mother had to run out to the store to buy food. When we came home from school, he was always there for us. Too many kids come home to empty houses today, because both parents have to work to make ends meet. That's why I took a part-time job when I was raising my daughter. I'd see her off to school in the morning, and I was there when she came home. The extra money I made helped put her through school and paid for her braces, and bought a second car for me.

Religion?

When I used to receive Holy Communion when I was young, I never doubted that there was only one religion, not until I was much older. I thought being Catholic was the only religion and the right religion. When I went to work after high school, I began to have conversations with people about religion, but never wanted to argue who was right or wrong. Because we had a business, I always remember my mother saying to my father, "Never argue with customers about religion or politics." And she was right. I wouldn't argue with people over religion, but I always felt that my religion was the best one. But now I don't feel that way. And I remember my father would put up the advertising cards from the Democrats and the Republicans in his barbershop to keep both sides happy during elections.

Did the nuns in religion classes have any effect?

I didn't have the Italian nuns from St. Joachim's. I had the Irish nuns at Sacred Heart Church for religious instructions. One nun liked me and begged my father to send me to Catholic school—but he refused. He always said that he paid taxes and that his kids were going to public school. She took me under her wing. She liked me. She was young and very pretty. She let me teach Sunday School in the basement at Sacred Heart. I didn't go to St. Joachim's in Chambersburg for instructions to make the sacraments because my mother was afraid of the canal that was still there between us and the Italian church. She was afraid of the water. We had a neighbor down in the pines who had lost a young son to drowning in the creek. Once they filled in the old canal bed, she wasn't afraid to let us kids walk up Hamilton Avenue to visit our relatives in Chambersburg, and to go to church at St. Joachim's. But the Irish nuns were nice to us public school kids.

What about your extended relatives?

Our aunts and uncles were like our second parents. They were good to us kids. They took us places, bought presents for us, fed us homecooked meals and protected us. I liked my aunts and uncles. They were an extension of our parents. My cousins say till this day that they wouldn't have gone anywhere, if it hadn't been for my father carting all us kids around in his old Model A Ford. It was a wonder that we could all get into it. He would take us down to the pines or to the beach in Seaside. It was depression time but we had fun down there. My father even used to include kids from the neighborhood in the gang who weren't blood relatives. We were poor but we were very well adjusted and very happy. We didn't even know we were poor. But later, as we got older and went on to high school, I felt deprived, especially when I didn't have money to buy a gown and go to the prom. And the strangers from the western part of Trenton looking down on us ethnics from South Trenton and Chambersburg. I sensed that easily. You don't meet prejudice until you leave the nest and go out into the world to make your way. As kids we used to hear name calling like wops, dagos, greaseballs. But you don't hear that too much anymore. The prejudice against Italians has gotten more subtle. But it's still there. Sometimes you'd meet prejudice even amongst us ethnics. If you'd meet a nice guy who was not your kind, and even if introduced by his sisters, his family would put obstacles in the way. They were afraid we'd start dating. They wanted him to marry within their kind. And when one of the girls did marry an Italian, there were problems in the family; they'd almost look down on him as if he were Black. Hopefully, that kind of thinking won't last forever. It was worse years ago.

Katherine

In no way was my choice of computer programming based on my Italian background. My family supported all of my choices, although they knew nothing about computers. And my Italian-American background does not affect my professional relationships.

Religion is probably less important to me than it was to my parents.

I am mildly interested in politics. Probably more so on a local level, because I do have three children and I am interested in what affects them. My ethnic background has not been a factor in my choice of a political party, but I am less active in politics than my parents.

Ann D.

I did not consciously select an Italian for a husband. As a matter of fact, he was the first Italian-American I had dated.

Is religion as meaningful to me as it was to my parents? Yes, even more so. Our choice of religion was an informed decision.

Mary R.

As I haven't yet settled on a career, it is hard to tell whether my background will have an effect on a choice of a career. Educationally speaking, my father, being an immigrant, believed it was very important for all us children to be educated. Five children will have college degrees, thanks to his efforts. He married a midwestern woman of Irish-Swedish descent, who raised and educated us. Their goal was for all of us to become leaders, people who wouldn't be afraid to say what we thought and to stand up for our ideas.

During my senior year in college (I was an economics major.), I decided to go against the business world route, which I seemed quite perfect for, and instead focused on writing. I don't know if it was my Italian-American background that had an effect on this choice. I think it was my parents' attitudes to-

ward my development that allowed them to support
me emotionally, as well as financially, in my endeavors. I still have a long way to go in my career goals,
and I have just recently decided to get a master's degree in family counseling, as this will keep me stimu-
lated and financially secure and still give me the
freedom to delve further into my writing. I have chosen family counseling and therapy because I believe
stable family dynamics allows one to take more risks
in life. And to succeed and be happy, one must always
follow her dreams. The stable family dynamics, although it is an "Italian" trait, actually has come about
in my family thanks to my mother's love and support
of my father's ideals. His family background is a difficult one because of their transplantation in America.
Had my grandmother remained always in Italy, she
would have been fine. Instead, coming to America in
her forties, she felt lost and instead of coming to terms
with living here, she clung more tightly to her Italian
past and its traditions. The result: my father and
brother have had a hard time being close. But each
has in his own family made major efforts at creating a
secure, close family bond. And both have, so far, succeeded. Again, however, I must add that some thanks
go to their wives who shared in their ideals. Between
my father and mother's values, I have seen the worth-
whileness in family bonding, and I am interested in
pursuing this as a career.

The effect being Italian-American had on my career to the present I know not. All I do know is that I
have, through my struggles, always been supported in
my choice. However, if I had chosen to be a waitress or
a cleaning woman to support myself for the rest of my
life, they would have been quite disappointed. Both
parents feel it is essential that we keep our minds active. So the struggle has been between using our
minds and allowing our emotions to play an important

role in our lives. The emotionality of the southern Italian is something I am just now beginning to comprehend. One, male or female, cannot live for career alone. One must, I believe, have close ties with worthwhile (those who respect and trust you) people. Perhaps, being Italian-American, I had to make sure both career and personal life were kept somehow in balance. But isn't this true for all young adults?

I most consciously will choose against an Italian mate simply because so far I have never been interested in any Italian males. I am, however, often attracted to half-Italian, half-Irish or half-Italian, half-Jewish males. I don't know why. Perhaps because they are similar to me. But the 100% Italian males whom I have known seem too cool, too cocky, dumb and proud. Yes, I know these are stereotypes, but they are true. At college, the 100% Italians played football, walked around like apes and spoke with terrible accents. They seemed overly concerned with their appearance and dress in shorts and Italian Tee shirts (sleeveless), with gold chains around their necks. The half Italian males, by contrast, seem more refined, conservative and more intelligent. Actually, I say more intelligent because they were more able to make light conversation. They could talk, were quick thinkers, and friendly. The 100% Italians seem to be less communicative, more extremist in their behavior. Maybe I fear their directness or their anger, although I don't know why I would, since I can be rather direct as well.

My background will affect my mate to the extent that he will understand what it means to fight and argue until the air is cleared. That, to me, is one of the most important qualities I hope to find in a man I am interested in. Not that I fight much, either. But I must be allowed to let off some steam periodically. And he will understand why that is necessary for me without being scared off.

Right now religion is not as important to me as to my parents. My non-Italian mother is the more religious of the two. My Italian father goes to church with her, though. We children do not go frequently—we're in the questioning phase of development.

Being in the searching stage, I am quite uninterested in politics. However, once I'm sure of what it means to be American and what I feel is important for a society, country or community to thrive, I might even become involved in politics myself—running for office or campaigning for someone. Or I might leave the United States. Who knows?

I believe in Capitalism to an extent because I believe everyone has the opportunity to succeed. The question is: Who is willing to make the effort? And who wants to struggle that hard anyway? I'm sure this has been transferred to me by the fact that my father is an immigrant who put himself through college and medical school. He, however, was a Democrat until he met my mother and got married; then he became an Independent Republican.

I am not active in politics, but my parents are.

Lucia Chiavola Birnbaum

At the outset of my fourth university year, the fourth year of World War II, I thought about the incongruity of remaining in college while the world was aflame, and I quit school. Shortly thereafter, I met and married a Jewish soldier from New York, a match everyone consigned to failure because of the cultural dissonance of an eastern Jew and a midwestern Italian Catholic.

The other side of cultural dissonance is the value of difference: the marriage has lasted—through our lives as graduate students, as parents of three sons, and as professionals. He is a physicist, an entrepreneur, and today an old China hand. I have remained an historian, with a belated knowledge of my own cultural heritage, that, in my case, has become the foundation of independent scholarship.

Independent thinking was not fostered in the climate of the cold war, nor was it encouraged by graduate school training. I was no more ready to question the accepted interpretation of United States history, preoccupied as I was with three sons and doctoral examinations, than the rest of my generation. Yet, as an Italian-American woman, with immigrant grandparents, who had attained a doctorate, I was part of the generation called the "best and the brightest," some of whom—at some point in the sixties, with careers in full sail—came to a dead stop, with no land in sight.

Mary Ann

My choice of a career was not affected by my ethnic background. My educational background and my first job after college led to my decision to go to graduate school and pursue a career in library science.

In my father's family of four girls and three boys, the girls were all encouraged by their father to become professional women, either self-employed or in positions requiring advance studies/training. My father wanted me to be either a doctor or a lawyer. Not feeling qualified to do either, I chose, instead, to obtain two master's degrees (Library Science and Art History) and a doctorate in Library Administration.

Even though I decided not to enter the professions that my father preferred, both he and my mother were totally supportive of my career choice. Unfortunately, both had died before I entered the doctoral program.

I have no children.

My father was Catholic; my mother, who was not Italian, was Protestant. I was brought up as a Protestant. I am only moderately concerned with religion, as were my parents.

As far as my interest in politics, *very* is too strong, *mildly* is too weak. I am interested in specific political issues and specific candidates. I have worked on the campaigns of several local candidates (often the ones who ultimately lost the elections).

I have no idea how Italian-Americans vote or how they chose their political affiliations. I tend to be a liberal Democrat.

I am more active than my parents were in politics.

Angie

In school I did feel more comfortable with friends who were Italian. I still do. Even in work. You don't have to say it out loud, it's there. The common background is your roots.

Did your Italian-American background affect your goals in education?

No. My parents always encouraged me. They felt very strongly toward education. They wanted me to go to college. It was my decision not to go. I wanted a business background, and I had just turned 17 in April, so I didn't feel ready for college. I wanted some office experience.

What were your school experiences like in relation to being Italian?

It was difficult, coming from an Italian background and going to an Irish-dominated Catholic school with others from different backgrounds. There wasn't any prejudice towards me personally, but the Irish were on top most of the time. In other words, there was favoritism toward the Irish.

Did you sense it with the nuns?

Sometimes. Not all the time. But it was there with certain students. They made you feel inferior. They felt superior. For tryouts for certain school activities, only certain ones were picked. The favoritism was subtle, but it was there. You could feel it even though it wasn't spoken out loud. But I didn't let it hold me back in any way. In fact I felt that I had proved myself a little bit more. That I could do just as well. I accomplished what I thought I could do.

Social mobility?

I was held back socially. We were raised strict. We couldn't go wherever we wanted. It was part of the Italian way, and I can't say that my parents were entirely wrong. At the time I probably thought they were wrong. But as you get older you get wiser, and you can understand better why your parents thought the way they did. I think that my father, being the parent of three daughters, felt that he had to watch us. He brought us up and he did the best that he could; he didn't want anything bad to happen to his children. He was very protective of us, and I really feel that he wasn't doing anything wrong. I think it was good. I didn't think that at the time, but I do now.

Selection of a mate?

I didn't think consciously or unconsciously about selecting an Italian or a non-Italian for a mate, or I wouldn't have married my husband. It would have to be the person himself. I really don't think I selected on the basis of nationality. It comes down to whom you are attracted to more than what his ethnic background is. Nationality played a bigger part in finding a husband with our mothers, because they had no choice. In those days a lot of couples were matched up. I don't feel I was restricted to looking for an Italian for a husband. But in my case and my husband's case, our parents were overjoyed that we were dating, since we were both Italian. They approved of our getting together because they felt there were too many problems when you marry into another culture, another background, another religion. You're multiplying your problems. Basically, when you marry into your own background, you have common ground, regardless of how different your personalities may be.

Did you seek out Italians for friends?

When I was in high school, I developed friendships with girls from different backgrounds. But I did feel more comfortable with friends who were Italian, and I still do. Even in work, other Italians and I have a common ground. You don't have to say it out loud, it's there. The common background is your roots.

Did you restrict your goals to business on purpose?

No. Basically, I enjoyed business because my father was in business. Even today I still have an interest in business. If I had gone to college, I think I would have gone into accounting. In the fifties, a girl was either a school teacher, a mother, or a nurse. I had a cousin who went to college. I don't know whether she got a degree or not, she worked in the court house for years, but she never went any further. I think today things are different. Second- or third-generation Italian-Americans had, and have, a better advantage to improve themselves than the immigrants did, and our children will have even more opportunities than we have now.

How does your background affect your relationship with your husband?

Not all Italian families are the same. But I feel very comfortable with my background. I think my parents did a good job of raising me and my sisters. We share equally the managing of the money. I get the food money and he pays the other bills. The mother is the heart and soul of the family; the father is the bread-winner. With two sources of income into the house, I think financial decisions should be a joint effort, so that we both know where the money is going. And we don't have assigned tasks. We see something that has to be done and we pitch in to do it. That's the way it should be. My husband helps with the laundry and even vacuums as well as takes out the garbage. Now that I'm working, we all have to help around the house. But when I wasn't working, I did it all. Yet—it shouldn't be that everybody helps because I'm working now. It should be that way all the time, with everybody pitching in and helping. If it needs to be done, it gets done. You don't walk away from it.

Did your background affect the way you raised your children?

No. But I wish I had raised my children a little bit more the way my parents had raised me. I think I was more easygoing with my children, and I wish I had been a little more deliberate with what I told them to do.

Religion?

I think that if I came from any other ethnic background, and I was Catholic, I would approach it the same way. All the Catholics from Europe generally think the same toward their religion, and they brought it here when they came over.

Politics?

Most Italians are Democrats. Probably most ethnic groups who came to this country are Democrats. Most parents were poor when they came here. The Democrats stood for them. The Republicans were for the well-to-do. That influenced me as far as being a part of the party that was for the working person.

Colleen

The only effect my ethnic background has had is that I knew—because my mother was poor—that I would have to choose a career that paid well. I did not want to work as hard as my mother did raising us. Consequently, I chose a career in sales at the Chicago Board of Trade where I am now a Vice-President for Security Pacific Bank.

Being Italian has not affected my career at all.

Religion is important to me, but perhaps I don't go to church as faithfully as my mother did. My father didn't go much. They divorced when I was four.

I am mildly interested in politics. I like to stay informed. However, so much of it is bullshit that it turns me off.

Probably a lot of Italian-Americans are Democratic. But I am a Republican mostly because I feel that we pay far too much in taxes due to the ineptness of our government-run enterprises.

I'm as about as active in politics as my parents were.

Nicole

Your parents were uneducated and yet you went to college. How was that?

When I went to kindergarten, I could not speak English. I learned it from my wonderful teachers whose English usage and pronunciation were impeccable. My teachers—all of whom were women—were Jews or WASPs with one notable exception: Mrs. Tess Cowell, an Italian lady with an American name. These women were brilliant. Probably, at a later time, they might have been doctors or lawyers. Back then the only career choices they had were those of secretarial, teaching or nursing. And I was very fortunate to have had such good teachers who were kind to me and even visited my home.

In elementary school and junior high (up to seventh and eighth grades) the neighborhood children attended the same school and classes. But at the end of eighth grade in junior high, the teachers and administrators assigned the students to one of three high school programs: Academic, Business or General, according to their mental abilities. I was selected for the Academic program, and from ninth to twelfth grades was no longer in classes with just neighborhood kids. In fact, most of my classmates were Jews and WASPs— just like our elementary school teachers. There were several Italians in my classes, but by-and-large, the make-up of the class was "American."

In my senior year, my classmates talked enthusiastically about the colleges to which they were applying or going. Naturally, they politely asked me which college I was going to. "College" was not part of my vocabulary. I never gave much thought to plans after high school. So I must have lied in the beginning. I must have invented colleges that I ostensibly was applying to. In fact, I did indeed apply to Beaver College, but I realized that the cost was prohibitive.

I walked to school each day with a friend, Evelyn. One day in May, as luck would have it, Evelyn said, "On Saturday, I'm going to take the entrance test for Trenton State Teachers College." I replied, "Oh, where's that?" She said, "I don't know exactly, but you take a bus on Centre Street and it takes you to the door."

I must have replied, "Gee, do you think I could go?" It sounded like a godsend to me—a real college where I could apply for admission, and it was nearby, too.

So I went with Evelyn that Saturday to Trenton State Teachers College. I really don't remember applying to that school, but I must have done so. The test that day was a written one followed by an oral part. In the orals, I had to read a list of words which were arranged from easy to hard. I was instructed to read them until I came to a word I mispronounced or could not pronounce, at which time the examiner would dismiss me.

I read the words well until I came to "epitome"—which I pronounced "e-pa-tome." I was sure I had failed when the examiner said coldly, "Thank you. You may go now." But lo and behold, I was accepted by Trenton State Teachers College. Evelyn was not.

I was going to a real college. I was happy with myself. I talked with my mother. She said something that was equivalent to "Go for it!" My father, however, was another story.

I approached my father gingerly. "Pop, do you think I could go to college? It's just down the street a little bit." (In reality, it was ten miles from home.) He said, "Why go to college? It's wasted on a woman. You're going to get married someday. Who needs college? Be patient until your husband comes along." I replied casually (although I must have been tense), "Gee, Pop, the college accepted me and I'm going to be terribly embarrassed to tell them I can't go. Will you let me go until my future husband materializes? When he comes along, I'll quit college. Okay?"

I don't know if my mother intervened, but my father said, "Okay, you can go, but you must be home by four o'clock."

So I was able to go to college to fill the interim between my single life and my married life, because my father was just waiting to get rid of me. I was his responsibility until I became someone else's through marriage.

This "future" husband never materialized, hence I completed the four years at State still single. I earned a college degree and I became a teacher, although I did not think I was going to become a teacher. In our third year, we had something called practicum, which meant that we had to go to a little elementary school for a couple of weeks of practice teaching. And I think the very first day that I taught, I knew then that I wanted to become a teacher. But up until that time, I was still excited with learning itself, and I enjoyed going to Trenton State. It was just great. Such a wonderful place to go to school then.

A footnote to this story: When I was graduated from Trenton State Teachers College, my father attended the commencement exercises. In fact, he sat in the front row. He was the first person in the audience to arrive. He was very proud of me.

Did you encounter any difficulties adjusting to college life?

As a commuter, I left my Italian home and entered an American world each day I went to college. Although I tried to keep the two worlds apart, there were times when they were on a collision course. Let me give you an example.

In my freshman year, I was given a course called "Folk Dancing." (Trenton State did not allow students to choose their own courses. A student declared his major at the start of his four-year stint and then followed a prescribed course of studies. I elected to be an English major.)

Folk dancing was fun and I must have shown some natural talent, because our instructor said to me after the second or third class, "I'd like you to try out for the modern dance group. Tryouts are tonight."

I did not know what modern dance was. (I probably thought it was ballroom dancing.) My two worlds were about to collide. A teacher's "invitation" constituted a command. One never said NO to a teacher's request. She wanted me to try out for a dance group after school hours, but my father expected me to be home about four o'clock.

What to do? I could not disappoint either world. And so I said to my father, "We have a very important class tonight." (I think I blamed it on astronomy, which was another mandated course.) He reluctantly said YES, and I tried out for the dance group and was home by eight o'clock.

I was chosen for the modern dance group and became quite an accomplished dancer according to my teacher and peers. We met at night once a week. All the time, my father believed the astronomy class was meeting to examine the heavenly bodies in the skies.

At the end of the year, the Girls' Athletic Association held a banquet during which time we girls, (never women), received awards, trophies, letters, etc., for athletic excellence. It was not my wish to attend, but here again I was told that I had to. So I went. One of the awards was a dance scholarship to study with Martha Graham, the supreme modern dancer in New York City.

When the award was announced, I knew that I'd have to do some inventive thinking, for it was *I* who won the scholarship, which called for me (the recipient) to study dance five days a week, for four weeks, in the Martha Graham Studio during the month of July.

Again what to do? I was sure that even my mother would not consent to my traveling alone to New York City, and for dance, no less! I could not refuse the scholarship, and on the other hand, I could not tell my parents about my scholarship. And so I invented another story. "Listen," I probably said, "there's a summer program at the college. By attending some summer classes, I could have a lighter schedule during the next school year. Can I attend? It's only for one month—July."

They tried to dissuade me. They used good arguments for my not attending. However, they finally said YES.

And so for four weeks, I left my house before eight o'clock in the morning to catch the train. I went to New York, got off the train, went to the studio, took my dance lesson, returned to the station, boarded a train for Trenton, and arrived home about four o'clock in the afternoon.

My parents never knew the difference. I pulled it off. I even carried books so that my departure each morning looked authentic. By fabricating the story about summer school, I allayed any parental fear that I would be harmed in the Big City, but I did suffer from guilt that my lie would be discovered. As I traveled to and from the dance studio, I worried that the train would have a collision. In my mind's eye, I could see a newspaper headline about a train wreck and a victim—a student from Trenton State Teachers College. What would my parents say?

Modern dancing was a nice experience. I grew to like it very much. In my senior year, I was the president of the dance group and because of the title, I was able to meet all the artists who came to our campus for performances. I became the dance expert on campus.

Rosemarie W.

Being a senior citizen, I am studying and practicing art during my retirement years. But as far as my working years were concerned, being an Italian-American might have had a negative effect *at one time,* as Italians were looked down upon, which made me work harder in my secretarial job. I didn't see it as a crutch, but only as an asset and still do. During an age when pizzas were not not popular and foods of Italian origin were unheard of, it made me a popular hostess. *Now* I'm more than happy of my heritage.

Religion is still very meaningful, but I'm not as dependent on it as my parents were, because it was where everyone met friends at church on Sundays and Holy Days.

I am very interested in politics, but not to the extent of concentration. I have so many interests that a day is not long enough. As for being a Democrat or a Republican, I cannot see where my heritage had any effect.

Stephanie

When I first went into the business world, having an Italian-American background did not have an effect on my choice of a career. However, as I matured and was employed by another Italian-American, I felt the clout. Continuing on into my career, which is the travel industry, I started to travel frequently to Italy to learn more about my culture from the people there, not what my family had taught me. I stayed in the travel industry with the belief that it would keep me in direct contact with Italy.

Being an Italian-American does have an effect on my career in the travel industry at present. I feel that I have the opportunity as well as the ability to teach and to educate the public about Italy, its people and its culture. However, I have found much jealousy and resentment from non-Italians for these efforts to educate them.

Had my family been more educated and aware of the importance of a college degree, I would have continued my education beyond high school. But the lack of money and the belief that I would be married stopped me from obtaining a college education.

As for the choice of my professional goals, I've always been supported, in a sense of speaking. I've never bitten off more than I can chew. I feel that I have climbed the corporate ladder the hard way, but I'm always more successful and wiser the next time around.

My Italian-American background does affect my professional relationships. Being in the travel industry and well-traveled to Italy builds confidence with clients and with those who know my abilities.

My social life has not been affected because of my being Italian-American. I've always been accepted socially.

Religion is not as meaningful to me as it was to my parents; however, it can be comforting to believe in what you were raised to believe in.

I am very much interested in politics. I feel it plays a very strong part in the quality of life we experience presently and will experience in the future.

If an Italian-American were in political power, I believe America would change for the better and there would be a lot more world peace.

I am as active in politics as my parents were.

Theresa Amato DiBuono

I was self-employed and my parents financed me, giving me all their support. They taught me how to respect everyone and to be a good listener. And being an Italian-American has helped me to help others with the Italian language. My family gave me an education and also taught me to explore Italian history. And my Italian-American background has strengthened my professional relationships.

My husband was a first-generation Italian also. His parents did not speak English. I did not consciously select him because he was Italian. It just happened. All sides agreed we had a marriage made in heaven. It's wonderful to be able to understand and speak Italian to all members of the family, children and adults.

Religion is as meaningful to me and to my family as it was to my parents.

I'm not interested in politics only because I don't understand it—very confusing. And my parents were not active in politics, either. They usually went along with some well-meaning neighbors.

Leonore

I think that because of my Italian background, I did not get proper guidance in high school.

Since we had Italian in the curriculum when I was a junior in high school, I wanted to take it the following year. When I checked my schedule for my senior year, to my utter dismay, I found Italian conflicted with a "much-needed" business subject. And no faculty members moved an "eyebrow" to accommodate or guide me when I told them I was striving to continue a very good record, and that I wanted very much to take that Italian language course. Today, no doubt, because we have Italian-American faculty, there is more flexibility in the curriculum. I graduated, got a job in a law office, and made arrangements to take evening courses. When I asked my principal, a dyed-in-the-wool WASP, for my transcript, he coldly informed me, while looking over my head, that I did not have the necessary prerequisites for college entry. I attended Essex County College and Seton Hall University.

My father was very supportive of a career for me, while my mother was lukewarm.

Catherine C.

I chose my major in college (history, B.A.) because of a love for American history. My teaching certification was also in history. What else could I do with my degree in the early seventies, other than teach, despite the different career choices besides teaching and nursing being established for women during those years?

My parents were very supportive of my decision to go to college. Although they never constantly urged or verbally encouraged my "doing my best" in school, I did earn good grades through my own drive and hard work. I knew my parents were proud of my choice and my accomplishments even though they did not outwardly praise me. It was a quiet praise. I did all my own selecting of colleges, sought financial aid, and even earned my tuition through summer jobs. My parents wanted to help, but I knew they really could not afford to. There were still four of the five children living at home. I commuted to school to cut costs. When I graduated, I was—and still am—the only child in the family who has earned a college degree plus graduate credits. I felt very proud about it, since my parents could not read or write English *or* Italian.

When I taught high school history and English, my being "Italian" was a great conversational topic. People were especially surprised to find out that I was born in Italy and became a United States citizen in the ninth grade. People find it very interesting. They always ask "What part of Italy were you from?" and "Can you speak Italian?" Of course, they assume I'm a great Italian cook.

Religion is very meaningful to me. I have tried to pass the importance of it on to my sons. They are being raised as Catholics. I'm not real active in the Church. My moving has prevented that, but I do go to church, observe religious holidays, say Grace at mealtime. I do not have crucifixes, pictures of saints, or statues around the house or garden. My mother was, and still is, more religious than my father. Being married to a non-Catholic, I feel like my mother; I'm taking responsibility for my children's religious upbringing.

I am not interested in politics. I follow candidates,

but I've never voted Democratic simply because Italians have. There is no influence of one party or the other regardless of ethnic lineage.

My parents were not active in politics. But my father to this day will vote Democratic. Whether it's for blue-collar labor reasons or Italian reasons, I'm not sure.

Louise V.

I think the biggest influence that being Italian-American has had on my career is how my exuberant personality fit in—or rather didn't fit in—with other scientists and engineers who tended to be more introverted and threatened by those who were different.

I am a research engineer. The Italian influence was subtle, but strong, having to do with keying in to enthusiasm and responding to encouragement. The emotional setting for my accomplishments was an extension of that which I had experienced at home.

When I was growing up, the country was enthusiastically responding to the challenges of the Sputnik satellite. During that time in history, Dwight Eisenhower and John Kennedy were Presidents and scientists were heroes. Both schools and television had special science programs. We used to wake up bright and early to watch the launching of the Apollo spacecrafts.

Actually, it was despite being Italian-American that I chose a career in science, as scientists were not any special role models in my family. It was the American culture at that time that nutured my interest. I also happened to have some talent in science, excelling in chemistry, physics and math to the point that I took extra classes. It was a high school chemistry teacher, who was also the advisor to our science club, who encouraged me to enter the Westinghouse National Science Talent Search. I studied how light reflects and refracts in a project that was good enough to win honors in the competition.

Simultaneously, I was doing well in my writing and had an essay published in our high school literary journal. On the encouragement of my English teacher, I entered and won a writing competition.

When I got to college, I majored in chemistry, graduating in February, 1973 from the University of Illinois at Champaign-Urbana. My father encouraged me to go into home economics, which I did try, but their nonrigorous approach to science turned me off.

My first job was in Cambridge, Massachusetts at a consulting firm where I worked in the chemical and metallurgical engineering department. This was my first exposure to engineers. Also, about this time, the Women's Educational Equity Act was passed by Congress. When I went to take supplemental courses in computers and statistics, the Dean of Engineering, who needed women for his school, drew me into a second degree program in chemical engineering. In May, 1979, I graduated with my second B.S. degree, this time in chemical engineering.

Upon graduating, I went down to Philadelphia, where I worked for Rohm and Haas in their research department.

I think the biggest influence that being Italian-American has had on my career is how my exuberant personality fit in—or rather didn't fit in—with other scientists and engineers who tended to be more introverted and threatened by those who were different. My first supervisor was Iranian and eventually our cultural differences caused me to move on, leaving the company for FMC in Princeton. This was one of the happiest times of my life. This company had quite a few more Italians. My officemate and project leader was Italian. While sparks did fly between us at times, on the whole we had quite a productive association. This era of content ended shortly after Reagan became President and the chemical business went through its wrenching restructurings. The research in my division of industrial chemicals was eviscerated with hundreds being laid off, including me.

To fill the gap, when so many professionals were chasing so few jobs, I went back to graduate school, getting my master's degree in chemical engineering from Columbia University in January, 1985. This was a tough and lonely time. I don't remember any Italians or Italian-Americans in the program, although there were plenty of Asians and Greeks and French. I didn't have any reinforcement of my identity as Italian-American.

My first job with my master's degree was with the Swiss firm, Hoffmann-LaRoche, but, unfortunately, it was before their "night of 1,000 knives." I was laid off in their reduction in force in February, 1985, after only seven months. It took nine months before I could find a job again. I went to a Swedish company called Pharmacia where I worked in their research department. On my trip to their headquarters in Uppsala, Sweden, they asked me to work there, but I declined as I had some difficulty working with, who to me, were nonexpressive people. In May, 1987, I gave a paper which led to my being hired by E. R. Squibb. That's where I am today. I have an Asian boss and we definitely have cultural conflicts as he is castigatory and I am more upbeat and enthusiastic. This is not the time of my highest content.

By my definition, characteristic Italian-American traits are expressiveness, exuberance and enthusiasm. I believe, from my experience, that these traits have intimidated scientific professionals from more reserved backgrounds such as Iranian and Chinese. The Chinese have tended to get offended when I have asked questions, as they expect you to figure it all out by yourself. My experience has also been that they have a narrow focus to their thinking—that any actions outside the immediate goal are extraneous rather than supplementing the dimension of a venture. My boss feels that writing reviews or articles for national publications is extraneous. So now I do it and don't tell him. I have not met one Chinese, or worked with one, who was a good team player in sharing the work, dividing the tasks, discussing the ramifications of the results. In short, I have never gotten any existential pleasure from my interactions with any Chinese. I make a point of discussing this as so many are in science.

I also feel something more subtle about the Chinese culture that is in conflict with the Italian. I haven't known a single Chinese to be celebratory. They never take time out to appreciate an accomplishment or acknowledge the progress made. They tend overwhelmingly to focus on what weakness or failing there is in a venture. In my family we are always having celebrations of this or that achievement.

I enjoy going to the Italian feasts and munching on the dried garbanzo beans. The processions are fun to witness. I enjoy the family sitting around eating sausage and green peppers and talking. I haven't been to a feast since I left home, although I live in New Jersey with a lot of Italians.

Until the past two months, I had not dated any Italian-American men. I don't know why, except perhaps that I encountered almost none in my studies and work environment. Now, perhaps, one can say that I am secure enough in my scientific identity to reintegrate with my Italian heritage.

I've been married twice. First to a Cuban and second to a Chinese, both of whom I met in college. I suppose my husbands were selected for intellectual compatibility and companionship in difficult developmental stages. In the first case, I was breaking away from home and seeking out my professional identity. In the second case, I was coping with all the rampant changes in the chemical industry, with all the layoffs and job turmoil. In the end we split because the disjuncture with the emotional side was too great.

Religion is as meaningful, if not more so, than it is to my parents. However, when I left home, I abandoned my childhood religion of Catholicism for its Protestant sister, Episcopalianism. The heavy emphasis on sin, guilt, confession and obedience to authority in the Catholic Church did not endear it to me. By comparison, I was gently drawn into the Episcopal Church, as it appealed more to the intellect and higher motives, especially the striving to be a good steward of the talents, skills and gifts granted by God. The Episcopal Church's stance is that of a coach to members as they seek ways to deal with life's hurdles. Granted, things don't always go smoothly, but apply your courage to a holding point and find a way to move on, using your unique abilities. I felt more comfortable with this approach as it tended to celebrate life (as opposed to the Catholic approach of castigation) and to integrate people's day-to-day experiences with theology and teachings from the Bible.

I also felt the Catholic Church trivialized Holy Days. At Christmas services there would be a birthday cake for Jesus replete with birthday candles, or kids marching around with flashlights. By contrast, in the Episcopal Church the kids were more supervised and the Holy Days were more participatory, in-depth festival celebrations. Christmas meant singing various Christmas songs before the services. Easter week meant the vigil and the washing of the feet. Palm Sunday meant reenactment of praising Jesus by marching with palms and singing Hosanas. Advent meant a pause for reflection on the meaning of the season. All in all, the Episcopal Church is a more contemplative, participatory church and is more inclusive of women. I am a chalice bearer and lay reader as well as having led various church groups.

I am mildly interested in politics. For the most part, Democratic, believing that concern for others takes precedence over greed. I support Mike Dukakis and voted for him when I lived in Massachusetts. On the local level, I've attended hearings on the issue of solid waste disposal/incineration and on new building in the area. I've written a letter to the editor of the Star Ledger, which was published. I vote. But being Italian-American has not directly affected my choice of a political party. And I'm probably as active as my parents in politics, if not a little more so.

Rosemarie T.

Upon completing high school, the options available to a woman at that time (mid-fifties) was to work, to get married, or to go to college. However, my parents, who were immigrants from Italy, did not believe that college was necessary for a girl. Being one of eight children, and the last of the brood, I stood a better chance than my older sisters to go to college. My brothers (two) would naturally go into the family construction business.

Since my chosen vocation was that of a teacher, and it had respectability as a profession, I finally convinced my parents that I should go. An older sister, who was instrumental in running the family business as well as my parents' personal finances, was denied going to Rider College during the mid-forties.

I believe that my interest in business was influenced by my heritage. Work ethic was very important, and to be successful, one should work hard and preferably have his/her own business.

Upon graduation from college, I went into teaching Business Education, completed graduate work in guidance and ultimately obtained a degree in administration and supervision. I had a desire to get into the family business in some managerial position, but women in Italian families did not usually "run" the family business.

My sister, who retired after 40 years in the family business, was not offered stock. When my father retired, she was not given stock or even a part interest in the business. She remained in the position of a "bookkeeper."

I probably had a desire either to lead or to supervise in some capacity. I periodically entertained the thought of going into business for myself. I also entertained the thought of becoming a lawyer; however, in both instances financial restraints prevented me from pursuing those avenues.

Our teachers union has an Italian-American male president. I have had many difficulties and personality conflicts with this man. I sued him for not representing me in a grievance, and during the ensuing hearings, it was proven that there was animosity towards me. He referred to me as "an assertive bitch." To this day, this man has difficulty relating to me. He has difficulty with women in authoritative positions within the school district.

Although I was married, I did not have any children. I did want children, but decided against it since my marriage was not solid. I will say that having come from a large family, I definitely did not want more than two children.

I have difficulty accepting Church doctrine and its ever-changing rules and attitudes towards marriage and divorce.

My parents and family are basically Democrats and so am I. But I am more active in politics. My parents were not involved at all. I have helped friends get petitions signed for delegates to national conventions, and I presently serve as treasurer for a candidate seeking re-election to the county legislature. I am more involved locally than nationally. I do have an interest in national elections and follow the news regularly.

Caroline

I came to America with my parents at age seven in midschool year (January) and was put into the same grade as I was in in Europe. I couldn't speak any English, so I couldn't keep up with the schoolwork and was made to repeat a year of school. Therefore, I always had something to prove, and I graduated a year older because of it. The kids of Princeton were better clothed than I was and it always made me feel out of place. Then when we moved to another part of Princeton, and I went to a Catholic school, it helped socially.

We all had to wear the same uniform, we were Catholics, my friends in school were Catholic, and the nuns promoted friendship among the students.

I never seemed to fit in with the Princeton ambiance, so I used sports as a conduit to make friends there. But since I was the oldest of the children in my family, I had to take care of my younger brothers after school. So I couldn't meet with the other kids because of family obligations. The other Italian kids in their section of Princeton were my early friends, but I had problems with the Black kids because of language difficulties. The language barrier gave me the drive to go on to accomplish more than ordinary. I was on my own during my school days (1949) to learn. But some teachers did try to help me, although I did most of it on my own and even had to teach my parents (mostly my mother) to speak English. Even today, my parents and I speak Italian to one another.

I used my spunky attitude to my benefit. And I saw what money could do for one's lifestyle in having the good things in life—and I wanted them.

Now I know that I can be on my own and I can still survive, after separating from my husband. He was dominant, so I focused on him and went "overboard" during the marriage. He was a very talented person and could do just about anything. But I've learned to live without having a man be the focus of my life. Now I focus on myself and what is best for me. Still, I admit that if Mr. Right came along, I would probably chuck it all to be with this new man and probably focus on him as I did with my first husband. But today I have a Mercedes and my own home and have supported other people living with me rather than having to be dependent for support on a husband. I like my independence, and I am enjoying my life now with a companion who lives *with me*.

Dale

They wanted me to go as far as possible in school on a graduate level. It was incredible support for that time period for a female child.

Effect of Italian-American background on your choice of a career?

My choice of a career was influenced more by my being Catholic than by my being of an Italian background. I was taught social responsibility in Catholic school. But my parents were also civic-minded. My father was active in Republican politics, with the Boy Scouts, the Holy Name Society at church. My mother also did extensive volunteer work. So my religious background had more influence than my ethnic background and reinforced my social commitment. My parents were prejudiced against everybody but Italians. The nuns taught me a different philosophy. They said that everybody was equal, everybody was good. So to gain my own impressions of others, I worked at various jobs at different geographical locations for and with Blacks, Jews and others, while going to college; and I came to believe that the nuns were right, rather than my parents. Other people weren't all bad or worthless, that they were like all other people, including Italians, some were good and nice, some were not. So I fought my parents' Italian identity prejudice against other groups of people. I went into a social work career after graduate school. I had brief experience as a social counselor, then moved into the administrative level of social work as an organizer and planner for social services.

Any effect of your ethnic background on your career to present?

No effect. But I do see being Italian as positive rather than negative. I was raised that way. My parents always said that I was lucky to be an Italian instead of being of another ethnic background.

Was your family supportive of your professional goals?

Yes. My parents were extremely supportive of my professional goals. They always said that marriage could come later. And it was not just for attending regular undergraduate college. They wanted to know what graduate school I wanted to attend. I was an only child. They supported my being on debating teams, and anything else that I did in school. This was the fifties. They wanted me to go as far as possible in school on a graduate level. It was incredible support for that time period for a female child. And even after I married and had children, they wanted me to continue my graduate studies and to get my graduate degrees.

Any effect of your background on your professional relationships?

No effect. No negative effect from an ethnic standpoint, but I have experienced negative reactions to being a woman professional. Because I'm a blonde, people say that I don't look Italian, and I confront them with the obvious fact that their comment is a put down.

Effect on social life?

With men I date it has a positive effect. There is a positive image to being an Italian female, since Italian fashion, sports cars and actresses such as Sophia Loren present such a positive image in the world today. Since my divorce eight years ago, I date an ethnic mixture of men, but haven't dated any Italian men, which is just a coincidence.

Background of spouse?

My husband was half Italian and half German.

Selection of mate?

There was no effect of my background on my choice of a mate. But before I married, I dated mostly Irish-Catholic men, since I was exposed mostly to Irish men in Catholic school.

Effect on relationship with mate?

My background did not affect my relationship with my husband. He was a military career officer and we traveled throughout the country. Our ethnicity did not play a major role in our lives. My husband was raised by his German-descent mother and his Italian side was not an influence in his background. And we lived away from our families all over America. I worked wherever we were. So our friends were mostly military and social workers and of different American backgrounds. My choice was to escape my parental influence by going into marriage with a military career man, knowing that I would leave my parents and the area where I was born and raised.

Effect of your background on your parenting?

My background had no real effect. Since we lived away from our families and on our own with our children, they did not receive any one-sided upbringing, but *were* affected by our military lifestyle. They are all college graduates and professional. They are religious, but I never pushed them into it, and they didn't go to Catholic schools as we did.

Religion?

It's as meaningful to me as it was to my parents. Maybe more so than what it was for my father, who was the typical Italian male in his attitude toward the Catholic Church. He was chief usher at the twelve o'clock Mass every Sunday, but it was done more as the right thing to do, since he had a high political profile in the community.

Politics?

I am strongly interested in politics. But I could never equal my parents' interest, since they were so active in politics, and were staunch Republicans. My father was extremely active in Republican politics in our hometown. And my turning Democrat disappointed my mother (My father was dead at the time.). In fact, she was horrified at my becoming a Democrat.

Catherine M.

I worked as a medical secretary for a short period of time in my marriage, until I became pregnant, I have not worked since.

After writing a book on the Italian community

that was the beginning of Madison's melting pot, and seeing and sensing the emotions and timing, I am in the process of forming a small company to continue tapping what is remembered by the old families. This will be done in a sequel to book number one, a 1990 calendar of photographs, a gold pendant shaped like the ten-block triangle of the old neighborhood with street and family engravings. The long-since-destroyed buildings are also being captured through sketches for notecards. These items have limited marketing areas, but will be received very well within the community.

My mother was born in Hungary; my father in Palermo, Sicily. My mother did not complete high school (1920s), but my father did and, being the fine athlete he was, went on to college and played football for a southern school. Professional goals and education were always stressed in our home. It was expected that my sister and I would go to college. She did, but I married young. I began my collegiate studies at the University of Wisconsin in my forties.

My parents gave us ballet lessons and piano lessons. Although we were not considered affluent by any means and lived in a blue-collar neighborhood, we had everything we wanted and always took pride in the way we looked and how we were accepted. We were both very popular in school and with our friends.

Socially, I find being Italian places me on a pedestal. Invariably, being Italian enters the conversation and remains the topic for long periods. It often begins with mentioning my father, then moves on to foods, Italian experiences. It is an ego trip, to say the least.

My parents have been devoted Catholics their entire lives, but my father is the more devout of the two. If you asked him to fill in for an absent altar boy, he probably could handle it with no problems. He will be 84 in December, and his memory goes on forever.

I can honestly say that if there were two people running for office, and one was Italian and both were equal candidates, I am sure that I would vote Italian.

I am more politically active than my parents, both of whom are loyal Democrats.

Sofia

My family was not supportive of my professional goals or my educational preparation. I was encouraged to leave school upon high school graduation. After I married, my husband encouraged me to attend evening classes at Rider College. I graduated from Rider with a Bachelor of Science Degree in Commerce.

I am presently retired from a civil service career with the State of New Jersey's Department of Labor.

My tendencies were to socialize with Italo-Americans, because, I suppose, I felt more comfortable having a common background. Presently, I socialize with people in my age group, regardless of nationality.

I am mildly interested in politics for economic reasons, and to curb the flow of ultra-liberalism. Because of our immigrant experiences, we have an inclination toward sympathy for the oppressed, but opposition to excesses in public welfare.

Carol Bonomo Ahearn

I returned to teaching in a school around the corner from where we lived so that I could be home

*when the children were home and nearby when
they were sick.*

Did being Italian-American affect my choice of a
career? Yes and no. Yes in the sense that my generation (second) was just emerging from poverty. My
grandparents were immigrants, and my parents were
very poor as children, but by the time I was born, my
father was becoming financially successful. (He didn't
marry until he was 36.)

His success was achieved in a method slightly different from most Italian-Americans. It was based on
success in the stock market. He was investing as early
as the 1920s. He got into the market because his
brother was a secretary to a stock broker and taught
my father what he learned from the stock broker.

How this uncle became involved in that line of
work is a mystery to me. He was what I would describe as more "American" than my parents. In other
words, more well-spoken and slim. These were the
words that I thought of to describe that uncle when I
was a child and these are the words I would still use.

This uncle was more middle class than my parents.

Though my father was financially successful, my
parents held working-class mores and life styles.

Because of their poor backgrounds and limited
education—neither went beyond the eighth grade—
they were committed to their children having greater
opportunity than they by pushing education as the
means to that end. On the other hand, they could provide little guidance about any great range of jobs. For
example, my father thought of lawyers as only crimi-
nal lawyers, not corporate lawyers.

My brother was encouraged to become a professional, which he did, and I, as a girl—although I

expressed an interest in becoming a lawyer—was encouraged to become a teacher, nurse or librarian (not a secretary, since my mother, by going to night school for 2½ years while working in a factory all day, became a secretary and I was expected to do better than she). My father discouraged my interest in law by saying that it was no place for a woman, associating with criminals as I would have to do as a lawyer, so I became a teacher.

This is a roundabout way of saying that economics and class influenced my career rather than my being Italian-American. This "story" could be true of anyone of any ethnic affiliation.

Again because of class, my sights were set low so that in half the jobs that I've had my abilities were underutilized. This fact is also related to my being a woman in that I took ten years off from work to raise my children (although during that time I attended an Ivy League university part time—my husband taught there and so they allowed me to take part-time study—and received an M.A. in English). When my younger child was in first grade, I returned to teaching in a school around the corner from where we lived so that I could be home when the children were home and nearby when they were sick. Although I was interested in a more stimulating job, I persevered with this until my younger child entered high school. By the time she was a junior, I was able to translate my teaching skills into other jobs.

I have always remained in the non-profit sector; as a college instructor (this was not a tenured position, but rather a pay-per-course situation, and by the time I received my M.A. in 1970, college teaching jobs were drying up), a curriculum designer at a medical school, a free-lance writer, a writer and video producer for an environmental agency, and now as a Senior Environmental Planner. (This job is a real stretch for me as I learn about the technical aspects of water quality control, and I'm enjoying the challenge. I've always enjoyed stretching and learning something new on the job rather than having to repeat the same thing over and over. And once I've mastered a job, I'm ready to move on to a new challenge.) I need a job that is inherently interesting, rather than one in which I'm just working for a paycheck. Trying out real estate gave me that understanding about myself. The very strong sense of putting myself last and my family first is connected to my being Italian-American.

I would still retain that same value system could I do it "over again," but I'd see more options for myself as far as the world of work is concerned so that I wouldn't have to sacrifice my own interests so much. But this is true of most women of my generation, no matter what their ethnic background.

My daughter is 23 and in retailing as a department manager for Macy's. She and I have talked about how, when she has a family, having children could be combined with this interest of hers: opening her own store, starting a catalogue shopping business, etc. Unfortunately, part-time work in this area will not be possible for her. In my opinion part-time work is ideal for a woman (or even a man), because it allows her to still be a homemaker, a role I enjoy. Maybe it will be possible for her daughter, but perhaps by then the idea of home making (by whomever) will be lost or role models non-existent. I hope not.

Family members were supportive up to a point, but my real work was considered to be what I did for my family, especially in terms of food and cooking, rather than my paid job.

But again my parents could be supportive only up to a point and this was limited by their own lack of information about jobs and by their view of what a woman should do.

As a younger teenager, I wanted to be a journalist, but I thought that meant being a reporter for the New York Daily News and covering accidents and murders in the dead of night—not exactly my cup of tea. Although we received the New York Telegram, I don't remember any female writers appearing on their Op-Ed page and no female columnists except for Hollywood gossip columnists and Emily Post, neither of whom interested me.

At about age eight or nine, I wanted to be a fiction writer, but I never came across books with Italian-American characters or ones in which a grandmother who didn't speak English lived with a family. In addition, I was basically taught at home—not explicitly, but somehow the message gets across—that we don't speak about what goes on in the family outside the home. This "suppression" would certainly inhibit any writing I might do in that what I felt most deeply about could not be written about; it would also give any fiction writing I might do a certain falseness because all the richness of my experience would be bleached out in a middle-class "white bread" type of writing. It took a *long* time for me to free myself from this prohibition, that it was a worthy topic. Probably Helen Barolini's *Umbertina* freed me from this. Finally, an Italian woman like me! And that was published less than ten years ago!

None of this, of course, speaks to the issue of the psychic toll of never disclosing to others what your background was like and what the implied message of that dictum was, i.e., that being different means inferior, rather than just different or circumstantial.

I find it significant that the present editors felt that these pieces should be printed under pseud-

onyms. Inherent in that position is the belief—probably accurate—that few Italian-Americans would speak
freely about their families if they had to sign their
names. An Italian-American woman sculptor I know
said that she felt free in her art only when her mother
died.

As I've become more confident of my values and of
my abilities, I find that I can socialize with people on
all levels of society, even the "old monied" people. People are people and share a commonality of emotions
and feelings despite accidental differences, so that I
can relate to such people in social situations. For two
years I belonged to a woman's debating club, which
had a cross section of people. It was very enjoyable.
My volunteer activities also bring me into contact with
all sorts of people. I sometimes feel like Will Rogers in
that I never met a person I didn't like. However, my
close friends come from the same socio-economic (not
necessarily ethnic) background as I—basically educated middle-class or artistic types or intellectuals.

I was brought up in the Italian section of Greenwich Village and in line with my parents' commitment
to education, I attended a private Catholic school on
Washington Square North. It was attended mainly by
Italian-Americans, Irish-Americans and the children
of artists who lived in the area as well as one German-
Jewish girl whose family was fortunate enough to em-
igrate during the war, first to England and then to
America. This girl, the artists' daughters (one father
was a writer, the other a painter), and two Irish-
American girls (one's father was a dentist, the other a
ship's captain) were my best friends growing up.

I gravitated to those girls whose horizons were
wider than my family's or the other Italian-American
girls. Their intellectual interests corresponded to
mine. The Italian-American girls seemed interested

only in boys—not that I and my friends weren't—but that seemed their only interest, despite the fact that one Italian-American girl in my class was the daughter of the most powerful Italian-American politician at that time. So it wasn't as if she were living in an intellectual vacuum.

I don't write this in a negative or judgmental way because I recognize that it's difficult to be anything other than one's historical or cultural milieu prepares one for. Just as the children I taught at the private school internalized their parents' views and attitudes towards life, so did the Italian-American girls with whom I came in contact.

I've never figured out what made me different from them. Was it my "artistic" temperament, my intelligence (my parents were told by my elementary school principal that I tested in the superior range), or something else? I don't know. I've often wondered about it.

That school I attended had a great influence on my life. It affirmed my interests in art and literature. My eighth grade nun encouraged me in my interests. In my eighth grade "autograph" book, she wrote that in my quiet way I would become a leader. This had a profound effect on me and my view of myself for the rest of my life. Me, a girl, a leader? An amazing concept.

When I left my Italian neighborhood and went off to a boarding college (my father wouldn't allow me to board out-of-state despite my being interested in a college in Connecticut), that nun's words stood me in good stead, because it was there that I came into contact with girls smarter and better prepared than I.

Her words reminded me of her belief in me. I became editor of our literary magazine and under my leadership it won, for the first time, a national award for form and content.

This was a particular source of satisfaction because a retired professor of the college had written to the present professor who oversaw the magazine that I couldn't write. She was not Italian-American (I never came across a teacher who was) and, frankly, I chalked up her assessment to discriminatory feelings rather than to an accurate judgment. So winning the award was especially gratifying.

I don't know if I was the first Italian-American to hold this post and that was what put the professor's nose out of joint, but I was, that year, the only Italian-American to head one of the major writing vehicles of the college, i.e., the newspaper and yearbook.

Religion was only a cultural thing for my parents. I am not religious in an institutionalized religious way, but I have a deep spiritual life. Also, the Catholic Church formed me in terms of many of my values of social justice, personal sacrifice, and altruism (others) as the basis for morality, as opposed to the self being the referrent for so many others.

I am very interested in politics. I ran twice for political office, once for the State Senate unsuccessfully, and once successfully as a state committeewoman.

My father described himself as an Independent, but in his later (more successful) years, he voted Republican on a national level. I don't know how he voted on the local level.

I also registered as an Independent, but in the first presidential election that I could vote in, I voted for Kennedy. His being the first Catholic, someone closer to my generation and the fact that he supported education—I was teaching by then—were all influences in my decision.

When I ran for office I had to declare a party affiliation, but, frankly, on the national level neither party now pleases me. I read Mario Cuomo's diaries and was very impressed with him. I felt that he was someone who spoke to me, whose policies I believed in. I even filed to be an uncommitted delegate to the Democratic Convention, but then didn't follow through in obtaining signatures because I had gotten a promotion at work and it wouldn't have been a good time for me to be away. It's just as well because not one uncommitted delegate on the ballot on Super Tuesday was elected—and this in a state with a very high Italian-American population. But this is understandable since most voters didn't understand that the uncommitted column was a way of pledging to no candidate so that a Cuomo draft would be possible.

I am still very disappointed that Cuomo isn't running. Maybe in 1992.

I am much more active in politics than my parents. On the local level, my parents didn't trust politicians. They voted, but they were not actively involved.

I remember that my parents admired Adlai Stevenson's verbal ability. Once again he embodied their belief in education. My father believed, though he never said it, that education would give us options in life that he never had. Within the limits of his world, he encouraged my brother and me to do a job that we would like, since we'd be doing it all our lives. Also unspoken was the reality that he had had to do whatever job would earn him money to support his family.

My father had a great belief in America. He believed that his son had as much of an opportunity to be president as the next person. But for himself, although America had been good to him (he worked very hard and succeeded), there was an underlying sadness associated with his early life which lingered throughout his lifetime.

At holidays, although he told stories about his successful business ventures, he also told stories about how, when he was 14 years old, he was riding the subway making a delivery for his boss and was laden down with all sorts of packages. A man turned to him and asked, "What's the matter, kid, did the horse die?"

Another story told about how one cold day, while sitting on his stoop crying because he had no mittens, a man came along and bought him some.

These stories engendered sadness in me for my father and a fear of being poor, an anxiety that persisted within me for a long time; and which, perhaps, still exerts its influence on me in that I am fearful about taking big occupational risks. But this may also be due to my being divorced.

Concerning attitudes toward money: I read the account of the FBI agent who infiltrated the Mafia under the name of Donnie Brasco. What struck me about the mobsters is that they could never get enough money. Not that they seemed to spend it, but they seemed happy only when lots of it was coming in. It was an extreme end of a continuum of attitudes toward money. I felt a part of that continuum (not in an illegal sense, of course, as they were in their attempts to satisfy that need), and wondered if there was a connection between poverty one generation away and attitudes toward money. I wonder about it because my concern is illogical.

It's difficult to generalize. I know Italian-Americans like myself who are concerned about money and others who are not. Maybe it's being middle-aged and thinking ahead to retirement, or maybe it's being a woman not brought up to think that she would have to support herself. But again I think of those sad stories of my father and wonder if he was really crying about not having a carefree childhood with parents too harried to express love.

Nikki

When I went to school, I wanted to be an American child. Maybe, in fact, I was even embarrassed to be an Italian. Maybe that's the reason that I did so well in school. Why I got straight A's. I was an American child. It was only in later years that I regreted not having learned more about my roots, and not having asked more questions. They, my parents, must have had novels in them to tell. The hard lives that they endured here.

Maria T.

I came to the United States as an immigrant on September 3, 1965, and I became a U.S. citizen on December 8, 1971. I visited Italy in 1974, and with the exception of a few other short trips, I have lived in Monterey, California for the last 23 years.

When I came from Italy, I taught Italian at the Defense Language Institute in Monterey. I also became an adjunct professor at the Monterey Institute of International Studies where I have taught Italian, and where I teach when a student requests Italian.

I have taught Italian at Monterey Adult School and at the Carmel Adult School.

I was born in Augusta, in the province of Siracusa, Sicily; and after attending the Classical Lyceum in Augusta, I attended the University of Catania, where I graduated in the summer of 1961. I hold a *Dottorato in Filosofia.*

I like to teach Italian and the Italian culture, and sometimes I feel frustrated when people don't take the time to appreciate it. I would like to teach more about Italy and its history, art, music, literature and government on a regular basis, but I feel that this dream of mine cannot become a reality in Monterey.

My parents were supportive of me when I was going to school. Now, I am on my own. I'm single and I make my own decisions.

I have many friends and acquaintances. Most of my friends are Americans or naturalized Americans. Although I know many Italo-Americans in the area, I don't have many friends among them. However, a friend of mine whom I see, perhaps a few times a year, is from Padova. We used to teach Italian at the Defense Language Institute. She still teaches Italian there, but I don't.

I attend some Italian social functions, celebrations, dinner-dances, meetings. I also see Italian movies when they are played in the area.

Religion is important to me, but not in the same way it was to my parents. Although I will never have that strong, unshakable faith my father had and my mother still has, I believe and I practice my religion. I attend church regularly and I have been involved in parish activities.

I am mildly interested in politics. I follow the news daily and some of the debates and the weekly reviews on TV. I am not active in politics, but I am a registered voter.

I wish we had a democracy in this country, in

which all the citizens would participate. I hope that changes will take place in the future to get more people involved, to awaken the social consciousness of the people. Things will not get better unless those who need changes in the social structure fight for them through active participation.

Rachele

Being of Italian-American background did not have an effect on my choice of a career simply because my present career, that of Fine Art Advisor, developed from years of study and work in the Fine Art arena. The arts have always been a part of our lives. My father was a sculptor. But this can be said of others who are not of my background. Most of my relatives would have preferred to have me choose a career in the sciences or engineering, because the arts do not offer rewards of a monetary nature. They value money over esthetics. My proficiency in the Italian language has a certain value in my field, but that, too, can be learned by an individual other than Italian.

My family was pleased with any success I had in life, not necessarily focused on my present profession. I earned my Fine Arts Degree at the age of 40 after my children were grown. I began working at the age of 14 while attending high school. My parents admired independence and encouraged me to provide financially for myself. Both parents worked. We lived with my grandmother who encouraged us to do well scholastically and to plan for self-sufficiency.

My background does affect my relationships in my profession simply because it is now popular and "stylish" to be of Italian descent.

My husband was an officer in the Italian Navy. I did not consciously select him because he was Italian. Circumstances were such at the time that they contributed to our relationship. It was a modern vision of *"Madame Butterfly"* with the events leading to marriage, children and divorce.

Having had the opportunity to live in Italy as I did, I learned more concerning my heritage than most Italian-Americans. It was a most enlightening and positive experience.

I do not believe my background has affected my parenting.

Religion is more meaningful to me than it was to my parents. I believe they did not approach religion in the spiritual context.

I am interested in politics, and I am also concerned for the state of politics in our country. I feel that we do not have the quality and expertise in our elected officials that we deserve. They certainly do not reflect the principles upon which our government was meant to operate.

My father was a Socialist and in his time there was a platform for Socialism. I feel that I do not have the choices which my parents had. In fact—I feel that I really do not have any choices at all.

Sister Margherita

I have always been treated with respect and dignity and I have always made my ethnic background known.

I joined the Religious Teachers Filippini when I was 13 years old. In June, 1935, during my Confirmation in St. Margaret's Church, Little Ferry New Jersey, Bishop Thomas Joseph Walsh stated: "Any young lady of Italian descent who wishes to join the Sisterhood should go to this group of Italian Sisters in Morristown." This impressed me. I was a graduate of St. Mary's School in Hackensack with Benedictine Nuns as teachers, and I had arranged to attend their novitiate in the Fall. I immediately changed my plans and contacted the Mother Superior at Villa Walsh. I visited her during the summer months and was interviewed. She said I should start high school at Villa Walsh. She would expect me on September 2nd.

It was Labor Day. My parents, six sisters, brother, and several friends were gathered at the dinner table. During the meal I announced my plans. I would leave at one o'clock for the convent. It is difficult to describe my parents' surprise and sorrow. But I was determined and, despite their objections, I left that afternoon accompanied by my mother and one of my sisters.

My career began with my study of Italian. Although my parents came from Italy around 1900, I did not understand or speak the language. I was fascinated by the language and culture. It was clear that I would succeed. At sixteen I received the religious habit and three years later made my profession. By this time my family was supportive of my goals. I earned my B.A. from Georgian Court College in 1943 and my M.A. from Columbia University in 1949, as well as my Ph.D. in 1960.

I taught at Seton Hall University part time and for about twenty years I was a professor of Italian language and literature at Fairleigh Dickinson University. My relationships were not affected by my Italian-American background.

I have always been treated with respect and dignity and I have always made my ethnic background known. I am proud of my heritage.

I have published 30 books and have received recognition throughout my career.

Kelly

My mother became a late-blooming role model for me when she went to college.

Did your Italian-American background affect your choice of a career?

No, I don't think so. No one in my family was a professional. My mother started going to college when I was in high school. There wasn't any role model to follow. I guess because my mother went to college, I realized that I could go. Somewhere in high school I declared that I would go to law school and be a lawyer. I went to law school, but I'm not a member of the bar and I ended up going into another area. My mother became a late-blooming role model for me when she went to college.

Effect of your background on your career at present?

My Italian-American background probably helps my career. In local politics an Italian last name does well, and I have aspirations to run for elected office here in Mercer County. So that's an advantage. In another sense I think it hinders, although I don't think it hurts me personally. Outside of running for office, I think that someone with a WASP last name has a better opportunity in administration, and probably in private industry, too. In Mercer County an Italian last name is a couple of points higher politically than a non-Italian last name. But not in the outskirts, not in the Hopewells and the Princetons, but that's not where you get elected in this county. You have to get elected in Hamilton, Trenton, Ewing, Lawrence, and the Italian last name helps there.

Was your family supportive?

Yes. I lived at home and they paid for my college education and most of law school, too, since I had gotten some grants. I worked part time, even though I didn't have to, but just to have some money of my own.

Professional relationships?

I guess because the major part of my job is political, my Italian background is favorable in Mercer County, maybe not in another county, but here, yes. Sometimes you'll get comments, "Oh, another Italian," from a non-Italian, and in the outskirts; but I've never encountered any references about the Mafia. I'm less sensitive to it, because I feel that I have an advantage.

How does your ethnic background affect your social life?

I think there's an effect. Not with friends so much, but the family dominates more. They take up more of your social time. There's less time for strangers, particularly when growing up. Everything was family oriented. We had a lot of family functions, and I always let them take precedence over something else. If you don't go, you don't show respect. I think I enjoyed it, though. If I had a choice, I'd rather have gone to a family function, because I always had a good time there. I felt comfortable. Presently, there isn't too much of a family situation anymore, except for my mother. My whole personal life has changed.

Did you consciously select an Italian-American for a spouse?

No, I did not . . . although he is. I met him in a bar. My girl friend from law school would always see him at a bar we frequented on Friday nights. He'd send drinks over to us, but he'd never join us. He would leave right afterwards. My girl friend actually liked him, and I was trying to get him to talk to her. Finally, at the end of summer, he came up and talked to us. He just kept talking to me and not to my girl friend. I didn't inquire as to his background. But I guess when you look at him, you can figure out what he is. We dated for five years. He was willing to date me during my three years of law school. He was in no hurry to get married. I guess I said, "All right, this is enough. I'm kind of bored, either we get married, or we break up." And he was agreeable to getting married.

Any effects on your relationship with your husband?

There is an underlying effect on our male and female roles. Most of the time it's not really a problem. He gives the baby a bath every night, and he usually dresses her in the morning. He does the vacuuming; but he does point out that I have to do something. "You're supposed to make dinner," or something like that, reinforcing his masculine world. He's a good father. He does pitch in and help me.

Parenting?

I think my background affects it in a different way. It affects it because I'm not allowing it to. I don't want my daughter ever to think that she has to stay home with the family. She's only three years old and even now I want her to go out and do things on her own. It's a reversal to make her more outward, to get her to be more social; to allow her to do things that we didn't do, what my sister and I didn't do. It's a conscious thing, yet in a way it's natural because of the way my life has evolved. Now I'll try anything, such as learning to ski. There was a time when you didn't do those kinds of things. You never thought about going skiing. I want my daughter to try everything. I want her to be exposed to everything. I want a more expanded world for her.

Religion and your parents?

I don't think religion was meaningful to my parents. And I don't think it played a role in my life. I don't really have any religion. I don't go to church. But I want my daughter to be exposed to religion. I think I was affected by my parents, because they were very negative toward religion. They had very bad experiences. It made me think there wasn't a need to pay attention to that area of life. I would not want to put my values on my daughter, or to give her any judgments. I want her to decide for herself. My husband thinks he's religious, but I don't think he is, although he does go to church on Easter and Christmas, and he does take our daughter with him. My daughter has been baptized. I conform in a sense. I do everything you have to do. I believe in my own personal philosophy and that the Church does have a role.

Politics?

I'm very interested in politics. When I was a teenager, I became interested in it. I just always have been. When I was about 13 or 14, I had a boyfriend whose father wanted to be the Superintendent of Schools in the city, and I helped him get literature out on his campaign. I was always interested in local and national elections. And I always thought that law was a good background, which was the reason I went into it and politics.

Effect of background on your choice of political party?

When I registered to vote in high school, I declared myself a Democrat, because I felt that I wasn't rich enough to be a Republican, not because I was Italian. But there was some background influence, since most working-class Italians are Democrats, while the upper-level Italians are Republicans. I never really did anything active as a Democrat. It was after I got out of law school and I started getting politically involved that I declared myself a Republican. I clerked for a year, but couldn't be involved with politics during my clerkship. I knew that once I finished, I was going to get involved with politics, so I started looking at the people who were on both sides of the fence, and I didn't like those who were on the Democratic side. I think that on the county level there is only one way to do something, and both parties are going to end up doing it one way. It's just a matter of approach, and I found that the Democrats were a little cruder and not as sophisticated. The Republicans I got to know did things more the way I would like to see them done. The types of people they dealt with were more like the people I wanted to deal with. I based it on personality. I liked the Republicans.

Anything you want to add?

Yes. One thing you asked me triggered something else about my Italian-American background affecting me socially. It affected me because I stayed closer to the family, and it affected me from an educational standpoint. If my family weren't so close, I think I would have gone away to college. I stayed home and went to Trenton State. I would have gone to one with a better academic reputation. As a commuting student, I didn't get involved on campus. I went home to my friends and family. I never really got involved socially on campus in any of the activities.

Angela

A "career" is what most young people have today. When I started a "career," it was a real necessity. When I married, I quit work on the birth of my first child and stayed home. But being Italian-American had no effect on where I worked then.

When I returned to work eight years after the birth of my third child, again my ethnic background had no effect. I became known as, and was called, "Mama" at my work place, my office, and I enjoyed the name. I berated anyone who may have been rude and referred to Italians with slurs or vulgarities.

My husband and my children were very supportive of me when I returned to work, and our children
were very proud of their Mom and Dad when we returned to school in 1959 to get our high school diplo-
mas. Then at work it was on-the-job training. I retired
eight years ago.

Presently, we belong to and are very active in the
Order Sons of Italy, and my husband, being of Sicilian
parents, belongs to "Arba Sicula," a national organization to promote the Sicilian language and culture.

Religion is not a great part of our lives. Though I
believe in God, and I pray to Him, and I was raised a
Catholic, I am no longer practicing my religion. But it
was not a big part of my parents' life, either. My ma-
ternal grandmother was the most religious one I can
remember, and I learned from her.

I am mildly interested in politics. And like many, I
complain about the system. Sometimes I write letters.
I vote, after I have discussed the issues with my husband. And we certainly look for those of Italian-
American ancestry when voting, but not as the main
criteria, only to assure ourselves that some of us are
not being left out of the political arena. Our many
committees for social justice are seeing to that. My
parents were not active in politics, but then, my father
left my mother when I was nine.

Carmella

I feel that my Italian-American background had
an effect on my choice of a career, because as a child I
always wanted to be "American," and when I was finally able to go to school at age 42, I became (what
else?) a teacher of English.

Being an Italian-American and involved in a teaching career has made me aware of how much information concerning the contributions of Italians and Italian-Americans has been omitted from our United States history books. It has also made me determined to disseminate as much material as possible about "us" to all I come in contact with.

My parents were illiterate peasants from Italy and held that "to raise babies a woman needed no education." When I was 18, working in a factory, my employer recognized my abilities and suggested business school. I had to plead and cry to get the $10.00 per month (which, of course, I earned) in order to begin to better myself. At age 16, I had been removed from school by my parents to go to work. The school authorities informed my parents of my potential, but my 14 siblings had to eat, too.

My Italian-American background does affect my professional relationships in that I feel much more comfortable with those of similar backgrounds and interests. All my colleagues are aware of my ethnicity because I strive to make them aware of the neglect which has continued even to the present time.

I am very much interested in politics, because it represents the seat of power which governs us as Americans and influences world events. And my awareness of the generations of neglected, qualified Italian-Americans has made me want to assist them "if they are qualified to govern." Up until two years ago, I was totally immersed in my education courses. In 1986, when I finally earned my M.A. in English Language and Literature, I finally had sufficient time and energy after the workday was over to join the Republican Party in my town. I am active politically and I encourage my children to be interested and active in politics in their respective towns.

Fran

My Italian-American background had no effect on my present career of teaching (a career choice made in high school), but it may have influenced my choice of a subject area: foreign languages. It seemed natural to have an appreciation of, and respect for, other cultures. Italian (Sicilian dialect) was spoken often between my parents and always when they were with their friends, so perhaps this fostered an interest in languages for me.

My choice of my previous career of full-time wife and mother was partly because of my being Italian-American, and partly a result of my being a product of the fifties when women had limited options, or didn't even realize that they *had* options. I graduated from college, taught for 2½ years, then resigned when I was pregnant in order to stay home and raise a family. I believe it was both society's expectations at that time (1968) and my Italian-American background that caused me to never even consider leaving the baby to return to work. I had four children in all, and it was definitely the "Italian" in me that wouldn't allow me to leave the children and go back to work. Emotionally, I could not have done it. I never trusted anyone to love them enough! When my youngest was in preschool, I did a small amount of tutoring for a local junior college. When she was in fourth grade, I returned to teaching. The position happens to be part time—ideal for the family-oriented Italian-American that I am.

My ethnic background does affect my professional relationships, but it affects how I relate to *all* people, not just those I come into contact with professionally. Because of it, I have a tolerance, acceptance and respect for most others. Perhaps sometimes too much of a tolerance, when I should be questioning or sharing my strong convictions more. However, because of how I was raised, I am basically a peacemaker. I am accommodating, not competitive, and not terribly assertive. I don't necessarily see those as bad qualities. I love people and attribute that to the love I felt as a child.

It definitely affected my social life in the past. My father came to this country when he was 21 years old, and my mother was five. My father was married at age 48, my mother at 33. My father was almost 51 when I was born, so not only did I have "old-fashioned Italian parents," as I saw it, but I also had "older" parents compared to those of my friends. My parents were very strict and extremely protective. I was not allowed to do many of the things that my friends were allowed to do. However, as a teen, I was allowed to participate in school-sponsored events and structured, supervised teen recreation programs. I just didn't have the freedom my friends had—even in college. I attended college in my hometown, so I lived at home and not on campus. This limited my social life somewhat. I had a curfew all through college and firmly believe that if I had taken a job locally, lived at home (which it would have been scandalous *not* to do!), and remained single, I'd probably still have had a curfew, even if I had been 30 years old. That's hypothetical, of course, but I base it on past experience.

Its effect on my present social life is evidenced by my love of people. Though I tend to be somewhat shy, I consider myself a warm, loving, caring and compassionate person who is sensitive toward others. I am a fairly open person who is both a giver and a receiver of support from my friends. I tend to respond emotionally to many situations and often operate on a feeling level. In general, I think, Italians *love* people. I'll never forget my friend's comment years ago when we were traveling through Europe together. She was referring to the responses received from people of various countries upon being asked directions. Though said in jest, she summed it up by saying: "The French point, the Spanish give you specific directions, and the Italians take you there." The warmth and open hearts that many Italians seem to have are indeed endearing qualities.

My religion is more meaningful to me than it was to my parents. Part of that has to do with the Catholic Church being a different church today from what it was when they were my age. I also think it became meaningful to me at an earlier age than was their experience. My mother's religion became more meaningful to her in her senior years. My parents attended Mass regularly on Sundays, and we attended as a family except for those Sundays when my sister and I were required to attend our Sunday School classes. They laid the foundation, and today my religion is very important to me. I draw strength from my religion, and it's also been an influence on my values.

I am mildly interested in politics. I'm not terribly interested on a day-to-day basis, although I'm certainly interested in what's going on in the world. I become more interested, of course, during important or exciting elections, or if something affects me personally.

My Italian-American background has had no effect on my choice of a political party. I tend to vote for candidates on an individual basis rather than becoming affiliated with, or displaying loyalty toward, any particular political party.

I am as "inactive" as my parents were in politics.

However, my parents never failed to exercise their right to vote. They were proud to be Americans and took their privilege of voting seriously. They never had an apathetic attitude toward getting out to vote, and as far as I know, they never missed doing so. I tend to take it seriously as well.

Dolores

I wanted to be a teacher, but as I went through college, I developed a real interest in law as a career. But *girls* didn't seem to go in that direction then, and as I thought about it, I kept hearing my *Nona* say, "A lawyer sells his soul." It wasn't bad enough to hear that, but it was always *his,* so I continued with education.

I feel that I have a good, strong foundation in setting goals for myself and others. If my grandparents and my father could have gone through what they did to come to this country and to build what they did, then I certainly can be strong enough to build more and continue being proud of my background. No matter how hard a task seems, if you want to do something, you can.

Being able to speak another language makes me feel proud and smart, because I am not ashamed of my heritage.

Rosina Raggio

I was that relatively unique Italian-American girl who went to the convent. At the age of 16, I entered the School of the Sisters of St. Francis in Milwaukee, Wisconsin and took vows in that order in 1948. I left the convent in 1973.

Italian fathers really don't like their daughters to become nuns. My father felt that I was cheating him out of his future grandchildren, and he used all sorts of dramatic and melodramatic ploys to change my mind. Though he ultimately came to terms with my convent life, he never really thought I was happy. I was told by my sister at a party for my 25th year in the convent, that he kept a suitcase in the trunk of the car packed with *lay* clothes. "Just in case she changes her mind." That suitcase stayed in the car and made trips to Milwaukee everytime my parents came to visit me.

My mother, on the other hand, felt that my going to the convent was her way of making it to heaven, and though she never really thought that I was good enough, she wanted me to be a *good* nun, so they could be proud of me. In the end, both of my parents were proud of the fact that I was an educated and active person . . . but *Dio Mio*! . . . those missing grandchildren.

When I left the convent, it was not to marry, but to find some peace and consistency in putting my professional life together with my religious life. I nearly married, but in the end chose not to trade my lively and satisfying single life for marriage.

I chose to become a nun because the life of the sisters in my high school in Chicago seemed exciting, interesting and concerned with what really mattered. I loved school and thought that as a teacher, I could make a difference. So from the very first, I wanted to be something "important." In the forties, one of the only professional careers open to women was teaching, and the selflessness of the nuns was an inspiration to me. It seemed natural to blend teaching and the religious life.

At the present time, I am very active in the Twin City Italian-American community. Meetings, festivals, parties, special events--I spend a fair amount of my free time socializing with Italians. As a single person, an ex-nun and an Italian (and I can't tell which of the three forces is strongest), I seek out community, family, *compari*. My Italian friends are a little like my mother, they define "family" as blood relationship. Having lived in the convent since I was 16, I learned to live and love a family of choice, and I am a kind of special "Aunt" to the children of several friends who are not related to me. In this way, I expand my life and fill it with the people and relationships I need—and want.

My sister doesn't understand this. She is still very "Italian" in that way. "Blood is thicker than water," she says.

I am not married, but when I left the convent and began to date, I found that I was attracted to Italian men, and I consciously sought them out. Unfortunately, there are not many Italians in the Twin Cities metropolitan area—not many eligible ones my age. So I gave up and began dating non-Italians.

I know that what I look for in a man I identify as "Italian," is probably what I loved in my father. (I'm aware of the Freudian overtones, but that's the truth.) My special friend has many of those qualities—gentleness, good sense of humor, sensitivity (he cries without embarrassment); he loves family life, he's quite physically and openly affectionate, a reader and an intelligent conversationalist. Though he has so many other non-Italian qualities, I, of course, am attracted to those that I recognize as "Italian."

Since I am not married at this time, I can only answer as a single person in a relationship. I believe that one of the attractions of my friend for me is my

"Italian" personality. His family is true WASP, having arrived on these shores in 1700 or so. He has almost no ethnic identity, and says he envies me my close identity with my Italian family, culture, language. Since knowing me, he has become more aware of his ethnic background. He is looking for his roots. He likes to attend Italian social events with me and finds my Italian-American friends interesting.

I have never had children, and I never will, but I often think about what kind of parent I would have been and have some observations on the subject.

As a college professor and counselor, I have always been inclined towards collegiality with my students, but I think that as a parent I would probably be rather direct and not so democratic.

I have seen my sister and reflecting on her parenting, I think that I would probably have attitudes similar to hers. My 28 years in teaching have given me some different perspectives, but I think that as a parent I would be pretty authoritarian. My parents were very affectionate, but not sentimental about us at all. I can't image my mother or father caring about whether or not we liked the rules or orders that they set down for us; they didn't ask our opinions often. They knew what they wanted the family—and us—to be. *Mama locuta est. Casusa finita!*

I observe that my sister and her children get along well, because her children know exactly where she stands—because she always tells them. They accept that. When my grandnephew visited me this summer, he seemed perfectly comfortable with the way I "parented" him. He knows how *Nana* works and so he understands his Aunt. He doesn't expect to be consulted about most of what he's told to do. But he got a lot of hugging and a lot of attention. That seemed to work for us when we were children and it seemed to work for him.

I am very interested in politics and as active as my schedule permits. My parents were also active in any organization that they belonged to. So I think my own political activity is the result of personal initiative as well as parental modeling.

I always feel that unless I am active—serving as an officer, chair, committee head—I'm not really making a contribution. My parents, especially my mother, were like that when I was a child.

In the convent I was not allowed to be politically active, in a public way, but I have always been involved in the politics of education. I feel strongly that I need to get into leadership positions if I want to have any impact on education.

I am already signed up as a Dukakis volunteer for the DFL Party, that is, Democratic Farmer Labor Party in Minnesota.

I have always felt that the Democratic Party is the party of the people outside the preppy WASP circle. If the principal issues of this campaign were ethnic, I would trust that the Democrats could deal with them. As an Italian, I have some sense that I am a minority and that my *compari* and I will get a better hearing from a Democratic administration. I don't feel persecuted, but I am aware of minorities who feel that way.

This may have more to do with being an ex-nun than with being Italian. Nuns are always for the underdog, for the minorities, for those who cannot help themselves. I don't think Italians belong in those categories anymore, so I'm not out to "help Italians" only. But I'd probably support Cuomo—maybe even Iacocca!

Teresa

Although I worked as a secretary after leaving

high school, I am presently self-employed as a dress-maker—4th generation, because it afforded me the opportunity to work from home while my children were young. I also attended evening college for ten years. There were tailors and dressmakers on both sides of the family—in Italy and in the United States.

I find that WASPs don't frequent Italian-American dressmakers. Although I'm tops in my field, my clientele is mainly Jewish. I think Jews and Italians have an affinity for one another.

My family was Italian immigrant artisans who believed in education, but who prided themselves in being able to create beautiful things. Since my three sisters and I were born between 1925 and 1935, we were encouraged to finish high school and then to marry. They (my parents) were appalled at times at the lack of culture in our education as youngsters, but they were very proud when we returned to school as grown women. Many of our cousins—male and female—went to college during the depression thirties.

I am President of the L. I. Regional Chapter of the American Italian Historical Association and Recording Secretary of the National AIHA. I feel comfortable in the company of academics and scholars who pursue the researching of Italian-Americans. Although I earn my livelihood in a craft and not as a professional, my working relationships are mainly with my clients who are 95% Jewish, while most of my friends in the professions are Italian-Americans.

I am mildly interested in politics, although for many years I was highly interested in politics. I like politics in Italy better; their way makes more sense to me. I'm a Democrat and my family was Democrat, although my parents disdained politics and were not active. My mother's family was active, mainly because we were close to Vito Marcantonio's family in Italy.

They were from the same village. My father was wise politically, but didn't participate except for voting every year, as did my mother. I vote, but don't participate at this time.

Elia

The Italian male appears to me to be self-centered and not caring of his wife's individuality.

I do not believe my background had any effect on my career choice. My career choice is not one any individual in my family has ever had.

My knowledge of the Italian culture has enabled me to better understand people of similar background.

My family encouraged and supported a professional goal and pertinent education. To be self-sustaining financially was encouraged. A college degree was encouraged as long as the education took place *close to home*.

I do not believe my Italian-American background affects my professional relationships; but it does serve to enrich me personally, yet it is not at the forefront of my social life, past or present.

My husband is not an Italian-American, and I consciously selected a non-Italian. The personality of the Italian-American male has never appealed to me. I have never appreciated the role I perceive the female to play who lives with an Italian male. The Italian male appears to be self-centered and not caring of his wife's individuality.

My Italian-American background does not affect my husband except to enhance our cultural understanding of the Italians.

Our son has been encouraged to maintain a close-knit family situation, with constant love and interest being reaffirmed.

Religion is not as meaningful to me as it was to my parents, but it is not rejected, either.

I am only mildly interested in politics. I have never been encouraged or motivated to be involved in politics.

Piccolina

During the forties, being of Italian extraction was not the most favored qualification for obtaining employment.

I'm a retired junior high school principal, having had a career of 33 years as a teacher, supervisor and administrator in the New York City Public School System.

My interest in teaching was enhanced by my mother and her family. Her aunts, sisters and brothers were teachers in Italy. She always spoke so fondly of them and was so proud of their accomplishments. After a visit to Italy as a child (during the Depression years), I became more determined than ever to become a teacher. I had met my aunts and uncles in the flesh. They were real and I was inspired by them. Teaching also offered job security, a good salary and a long summer vacation. All of which would help me to visit Italy again and again to become closer to my mother's family. Today, my Italian cousins are teachers. My brother's daughters, growing up in the same household with me and their grandparents, are teachers. They are proud of their Italian heritage. They, too, after a visit to Italy during their teen years, returned with very positive attitudes toward their heritage and its culture.

As an Italian-American woman I had to work harder than most to prove that I could achieve my goals and objectives. During the Depression, to become a teacher of Italian—since I wanted to teach this beautiful language and culture to others—was no easy task. My parents could not afford a college education for me. Fortunately, living in New York City and attending the right high school (and achieving exceptional grades) gave you the opportunity to be admitted to a tuition-free college. This I was able to do. I passed the entrance exam for Hunter College High School (a very special high school), and upon graduation with good grades, I was admitted to Hunter College where I majored in Italian and Secondary Education. I graduated with a B.A. degree *cum laude* and membership in Phi Beta Kappa. During the forties, being of Italian extraction was not the most favored qualification for obtaining employment. Your only hope was Civil Service. When the Board of Examiners of New York City Schools gave examinations for teaching licenses, I applied. It was a slow climb up the career ladder, taking qualifying courses and examinations for each position I wanted. With years of teaching experience, courses, exams, interviews and competing with other qualified candidates (in spite of some discrimination and dirty tricks), I obtained a junior high school principalship and became one of the first, few Italian-American women to be principals in the New York City Public School System in the early seventies. I, of course, was very active in many Italian-American organizations and the Italian-American community during that time and still am. These groups were supportive, helpful and inspiring. Today, as a retiree, I am more active than ever.

My mother—more so than my father—was supportive of my educational preparation and professional goals. Although, economically, things were very tight at home during the thirties and forties, both parents saw that freedom from economic problems lay in a good, solid college education. My mother insisted that I complete college without working during the day and going to school at night. She worked as a seamstress and dress factory operator to bring money into the household. She was not in the best of health, but her desire to see that my brother and I completed our education was paramount. Much hard work and many sacrifices!

Due to my teaching of Italian and being a supervisor of foreign languages, I became active in many professional, social and cultural Italian-American organizations. I was determined to bring the positive achievements and contributions of our people to the attention of the American public at large. I fought against discrimination and negative stereotyping of Italians and Italian-Americans by writing letters, participating in protests and panel discussions. Today, after a career in education, I'm president of the Metropolitan Council of the National Italian-American Foundation in New York; New York City Representative for *ITALY/ITALY* Magazine; a board member of ITALIAN HERITAGE AND CULTURE MONTH COMMITTEE and of many other similar organizations. My happiest and most rewarding experience was being Dinner Chairwoman at a dinner honoring Associate Justice Antonin Scalia—first Italo-American on the U.S. Supreme Court—last November in New York City.

My ethnic background affects my social life a great deal as I participate in most of the social functions given by Italian-American organizations in New York City, Washington, D.C. and Italy. I attend dinners, participate in conferences, go to luncheons, receptions, fashion shows, concerts, tours and trips to Italy that are sponsored by these groups. I have met many outstanding and distinguished Italians and Italian-Americans at these social functions from the President of Italy to the Governor of New York and various celebrities.

As a middle-of-the-roader, and at times, as a conservative, I have found that the Republican Party meets my political philosophy more closely than the Democratic Party.

Italian-Americans are hardworking, individualistic, family- and church-oriented, nationalistic, patriotic and ambitious to be successful and independent—qualities that I find are more associated with the Republican Party of *today*.

I am active in politics as far as supporting my party's candidates with the vote and with contributions. My parents were not active in politics per se, but very much interested. They always voted.

I first became aware of being Italian-American during World War II—being in college at the time—when great anti-Italian feeling and prejudice were everywhere.

I intend to carry on past traditions, particularly religious holidays, family reunions, Italian cuisine, and maintaining close ties with friends and relatives in Italy.

Lisa

My choice to work in the arts represents a hard-won struggle to extricate myself from the pressures and restrictions of my family, my upbringing and my education. Any guidance I received was intended to direct me into other "safer" and more secure, less threatening professions—education, for an example.

My family always discouraged any inclinations I had from childhood toward the profession I now pursue. In the performing arts (I am an actress, singer, middle-eastern dancer, director, producer and writer.), freedom of expression is essential and self-expression of any kind in my younger years was squelched by my family; an attitude which was reinforced by the nuns in the Catholic schools that I attended until I graduated college. So much for the intimate aspects of being Italian-American.

Forces from the outside have also affected my career considerably. When I was growing up, no role models (or hardly any) were visible in the media (Annette Funicello? Anne Bancroft, who changed her name?); and even today, they are just beginning to emerge. As a result, I am often passed over because of my ethnicity. I am not "whitebread" or "P.G." (meaning Proctor & Gamble material). I don't have the overall WASP look and therefore do not blend in with the images that are preferred on TV in commercials, sitcoms and soap opera by those controlling the purse strings of the industry.

I produce a TV show in a magazine format and I'm employed as well in the theatre, films and cable television. As a result, I have become a "professional Italian-American." I also understand thoroughly our past history and our present image in the media. This can't help but affect how I view the world.

I have had serious relationships with men of other ethnic backgrounds, but I prefer Italian-Americans, even over Italians, *especially* over Italians. A similar background makes it easier to relate.

I am only mildly interested in politics. Since I am an artist, and while even art is political, I leave politics to the politicians. I am traditionally Democrat, but I rarely vote, although I would vote for Cuomo.

Toni

So besides nationality, it was religion as well that held the Italian back in Princeton. Being an Italian-Catholic there was like being a leper.

Let's talk about your background.

I was born in Princeton, New Jersey. I lived in Princeton all my life, went to school and married there. My father came to this country when he was 11. He moved to Princeton in 1911. My parents married in 1920. My parents lived there till my father died in 1950. My mother still lives in Princeton. We had an apartment on Witherspoon Street near the bank, near Nassau Street. We also had an apartment on Nassau Street. It was not an Italian section. The Italian section in Princeton was located at the lower end of Witherspoon Street near where the hospital is presently located; Leigh Avenue, Lytle Street, Henry Street, Clay Street, that was the Italian section. It was adjacent to the Black neighborhood. John Street was the Black section. And in those days, I think the Blacks and the Italians got along fairly well, because they weren't the Black militants that you had in the sixties. The Black population was more established, and they (the Blacks) had more status than the Italians did. They may have been treated even better than the Italians. These Blacks were from the old families brought up from the South with the wealthy White land owners who moved up to Princeton in the 19th century. So these Black families lived in Princeton for generations. At first they lived in the homes of the wealthy, then later they established their own homes.

Did being Italian-American have an effect on you in school?

I think so. I never lived in an Italian neighborhood as such, but as far as being an Italian, I had much more status than most of the other young Italians. My father was a businessman who was well respected. He was intelligent, made a fine appearance and was active in politics. The Italians in the community looked up to him. He would take them for their citizenship papers, and my mother would type papers for them, if they had any kind of problems with the law. If they had financial problems, my father would take them to the bank and help them get loans. But despite that, I sensed the prejudice as I was growing up. With my name in particular, first and last. I hated my first name. Nobody could spell it correctly. My last name was no problem. I remember in Catholic grammar school, the nun told me I was misspelling my first name. My parents had taught me the Italian spelling of my name. You can imagine, my being a fourth grader, how sensitive I was about that, misspelling my own name. That was done with quite a dig; that was hurtful. Teachers have their ways of letting their prejudices be known.

It was funny, I couldn't really identify with the Italian community. I was an only child. I was well dressed and clean in grammar school. The other Italian kids were not always clean. A lot of the girls came to school with head lice. And I can remember myself cringing when they would be sent home. I can still remember that. Without it being said, I could sense it; I got the feeling that they thought all Italians were dirty. My mother was very fussy. She made sure I was clean. It just seemed that the only ones who got sent home were the Italian kids. Remember, this was Catholic grammar school with those lovely God-fearing nuns, those demons who were the Irish Sisters of Mercy. It was an indirect stigma that I felt. In Catholic school it was just the Irish and the Italians. And growing up in Princeton, there were two lines of work; the Irish men got the janitorial jobs at the university, while the Italian men were the gardeners on the grounds. The Irish children didn't seem to have that much drive or ambition. I noticed that. In fact, from my graduating class from St. Paul's Catholic Grammar School, I was the only one who went on to college from the girls, and there were only two boys who went on to college—and they were Irish. That says quite a bit in terms of drive and ambition.

Did being Italian-American have an effect on your career?

After I finished college, I went to work. I commuted to New York City. I don't think it had an effect. It was during World War II, and they were hiring women to do men's work, so that wasn't a factor. Being an Italian-American woman wasn't a problem for job choice. And the college that I had attended, which was Douglas, had a large, diversified student body—all female. There were lots of Jewish girls. I identified more with the Jewish girls, because we were in the minority, and the Jewish girls had a tremendous amount of drive. So I don't really feel that being Italian was any great handicap at college. But it was more the social slurs, I think.

I went to Princeton High School. I was in the academic program. I can't be specific about it, but I had a feeling that Italians were not part of the "in-group." Except there were a few Italians who were brought into the Presbyterian Church. There was a time when religion became an issue as well as nationality, and in order to get jobs, they (the Italians) joined the Presbyterian Church. So by being Protestant, these people got jobs. Several Italian families did this early on around 1900. One of the daughters of one of these families, who was a contemporary of mine, had an inside track on a lot of things that were going on in Princeton. She had the right religion. So besides nationality, it was religion as well that held the Italians back in Princeton. Being an Italian-Catholic there was like being a leper. I didn't feel the social slurs in college quite so much as in high school in Princeton, and later, after I got married and moved back to Princeton with my Irish-Catholic husband from Scranton, Pennsylvania. Whenever I told him about the religious prejudice in Princeton, he just couldn't believe it.

He was working in a prominent insurance agency in Princeton, and we were invited to a buffet dinner party on a Friday night. The main entre was turkey. That was in the days (the forties) when Catholics didn't eat meat on Friday. And what did my husband and I do? We ate the turkey. We could have passed it up, but we didn't. We didn't have the courage of our convictions, I guess. In retrospect, I think that was a direct social slur; do it our way or nothing. Another

associate, whom my husband worked with, the director's son-in-law, whom my husband was also friendly
with, invited us to his home as well. And while we
were there, his wife told a story about someone who
had just gotten engaged to be married, and wasn't it
great, except that she was a Catholic. When her husband pointed out to her that my husband was a Catholic, the wife said to him, "You're a Catholic!" as if he
had suddenly gotten AIDS or something. It was worse
to be a Catholic in Princeton than to be of the wrong
nationality. Getting back to the turkey thing, when we
went home, (we were living with my parents then), my
father asked us how everything went and what they
served. When I told him that they had served turkey,
he said, "And? . . ." When we told him that we had
eaten the turkey, he was disgusted with us, as if to say
that we had no guts. It made us feel sheepish, that if
this man could hold his head high, why couldn't his
daughter and son-in-law do the same thing?

Another social slur happened after my first baby was
born, while I was still living with my parents. I had
joined a group of young mothers, such as myself at the
YWCA. We met a couple times a week. The director of
the group, whose husband was a prominent university
and political figure in the community was asking us a
little about ourselves, and since they were all attached
to the university in some form, when I said that my
husband worked in New York in the insurance business, she looked at me as if I were a misfit. Here I was
born in Princeton, raised in Princeton, schooled in
Princeton, had a college education, and because my
husband worked for an insurance company in New
York and didn't have an attachment to Princeton University, it was unthinkable. It was so pretentious.
These girls who worked for the university in the offices

were paid minimal salaries. The prestige was supposed to be compensation enough, off-setting the small wages. It was the same for the professors, since the state colleges paid more than what they made at Princeton.

Did you continue with a working career?

I had worked for an insurance company, doing statistical work. My major was in sociology. I wanted to go to social worker school. But I went back to college, Trenton State and Rutgers and got my master's. I can't really say that my Italian-American background had a big effect there.

Notice any social changes toward Italians when you went back to school?

I didn't have any social stigma directed at me, but I felt them in regard to others. I am a sensitive person, maybe it comes from being an only child. I went back to work, after twenty years, as a social worker involved in a child-study team. There were slurs made. The director and administrators would say, "Well, you know, they're Italian. They're not always clean." The director of the team said something about Italian girls never having learned to take care of themselves hygienically when they have their periods. So-called educated people making these statements, painting all Italian girls with the same brush. Saying that they were taught to use rags during their periods and that they had to wash them out. The director was so bigoted against a lot of people, making comments like, "What do you expect." A horrible indictment of people.

Another thing, when we moved to Pennington (We

have Irish- and Italian-Catholics here.), we would attend social activities with the neighbors. And I hated it when they'd say, "Eyetalian." We had a picnic and there were black and green olives, and one woman said that she didn't want any of those *Eyetalian* olives. It tells you something about the person.

Getting back to high school, we're working on a fortieth reunion, going through a list of names. We spotted one that was very Italian—first and last. One of the women there said that she thought he was called Sandy. Another one said, "No wonder, with a name like that." Forty years after graduation and the prejudice is still there. The woman who said it was a red-headed Irish girl who slings hash at a local diner, and she's putting other people down.

Another incident I remember; I got tired of working in New York City, so I came back to Princeton to live at home. There was a woman scientist who was a customer of my father. I guess she had met me already. She knew I was looking to branch into something else, and she said to me, "Why don't you take up sewing? Your father's a custom tailor." My mother was a dressmaker. My parents had an established business in Princeton. Even though I had a B.A. degree, I was supposed to take up the needle and thread and be a seamstress like my mother. I should go back to my place and do what was expected, being a woman from an ethnic background.

Did you live on campus or at home while attending college?

I commuted to college between Princeton and New Brunswick. I couldn't afford to live on campus. If my father would have allowed me, and I had the money, I would have lived on campus. It was a combination of the two. He didn't want me to leave home. You know the Italians. I would have loved being on my own. That was one of the dreams that didn't happen.

Any effect of your background on your choices?

I honestly don't think it had any effect. I went to the college I could afford. I certainly wasn't bound for Vassar. But my father did want me to live home while I went to college. So that was the old-fashioned Italian thing.

On your goals in life?

No, I don't think it has an effect. But now I have an Italian first name and an Irish last name. My husband used to kid me that it was like the east and the west coming together. When you put my name on an application form, it does make someone do a double take. But I don't think my ethnic background has limited me in what I wanted to do.

Satisfied with your choices?

I wish I had had more social experiences before I married. I was 24 when I married. If I had lived on campus, I would have met more young men of diversified backgrounds. There would also have been Italian fellows, you know, the whole gamut. So not living on campus in college did have an effect. Living on campus would have been a positive social experience. That was one of my big disappointments. It did affect my choice in marrying. It limited it.

Friends?

I had no Italian friends in high school and few in college; and those only because they were in my same classes, not because I sought them out. I don't think today it makes a difference. But I do have two colleagues whom I work with, a woman in the same field and a child psychologist. I enjoy them and somehow we're on the same wavelength. There is a connection with the woman and the man. But I don't do that with all Italians. I think with me it's the level of education. There is a class factor involved. I didn't like to be identified with some of the Italians in Princeton. You know, the Italian women who would wear the black dresses and the black shawls. I used to cringe at the sight of all that black.

While dating, did you look for Italian men or non-Italian men?

I wasn't allowed to date when I was in high school. Because I lived in a college town, my father was very strict. I didn't get a spanking, but the rules were there and no daughter of his was going to date a college student. Finally, I did date a student from Princeton. He came to the house and showed the proper amount of respect to my parents. I didn't feel I was free to be as social as some of my other friends. I guess I could understand where my father was coming from. But I never dated an Italian man. The Italian fellows who grew up in Princeton, the ones I knew in high school, weren't all that ambitious. Not one was in the academic program. They limited themselves to the commercial and industrial programs. I have to admit that maybe I was a little snob at the time. I really wasn't attracted to them at all. I went to a girls college and met my husband when I was working in New York City. I have never even dated an Italian fellow.

Also, in those days, Princeton didn't have the Italian grocery stores where you have the provolone cheeses and the other nice foods. My father would go down to Butler Street in the Italian section of Chambersburg in Trenton. He'd take me with him during the holidays to get all the ethnic goodies. Even then as a child of maybe 12, I got a sense of the community that they had down there. Of course, my father knew a lot of the people living there. I can remember that it was a homogenous community, and I didn't know what that meant at that time, but I felt it. I wished that I had that type of an ethnic background. Here I was, plunked down in a community like Princeton, with the social elite of the WASP and the university. Where did I fit in? Where was my identity coming from? Who was I? I was a little Italian girl who enjoyed using her mind, maybe even socially isolated, who couldn't really see herself as a part of the Princeton Italian community, either, because we didn't live there, and I was never a part of the *other* community in Princeton. I had to go my own way. I remember sitting on one of those brownstone porches in Chambersburg in Trenton and seeing all those kids playing around in the street, and when the women would come out in their aprons they would talk to one another. Everybody seemed to be doing the same thing, and they knew what they were doing. They felt accepted and a part of their community. It was the *sameness,* see, the *sameness.*

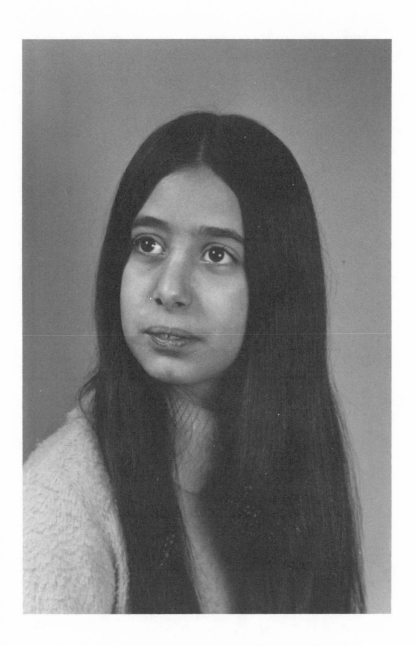

BOOK FOUR

WOMEN IN AN ETHNIC ENCLAVE

A SENSE OF PLACE

This urban ethnic enclave is located in a major New Jersey city, and it has remained intact as an Italian-American community for over 100 years.

The community was formed when Italians, many from a town outside of Naples known as Casandrino, migrated to the United States at the turn of the century. Many came to work either at a wire factory located in the community or at one of the potteries nearby.

Presently, the area is in transition with new Italian immigrants and an influx of Hispanics and Blacks on bordering streets. These streets, once dominated by Italians, are referred to as the "fringe" of the neighborhood.

People from the suburbs are attracted to the area for its specialty shops and many restaurants. And a lively, unique establishment of newly arrived immigrants from Italy blends the old and the new with offerings of Cappucino and espresso at cafe-like tables, imported candies and other Italian items, as well as tapes of Italian movies and video games. The suburban Italian-American grandchildren return to purchase goods and services, to visit, and to participate in community activities such as the annual street festival referred to as the "Feast of Lights."

The streets form a mosaic of neatly kept, mostly row or semi-detached houses. Some of the semi-detached houses have portico porches, side walkways or driveways to the backs of the houses. The postage-stamp-size backyards are neatly manicured, with many utilized as vegetable gardens. The porches are adorned with hanging plants and sometimes overly crowded with outdoor furniture. Small and unpretentious on the outside, the houses are deceiving. Their interiors contain remodeled kitchens and baths as well as converted cellar dens, and they are either modernly furnished or filled with antiques and family memorabilia. Most houses include a living room, dining room, kitchen, pantry area and three upstairs bedrooms. Some forego the dining room for an enlarged open living room. The stairway to the second floor is usually situated at the end of the double living room or dining area.

Although the neighborhood boundaries are shrinking with the influx of non-Italians and other ethnic groups, which may suggest its future demise as an Italian-American community, operating in tandem are renewed interests and trends that may stabilize the ethnic group identity.

There is an expressed interest in the community and a renewed appreciation for the old culture. The younger generations are buying homes or renting apartments in residences of parents or grandparents. One woman (Rena) bought her husband's grandfather's house after his death and restored some of the original aspects of the home. A previously covered fresco on the ceiling is displayed once again as are rediscovered old prints and paintings, including the original used as the model for the fresco.

She comments: "The houses really have character. I can afford to live somewhere else, but I love this house. I think the second generation had to put up the paneling, the aluminum siding, to fit in, you know. Now they're tearing it down and appreciating the value for the old things, the culture underneath."

Rena also hosted a "Renaissance Evening" at her row house for about 40 people. A trio of musicians promoted the Italian culture by performing at the houses of selected guests. A singer and musicians, both residents and former residents of the community, mingled with the guests and performed songs accompanied by piano and mandolin. Song sheets were distributed for a sing-along of Neopolitan folk songs. A cocktail party of Italian wines and appetizers preceded the performance, which concluded with the serving of Italian espresso and pastries.

A sampling of younger-generation women expresses a shared sense of history as they tell about their roots in the community:

> This house was my grandmother's. We're the caretakers. My brother lives nearby, my mother two doors away. People have been around for so long. You can go into the next block and people know who you are and where you belong.

* * * *

> I have my mother and father, my sisters, all my friends, my girl friends are here, except one.

* * * *

I was born in this house. When my parents died, I stayed. Now, I'm living here with my own family. My husband always wanted to live here, to have roots here.

* * * *

My mother lived up the other end and all the family. We all stayed together. My aunt was there. My grandmother. My other aunt. My mother across the street, then me here. Our family lived on the same street. My sister lives on Michael Avenue. So we all stayed close together.

* * * *

I think people here are more family oriented—with family as well as with neighbors. They support one another. I noticed when I was growing up, if someone was sick, a neighbor was right there with them. Consistently always there when anyone needed help. It's always been like that.

* * * *

Let's put it this way. The kids are different in this neighborhood. They are more close-knit. They stick up for one another.

* * * *

It's a very tight-knit community. There's a closeness here and a feeling of nostalgia. There is more togetherness here.

* * * *

Here there's a sense of identity, a sense of community. In the suburbs, people don't care about other people.

* * * *

People are out on their porches and they watch. We don't have robberies. I imagine there are a lot of robberies in the suburbs.

* * * *

I can walk around here at night. I don't know if it's psychological or not, but for me, it's safe here, and that's why I feel safer.

* * * *

It's different here; it's different from the suburbs, because it's a real community. People know each other. When you walk down the street, you can walk in safety. I never lived in the suburbs, but it doesn't look to me like you can walk around out there.

* * * *

I can walk around here. It doesn't offer you privacy, but you know people are watching. I feel secure here. Take the suburbs, for example, you don't see people out front. And when you're not familiar with the neighborhood, you're scared.

* * * *

I would say that the people in my family are our best friends, and to know that they are close gives you a good feeling. I lived down in Atlanta, Georgia for two years while my husband was attending school there, and we couldn't wait until we came home.

* * * *

There are a lot of young people buying the homes. The older people die, and the younger people are moving in. There are a number of changes. Some of the people who are coming in are really downgrading some of the properties here. The ones who are renting homes out. They don't care who they rent them out to.

* * * *

A single, third-generation woman (Anita) from New York City, who recently purchased a house, explains why she enjoys living in the community:

First of all, I needed to buy a house and looked for it in the suburbs. . . . I began to think about what kind of atmosphere I really wanted to live in. I'm making use of the neighborhood. I don't know whether the people who live here and were born here make as much use of it as I do. Most of my friends enjoy coming here and walking to restaurants. . . . It's funny, most of my friends who live in the suburbs prefer to come here. There's more activity. So many nights we've sat on the porch. I've had three or four porch parties.

Anita explains that no place but here could anyone understand her appreciation for her father's fig tree that she transplanted from his home in another city. She describes the tree planting incident:

> There's a lovely old man just one house over who is 93 years old. He's a delight. I have a fig tree in my backyard that I transferred from my father's house when he died. The day I moved in, in the dark of the night, my sister and I are out there digging a hole, and I said to her, they're going to wonder who is moving into this house. Here comes a woman with a tree under her arm. We dug the hole and planted the tree. Anyway, he came over to me one day, the 93-year-old man, and he explained to me what was wrong with my fig tree, and why I wasn't getting figs, and that he would help me, you know, cut off the saplings. I didn't know anything about it until this 93-year-old man came over. You know he came to America in 1909.

She continues with:

> If I don't go to work one day, sooner or later in the day my neighbor will call up and she will say, 'I noticed your car was out front.' She's 75 years old and she has a pacemaker, but she cares, you know. It's very nice to have that. It doesn't offer much privacy, but I feel much more secure here. People know me and they care about me.

> I had taught in Newark for two years, when I first got out of college, and then I went and lived in Italy. Actually, I just went there on vacation, but ended up staying.

> I had interviews with the armed services to teach. I hadn't gotten an appointment. So

once I got to Naples, I registered with the American schools there.

I lived right in Naples with a real Italian family. That's why when I moved here, I felt as if I were coming home!

* * * *

DIVINIA

Divinia arrives for her interview at her granddaughter's house on a Sunday afternoon. She had her hair done for the occasion. She talks as her daughter and granddaughter prepare dinner.

Divinia came from Italy when she was 14 and married at age 16. She explains that she and her husband shared all household tasks, and that they both had to work to support the family. Their offspring helped to support the family, dropping out of school as soon as they could. The older children also cared for the younger ones. She tells how the family, all dressed up on summer Sundays, walked to visit relatives or neighbors. It was her job to starch and meticulously iron the children's white dresses and suits for the occasion. The family would drop in unannounced from house to house where they would eat, drink and dance. The young married couples danced to the music of recordings while the children played. She remembers baking bread each day. The children would take the loaves of dough on a wagon each morning to the local bakery shop for the baker to cook in his large ovens. Often, her husband prepared dinner and tended to the children. She explains that her husband was very strict about the children's behavior. He was the more authoritarian parent, but she considers herself to have been the more influential or dominant of the two.

Divinia had only two years of schooling in Italy. As a child she worked on a farm tending sheep and doing chores. She speaks about attending the community's Continuation School for Girls as a teenager. There, she learned domestic skills only. An intelligent and articulate woman, she taught herself to read and write English. She prides herself on reading the newspapers each day. And now that her eyesight is failing, she listens to the news on the radio. She had to work to help support her family as a young child, and also as a young mother. She explains that she never had the opportunity to attain a formal education.

Her daughter, Maria, describes her second-generation family quite differently. She and her husband both worked. She had her responsibilities and he had his. They rarely, if ever, engaged in activities together. He generally went to the men's club and she had her family or girl friends to spend her evenings or spare time with. When it came to the children, she was solely responsible and he referred to them as "her children." They never discussed childrearing and only on rare occasions shared in any of the children's activities.

Maria tells how her husband's family controlled their early married life. Her husband lost an opportunity to travel as a musician with a well-known singer because he abided by her father-in-law's wishes. At that time she had two baby girls. The family's suitcases were packed and placed in the hallway of the father-in-law's house where they lived. The morning that they intended to leave, the father-in-law carried their suitcases upstairs to their room and demanded that his son stay *home* to raise his family. His authority was never disputed. Maria explains that her husband never discussed the incident, but "it changed him forever."

* * * *

CAMILLE

Camille, a young woman, explains that she lives around the corner from her parents. Their backyards meet. Her grandfather came to the United States from a village near Naples to work in a local factory. She relates his story of disillusionment that the "streets were not paved with gold" as he thought and the American women looked like "painted clowns." Remembering a young girl from his village, whom he knew only slightly, her grandfather wrote his parents to arrange for their marriage. Her grandmother arrived at age 18 to marry a man she hardly knew. The young woman explains that her grandparents purchased a house in the early 1900s. The grandmother's sister bought a house next door shortly thereafter. When their children married, they also acquired houses one next to the other, forming a chain of family households. At one time, seven individual households of the extended family occupied a half-block section of the city street. Other extended family members lived either across the street, down the street, or around the corner. Only one of the original family houses is now occupied by a nonfamily member. However, three third-generation families have extended the family's occupancy on this city block. Most other members of the family live in the community with the exception of four married cousins who live in the suburbs and two married cousins who purchased their houses nearby in the city. The single fourth-generation women of this family, ages 19 to 31, still live in family households.

The grandmother and her sister, *Zia,* who were usually dressed in black, spent most of their married lives together, sitting outside on their porches when their chores were done, or in and out of each other's houses. Later, when the grandmother got a television set, they would watch the soap operas, while commenting on the lack of morals of the women in the soap operas. *Zia* was widowed early in her marriage and had only one son, so she was surrounded mostly by her nieces and nephews, and later her grandnieces and grandnephews. Two of her nieces still live on the same street and seem to have repeated the older women's pattern of living.

* * * *

ROSEMARIE

Rosemarie, a 22-year-old mother, discusses her family's generational residency in the community and also illustrates the traditional allegiance to the family. She explains that when her grandmother died, leaving a family of ten children, her grandmother's sister married her grandfather to keep the family together.

"My grandmother and grandfather live over there (pointing to the corner outside of her window), and they lived there all their lives. My mother and all of them. When my first grandmother died, my grandfather married her sister. She came from Italy. She was going to be a nun. She married him because he had ten kids and my grandmother had died. She accepted it. They didn't know each other, but that's how the tradition was. She was sent here. She took over the family and had three more children with my grandfather.

"My uncle went with his father (my grandfather), to Italy to bring back his aunt, who was to become his stepmother. This tradition was customary in such a family crisis. The sister was related to the children by blood. She would love and care for them as her own. Everyone loves my grandfather and step-grandmother. When my family gets together for social events, we are about 200 and usually gather at a hall or a restaurant owned by one of my uncles. My grandfather became ill recently and was not at our Thanksgiving dinner. His presence means a lot to all the other grandchildren, too."

* * * *

Il Circolo Feminino

(THE WOMEN'S CIRCLE)

While the men were out of the house, the women also had their unique peer group activities consisting of family and friends. They sat on porches or chairs on sidewalks under shady trees in the summertime. Part of the daily routine was to join the women's circle after cleaning the house or cooking. A second-generation woman tells about the women's activity in the neighborhood as she remembers:

> ... years ago, all the women out front would sit ... my generation. That was our entertainment at night. ... We would go out and somebody would dance and somebody would sing ... my mother would make the homemade bread in this neighborhood. And her loaves were about a yard long. And the neighbor next door always had mayonnaise in her house and one of the neighbors, she always grew tomatoes. So we used to sit out and we used to bring out the bread and the tomatoes and the mayonnaise. And we all had a sandwich.

Camille tells about one group of women, called the "Shady Tree Club," who would sit and talk under a tree after their morning chores until it was time to prepare lunch. After lunch they would congregate until dinner. Their husbands would go out after dinner and the women would gather again until dark while their children played. When the tree became afflicted by blight and had to be destroyed, a mulberry tree was immediately planted in its place. The mulberry tree was selected because of its quick growth even though the women knew it would be messy. They shared the task of washing down the sidewalk when the purple berries fell. There was one bench under the tree and one bench against the front of the house. Chairs were brought out if extra seats were needed. The social circle was not limited to the women who lived on the street. It was also frequented by the women's relatives or friends who walked from other streets in the neighborhood. The core members of the social group consisted of about ten women, four of whom were sisters. The tree still remains on this street and people still sit outside, but the activity is not as regulated as it once was.

* * * *

A unique "sewing circle" of second-generation women still exists. For over thirty years a seamstress has operated a dressmaking business in a house basement. Before she had her own house, it was operated in the basement of a friend's house.

Customers may come with clothes to be altered or for fittings by entering the backyard from the side entrance of the semi-detached house. The cellar door is always open for customers to step down into the renovated basement. Ironing boards, racks and machines are draped with various articles of clothing. The seamstress does the major work, but there is a regular group of women who visit and talk. While they are there, they help by pulling out hems or taking out pins. The seamstress delegates the tasks. The women do not get paid for their services and that is not their reason for helping. They go to socialize. They enjoy customers and like to hear about people's business. Payment is in the form of reciprocity for the helpers as well as for the seamstress. The seamstress charges very little. A stack of alterations may cost less than ten dollars. The helpers get free alterations or something made for someone in their family. For instance, the seamstress made draperies for one woman's daughter-in-law, who paid a minimal charge. She was told by her mother-in-law to remember the seamstress at Christmas and other holidays and was also told what little gifts the woman would like such as a jar of rum cakes from the neighborhood gourmet shop.

The women take personal interest in the customers, especially the younger women and teenagers. There is usually a lot of talk about the women's dresses for special occasions. They comment on the details of who is wearing what, where they are going and with whom. Special attention is given to prom gowns or dresses for a wedding party. They comment about the girls' boyfriends and about individual family wedding arrangements. The teenage girls have costumes made for a high school gymnastic competition. The costume design is judged as part of the competition, so when several girls' teams have their costumes made by the seamstress, there is a lot of excitement and talk about which is best and who should win. The women go to the Girls' Sports Show and take pride in watching the performance of which they have had a part. The women plan theatre and bus trips several times a year. They also help organize, under the seamstress' direction, trips to Italy every few years.

The third-generation woman who had the draperies made tells about how the seamstress and two of her helpers came to hang them at her house in the suburbs. The young woman entertained by serving coffee and desserts. This personal gesture of hospitality was appreciated and expected. This kind of reciprocity is always a topic of discussion for the "sewing circle."

* * * *

JOAN

Joan lives in a row house. The two-step porch entrance leads into the living room and open dining room. The living room includes a television set and comfortable furniture. The formal dining room is used for family purposes such as homework, and Joan's craft projects. The kitchen is remodeled with an island countertop, a dining table and chairs.

She comments:

> I remember when I was growing up, no one had a clothes dryer. Monday mornings they would be out in the backyard hanging their clothes. It was nice, because they also had their little coffee claque while they did the clothes.
>
> They still do it. They get up early in the morning. They're out there sweeping the sidewalk, washing their porches.
>
> People get together more so outside. In summer, I recall, was when the majority of the people used to sit out on their front porches years ago and socialize. They would bring out their little lawn chairs and just sit out there for a few hours.
>
> They still do that. But there are quite a number of people who have passed away. At my mom's house, during the summer, there are still people who sit out there on the sidewalk.

The only reason why I'm still in this house is that I don't have to work. If I moved, I would definitely have to work. But I have this part-time job. It gives me a little extra spending money. I'm helping my cousin out in a doctor's office. She's a nurse there. She needed some help. Otherwise, I think I'd still be home. I can't say exactly why I work. I do enjoy it.

I really consider myself to be a housewife. I like being home. I do. I really enjoy it. Running whenever I could. Doing whatever I want to do. Some people can't stand staying home. But not me. I like it.

Everyday is different, because I work for a doctor and a surgeon. You never know what's going to happen. Some days I go in at 9:00, some days at 10:00. I go in whenever I'm ready. Leave whenever I'm finished, whenever the patients are done. I go out to lunch, maybe for a couple of hours. I go back to work and then I go home. Go to the store. Cook dinner. Take care of the kids.

My husband helps me a lot. So do my children. They help me clean. Of course, my laundry is never caught up. If they didn't help me, then I don't think I would work at all. I have their support. I have three men in the house. They all wear two pairs of socks a day. Two pairs of socks! I'm never caught up. I'm not the type to wash and throw things into the dryer and take them out. I iron everything, even the socks. When I first got married, I ironed everything. I didn't iron socks, though, but underwear, sheets, all that stuff. I ironed everything. So I'm never caught up.

I taught my husband how to iron. He ironed for three hours one night. He set up

the ironing board where he could watch some
ball game on TV and ironed for three hours!

* * * *

MARY ANN

Mary Ann lives in her grandmother's house across from the community park. It is a row house with two outside entrances from the sidewalk. One enters into a long hallway leading to the upstairs and a dining room. The ground-level entrance leads to the living room and TV room. The furniture is den-style for family comfort. The dining room is furnished with antiques and is more formal. A lace tablecloth completes the decor. The kitchen was remodeled and is functionally modern. A clock with chimes and seasonal decorations complete the setting. A picture of *The Last Supper* hangs on the side wall.

I was born here, *Mary Ann begins,* two doors away. My brother lives two blocks from here, and my mother, two doors away. My childhood memories are of both grandmothers. My grandfathers died when I was little. My father had one brother, my Uncle John. He lived here with my grandmother, my Aunt Dollie and their son. We lived two doors away. Then there were all my father's aunts and their children who came to visit. I visit regularly with my mother, my uncle and the ones who live in the neighborhood. I have three sisters and two brothers. My brothers and sisters have children. We're a crowd.

When I was little, I always thought Italian women were old and had Italian accents or spoke Italian. My older brother and sister speak Italian. I wish I did. I understand. As kids we were forced to understand, especially when my grandmother, or my mother and father spoke it when they didn't want us to understand them. I remember my father's cousin. She spoke Italian so fast to my older brother and sister. When it came to me, I just stared at her.

My mother's mother is from Calabria. My mother's father—Abruzzi. My father's mother and father are Neopolitan from the village of Casandrino.

My mother's mother was not educated. She was a peasant. I guess a farmer. My father's mother came basically from the same type of family, but she was educated. She was a midwife. She studied at the University of Rome. She was very literate. And she was the neighborhood midwife around here. Later, she cooked at my father's restaurant. She crocheted a lot. Just a typical Italian woman, but she was educated. She used to show us her certificates. A lot of people referred to her as a doctor. She died in 1970.

I know more about my father's family because it was bigger. None of my grandmother's sisters came here, only a few of her brothers. Uncle Walter lived with us, also. Then there was Uncle Domenick. He fought in the First World War and ended up in a veterans' hospital. Uncle Joe went back to Italy and my mother lost contact with him.

My mother's mother wasn't educated. She took in laundry. My grandfather died when I was little. I remember my father saying that he did factory work. My father said they had land down near the shore, but that they lost it during the Depression.

People have been around here for so long.

When my boys go out to play, or go into the next block, people know who they are. If they see them where they don't belong they'll say, 'I'm going to tell your mother.' Everybody sort of knows everybody, or knows where they belong, or could find out without too much trouble.

I compare here to where my sister lives in the suburbs. She knows her immediate neighbors, but not those at any distance. Here—for a four-block radius—you still know people. I remember when we were kids, we would walk down the street with my parents and say hello to everybody. People were always sitting on their porches. It's kind of the same thing now. Especially certain times of the year. Summer—they have night games in the park. September—it's the Feast of Lights. People who know I'm here come to watch the fireworks. It's just a feeling of knowing. I probably know at least one family on each block. That is definitely different. A lot of areas in the city, people got out. Here—they seem to stay.

I'm the only one left. My three sisters and one brother have moved. I don't know how long my younger brother will stay. I felt the need to stay. My father used to say that if this house were fixed up, it would be everything I want. My mother used to say, 'You won't be sorry if you raise your kids here. You got the church right here, the school, the hospital.' It's true. We don't have driveways. The kids can ride their bikes on the sidewalk. I can let them go to the park. I don't have a yard, but they have a park and a school across the street. They can develop a sense of responsibility by living here. My sisters can never send their kids to a corner store. Mine know the neighborhood merchants and their personalities. My older son used to go to Charlie's Bar and pass play money to buy peanuts. Charlie would go along with him. My son would tell me about it, and I'd tell him that you can't buy peanuts with play money. 'I know, Mom, but Charlie doesn't know that,' my son said. They're more secure. I'm more secure. Sometimes, I worry about all the people, the noise, the ball games. You might think it's a World Series with these kids. I wish they'd just let the kids play. A lot of people go over to watch the games. I let my kids go. They're used to being around people. Their school is small. There's one group for each grade. If they go on the corner, they'll get chased back home. A lot of people will yell if annoyed, but mostly because they are concerned for the kids.

This is home, and if there's something else I want, I can go out of the neighborhood to get it, but this is home. If I need the beach, I can go. There's more than just a house. My sister moved. She's got a nice house, but to go anyplace, she has to use her car. Get the kids in the car. They can't ride bikes. I think they're missing out.

There's not as much interaction among neighbors as when everyone used to sit out front. I think people still care. This block, in particular, is for the most part pretty much the way it was. The outside life changed a bit, but the caring is still there.

Last year some Black kids came to play basketball in the park. The neighborhood kids pulled the backboards off. No overt violence. They just let them know they were out of bounds. During the riots there was trouble. The house on the corner is a rental. Some

Spanish people moved in. The reception was
cool. Nobody said or did anything. They didn't
stay long. The day they moved, people stood
and watched them. I did it myself. I don't
know why. I have Spanish friends and a Black
co-worker. I invite them to my house. But that
day—it was like—no, you don't do this here.
The landlord is an Italian, but a more recent
immigrant.

The new Italian immigrant is different. I
don't identify with them in the same way. The
sense of loyalty and dedication just isn't
there. It's a get-rich and get-out idea. I've
seen it done. They leave it for us to clean up.
They go back to Italy. These new immigrants
are more transients than immigrants. Our
grandparents came here never to go back
again. It must have been a compelling force. I
don't know what it takes to do that. I can't
imagine my husband coming home and saying
to me that we're leaving—never to see my
mother again? I see my mother just about everyday. I see her sometimes at lunch and at
night. Usually, we go there, or she comes
here.

Holidays are spent with close friends and
family. Vacations are with the family. My
mother has a house at the beach. We congregate there. My mother and my sisters who do
not work spend the summer there. I spend my
vacations and weekends there.

Working women are accepted and toler-
ated, but it's still viewed as better if the
mother stays home with her children. It's indirect, but you know it.

I'm an Income Maintenance Specialist
with the State. The night before, I lay out the
children's clothes. In the morning, I get
breakfast, wake the children, clean up the

kitchen, get the children out of the house, get dressed and go to work. My husband's out by 7:30. So I'm usually alone here with the kids. He finds his moment of relaxation by getting out. He escapes. I like quiet in the morning, but I don't get it. I try to get home for lunch to tidy up a bit, start supper, shop for dinner, check on my mother. It gets to be too much, if I don't. I go back to work, stay until 4:30. The kids are here when I get home. Then there's homework and dinner. Afterwards, the kids have their chores, clearing the table, loading the dishwasher. Sometimes, my husband helps out. Then the boys watch TV, play upstairs making forts, jumping on beds. If my husband's home, they're usually quiet. If I have the energy, I stay up till 10:00. Otherwise, I just go to bed. Everyday you have to do the same thing.

As a parent, I have more rules than my husband, but he gets more reaction. Maybe my words don't sound to them the way they sound to me. My husband has a loud voice, but he can show tenderness, too. I do more touching, hugging and kissing than he does. Sometimes, I don't praise as much as I should. That's because I expect so much. My husband lays down the law, but I am definitely the more dominant parent.

I enjoy going to church. My grandmother went whenever she could. My mother went everyday. But for me it's more existential, more on a personal level. It's more important to me to be a Christian than a Catholic. We never read the Bible. There was no exposure to it. I read the Bible a lot now. I wear St. Joseph and St. Francis medals. *The Last Supper* is hung in my kitchen. Crosses are in all the bedrooms. The house is blessed. My children wore medals as babies, and I considered it a bad omen if they got lost. And we were always taught to fast or abstain. As far as rules and doctrine, I will always abide by them—it's philosophical.

The Feast of Lights is not what it used to be. Of course, I can't see it through a child's eyes, anymore. But I see no shame in making something commercial out of a religious observation. The church was packed for this year's religious procession. And people still do housecleaning and prepare for the feast, because you get a lot more visitors. We watch the fireworks from my porch. Somebody always comes in to use your bathroom, relatives, friends, even strangers. I remember my mother let some girls in, and they wrote their names on the mirror!

* * * *

JEAN

Jean lives in a row house with an enclosed portico porch. The aluminum-covered frame dwelling is situated across from the small community park that offers a bit of greenery in contrast to the starkness of the urban streets. Although the house is clean and sparsely furnished, creating a functional atmosphere, it has the warm, friendly feeling of family life.

She comments:

People say that there's more closeness between neighbors. Of course, the homes are closer, too. That makes a lot of difference. I know of people who have moved out to the suburbs—and have moved back. They didn't like it because people weren't as friendly.

My husband likes it around here. That's why we moved here. I do like it here. I love my neighbors, but if I could move and afford a bigger home, I would move. I wouldn't stay here. If I could speak for myself, I'd prefer to live in the suburbs. We've been here ten years, and it hasn't changed much.

I remember my grandmother saying that her father put her on a boat when she was 16 years old, all alone. He had relatives here and sent her to them. Why? I really don't know. When she got off the boat, it was a prearranged marriage at 16, with her future husband waiting at the dock. She talked about it all the time. That's the way things were done. Not now. Years ago, you just did what was said and that was it.

I have a part-time job that a friend got for me. I can walk to work and be home, if I really need to be. My family comes first.

Before 8:00 in the morning, I have two loads of wash done. I'm up at quarter to six, but by 9:00 P.M. I'm dragging. That's my day. It doesn't bother me. My husband helps me when I need help, when I ask for it. I've always said that whenever I need him in a pinch, he comes through for me, but basically I do most of it myself.

* * * *

CONVERSATION WITH LENA (MOTHER)
AND LISA (DAUGHTER)

Lisa lives in a second-floor apartment owned by her parents. The apartment house is located on a typical busy urban street across from the parish church where double parking is a common occurrence in front of business establishments.

Lena, her mother, still lives around the corner in a row house in which she was born.

Lisa: This community is a family neighborhood.

Lena: People watch out for one another, and they're very helpful. There is a sharing. It has family characteristics.

Lisa: The community itself is like a family. When I walk from my place to my mother's house with the laundry, people say, 'Hi, ya! Let me help you with the basket.' It's like the old generation.

Lena: The new people moving here don't fit in. A young couple moved into the apartment next door. They're not helpful or considerate.

Lisa: A person not born in this neighborhood is different from a person who is born here. I enjoy the noises and the church bells. They mean something to me, but the new people complain about them.

I may move. I live in my parents' apartment house around the corner. I would move because of space and also for the baby.

When I do get a house, it will be in the suburbs. The reason for not getting a house yet is that I want to be close to my mother, being married and young and having my husband out a lot at night. I'm close to my parents. It's better than an apartment complex. But I will miss the whole atmosphere when I move. I don't know how I'm going to adjust.

My husband is Irish. His family is from the neighborhood. His family was here from when the Irish immigrants settled here. He likes it. He likes Italian food. He fits right into the city life. But there are times when he has to have peace and quiet. He's an attorney.

Lena: Over the last five years there's been a great deal of change. New neighbors. Loss of friends through death—whatever. Both my parents are gone. My mother died just this past April. This is her house. It's still a home. I never had any intentions of moving. Maybe I never will. I don't know. The newcomers aren't as sharing and considerate. People here were always considerate of their own homes and their neighbors' homes. Whenever it snowed, you not only shoveled your sidewalk, you shoveled your neighbor's sidewalk. This newer generation takes things for granted, like it's your job to shovel their sidewalk. The sharing is gone. And they leave their dogs out day and night. They don't care if it bothers you. This time last year I had no intentions of moving. This year—if I could find a nice little spot to live, maybe I would move.

Lisa: Socializing is mostly outside in this end of the neighborhood. We never went in and out of people's houses. If there's a death in the family, a birth, or something else, they will run in with a pot of soup or a bowl of macaroni. They will stop in at Christmas and wish us Happy Holidays. No gifts are exchanged, just friendship, and a cup of coffee.

Another example of old neighbors versus new neighbors: If your clothes are out on the line and it starts raining, the old neighbors will yell, 'Lisa, bring in your clothes, it's raining.' But the new girl next door could be standing right at the window and would never think to yell to you to get your clothes. Not that it's bad; it's just their way of life.

Lena: My parents were born in Italy. My mother came here when she was nine. My father was a little older. America was their new country. It gave them their livelihood.

Lisa: My grandfather was proud to come to America—to become an American citizen. He went all the way with being American, even as far as the language.

Lena: My parents, especially my father, believed in education. He respected the American flag, and we were not permitted to speak Italian at home. When people came into our house and rattled off in Italian, my parents would answer them in good English—not broken. The people would be left with their mouths open. And we were the only ones who graduated from high school around here. My father would not permit us to go out to work, like our friends. We had to finish high school. College would be up to us. He pushed education. He read the newspaper from front to back and could tell you everything in it. He loved the opera and all the finer things in life.

Lisa: My grandparents came from the same town in Italy, but they didn't know each other. This hilltown they were from was between two mountains about three hours from Naples. My grandmother washed clothes on the rocks in a mountain stream and carried water on her head on cobblestone streets. She always said that was why she was short. It pushed her down! They came here for a better life.

Lena: Two years ago we visited Italy and saw the house that my father was raised in. We couldn't find my mother's house. My father's people lived right in the middle of town, but there's nobody from his family there now. He tended sheep. The lady who lives in the house now was so happy to see my mother and father. She invited us all in for supper. They have tile floors and tile walls. They're very clean, very humble, very poor. Still—I felt so proud to be Italian.

Lisa: We were so proud when we came back from Italy. We saw the works of Michaelangelo and DaVinci—and all the splendor.

Lena: You come back with a bigger chest—and just walk around with this pride.

My mother went up to only the second grade in Italy. My father went to night school when he came to America to learn English. He was mostly self-educated—and cultured.

When I was in high school, I was a straight A student. I was chosen to work the IBM key punch machine in class. When I went out into the field of work in 1941, it helped me land a job with General Motors. I worked eight years there in the IBM Tabulating Unit on computers. After the war they went back to the old way of doing things and asked me to stay on as a bookkeeper, but I refused. I wanted to stay in the computing field. I went to work for the State.

Lisa: My mother should have a degree in IBM computers. I have a B.S. in Education. I wanted to go to Temple University to get my master's degree in early childhood education, but going myself to Philadelphia . . . that held me back from going there.

Lena: I always wanted to go to college. I wanted to be a teacher. My father would have supported my going. But I loved what I was doing. I never pursued the college thing any further. I never said to him that I wanted to go. I have worked ever since. I stopped when my daughter was born. I went back to work when she was two, but only because I lived with my parents, and my mother could take care of her. My family and my home came first, then my job.

Lisa: My mother was the only woman in the family who worked. And she was the one who did the Thanksgiving, Christmas holiday get-togethers. All the baking. She did all these things, plus working.

Lena: I always said that when I went back to work, my husband would never go into a closet and say, 'I don't have a shirt or socks to wear.' He has never said that until this day.

When I got married, I looked for a man who respected women. I figured when a man respects a woman, he loves a woman. You know, kindness, loving, giving, good old-fashioned manners.

Lisa: I think that communication, in whatever form—talking, listening, understanding—is important in a marriage.

As for religion, it comes down to a more personal level for me. I have a lot of religious articles around the house, but I don't expose them for decorative reasons like my mother does. It's something private and humble, but they're around, in the corner of the hutch, and I don't care if someone else knows it.

* * * *

DAWN

Dawn lives in a third-floor apartment in a large, single, Victorian building, which sets back from the busy street. It's a commercial area that includes a bank, real estate and doctors offices and a funeral parlor. A security bell system calls the tenant to the front door. Once at the third-floor landing, one enters into a hallway/foyer that is charmingly decorated with a table, sewing machine and dress mannequin. In the kitchen, the table is covered with a floor-length calico cloth and glass top. The living room and bedroom are decorated with white wicker, antique collectibles, posters and prints and piles of cushions. There is a Greenwich Village aura about the place.

> People sit on their porches in the summer, *Dawn begins,* but in winter they hibernate. Yet here you know people. When I moved into this building and put my name on the mailbox, they would say, 'Oh, you're so and so.' And when my husband moved in, they said to him, 'Oh, your sister is married to so and so.' I don't know how they know so much, but they know. Sometimes, I wish I could be anonymous, but that's only once in a while. I really like it here. I like the fact that people know one another. You can walk down the street, in the park, there's thirty-five people whom you know. And it's nice that you can walk to get whatever you need from the deli, the bakery, the liquor store.

There is also a safety factor here, because everybody knows you. My husband says that people around here still think it's like it was in 1930. My husband's grandmother lives in a three-story house with a basement around the corner from us—all by herself. When she goes to her daughter's house for a visit, she doesn't leave a light on in her own house— and stays away for days at a time. I'd be scared to death to go back into that big empty house.

I don't want to live in the suburbs. I prefer living in a city or a little town. Where you can still walk to get to where you want to go. You don't have to drive your car to go get a loaf of bread. We don't have any yet, but if we do, I don't think this is a good neighborhood for children. We're in the *fringe* area. It's the border between the *community* and the rest of the city. We're close to the train station, where it's not safe. They call people on the fringe *them* and refer to people in the community as *us*.

They split this community. On this side it's half Spanish and half Italian. On that side, it's sort of us and them. I feel that the Italians across the street are not sympathetic to the Spanish on this side. They'll pass remarks that *they* live three families in one house. My grandparents lived like that. If you have nothing when you come here, three families share a house. I resent it, because their grandparents lived like this. On Sunday there are men all dressed up on the corner talking in a foreign language. And if you're not real sure of the area, you don't know who is Spanish and who is Italian. The similarity is so close, you know. I feel like the Italians won't give the Spanish a break.

The conversation returns to a more personal level and Dawn continues:

> We lived together before we got married. And we never discussed it with our parents. We just lived together. They never discussed it with us. Probably didn't want to. But they were fine. I'm sure my parents would have preferred our getting married. We adjusted. They adjusted. My brother lives with his girl friend. My parents have coped rather well. Things I thought they'd never be able to accept. Years ago I wouldn't have thought they could be so understanding. They could have said, 'We're not seeing you anymore.'
>
> They never did confront me about it, and never acknowledged it. Sometimes I would laugh. My father would ask my mother, 'Why does *he* answer the phone when she's not there?' He would beat around the bush. That's his way. I would tell him I didn't want to play games, that he knows who lives here, and who's paying half the rent and expenses.
>
> It's amazing, they've accepted things that I never thought they could. First, I was divorced, then I moved in with someone. My father thought my divorce was a real disgrace. Then when we went away together on vacation while my mother was in the hospital, he went bananas. But he didn't say anything to me, because he knew I would not listen.
>
> When we did decide to get married, we went to the Protestant church on the corner. I didn't think we would be accepted at the Catholic church.
>
> I always went to the Catholic church, although there were things that I never believed. Practices that I never believed in. The Protestant religion is probably more to my

way of thinking. If I have children, I will raise them as Protestants. And I will take them to church.

Once again Dawn shifts from one topic of conversation to another and begins to talk about her family:

My family is really not educated. We're the first generation to go to college. My mother's brothers, my father and his sisters, none of them finished high school. In my mother's family, only one person graduated from high school. My mother went to 10th grade and my father went to 9th grade. My parents dropped out of school to work, to help support their families.

This friend of mine, who's in her thirties, when she was in her late teens, going to Rider College, her grandmother, who was very old, said to her, 'What are you going to college for, to have babies and change diapers? Are they going to teach you that? Then you don't have to go. That's all you need to know.'

My husband's family has college graduates in it. I take night courses now. I work and I have a small florist business. I do weddings and things like that.

I work primarily for the income. But also for my own satisfaction. If I didn't need the money, I would still do something. Even if I hit the lottery, I would do something that I like to do. I like to work.

I am not one to clean. We share the housework. But I don't think we're the norm. We're so busy. I work, sew, have my florist business. My husband commutes to New York City. He walks to the train station. Living here makes it easy, but he has a long day.

* * * *

RENA

Rena's row house stands out from the rest because of the dark, ornate front door, which opens into the living room. And the first thing that a visitor sees is a refurbished ceiling fresco with its biblical quality and Sistine Chapel effect. The house is furnished with collectibles and antiques, including a massive piano that fills most of the dining area. In contrast, a child's table and chairs are situated in front of the TV set. Family and friends visit frequently and informally.

She comments:

> I had my grandmother and grandfather on the same block, and two sets of great-aunts and great-uncles, and another grandmother nearby. My husband lived with all his family. Three families lived in one house, three sets of parents, a grandmother and six kids.

> The Italian woman basically cares about her immediate surroundings and doesn't concern herself about the larger world around her. Her world is her family. That's it. She kind of shuts the door. Well, I don't. I get involved, in this or that committee. But since I've had my son, I've slowly gotten out of some of that. Yet I'm always with a cause. I detest milk-toast women with no spunk, or who don't even read the newspaper. Don't even know what's going on in the world.

The Italian-American is not as mobile as say the WASPs or the Jews. But I've traveled extensively and so has my husband. We went to this policeman's retirement dinner and the PBA president's wife had never been to Florida. She looked at me like—Who is this young twerp? The woman's in her fifties. She's never been anywhere.

I think it's harder for Italian-Americans to move away or to travel. I think it's guilt. A lot of them have never been out of the community—even to New York City, which is only about 60 miles away.

My husband cooks breakfast on Saturdays and Sundays. During the week, I cook supper every night. All he knows how to cook are bacon and eggs. And when he cooks, he expects me to clean up. If I'm really tired or if I'm premenstrual, he'll pick up my slack. If I really get behind, he'll clean the whole house for me spic and span. I have friends whose husbands are different. One of my girl friends' husbands has never changed a diaper in three years. If the child has a bowel movement, he'll get disgusted.

I have a three-year-old son. I do expect him to have some responsibility, because I am not his valet, or his maid. I expect him to pick up his clothes. But my mother says that's what you're there for. I resent that. I have an aunt, my role model, who has two boys, and she does everything for them. She picks up after them. That's very Italian. There's no reason for that. Italian women *spoon-feed* their children. I'm still feeding my son with a spoon when he doesn't eat, because I have that Italian guilt. He has to eat! We were at a friend's house and she asked him why he wasn't eating. He said, 'I have nobody here to feed me.' I almost died, I was so embarrassed. That's from my background. That's all it's from.

I try not to pick up after my son. I make him put his things in the hamper. My grandmother and my mother think differently. I have three sisters who are Italian princesses. They don't even know what it is to pick up their underwear and put it into the hamper. They don't know what it is to iron or wash clothes. They've always had my grandmother or mother take care of them. That's typical. They're really malcontents. Maladjusted. No one is good enough for them to marry, or they're afraid they might have to raise a family, or care for a house. It's hard work. It's not some glamorous thing. I think the second generation does that to their children—gives them an overabundance of material things. Then they don't know how to face reality. They're really immature.

Italian mothers doted over their sons because they never got the love and admiration from their husbands, and it was one vicious circle. I would never make my son that way.

I sell real estate, but I'm not career oriented. I had my child at 27 because I wanted to. I could put him in day care, but I want to be there for him. I don't have a nanny. I want to be the one who stimulates him. I do take him to the Montesori School a few mornings a week. He's bright, so he needs something extra. The school's about 20 miles away. I usually spend the time with the other mothers, shopping or out to breakfast or lunch, until it's time to take him home.

I want my son to learn the Italian language and the Italian culture. He doesn't have the advantage that I had—an Italian grandmother. Exposure to art and travel—it's important. My grandmother brought us to Italy.

I read to my son all the time. His favorite book is by Tomie de Paola, *Strega Nona,* about a Calabrian witch and her magic pasta pot. I'm a 24-hour parent. He's attached to me. He stays with only two people, my mother-in-law, or one of my sisters. I've never had a stranger baby-sit him. I would be appalled to think of some 12-year-old baby-sitting him. We have the freedom of our extended family.

We help one another out in a crisis, financial or otherwise. Our parents and my grandmother have keys to our house.

Would you believe, we have had family join us on our honeymoon? My husband's cousins surprised us while we were in San Francisco. One cousin and his wife were nearby on business, another cousin thought it would be nice for all of us to get together, so he flew out. They surprised us by showing up in the hotel lobby. It's crazy, but you have to understand the closeness of these cousins. They just wanted to be all together—honeymoon or not!

My husband's good, he wouldn't hurt me. That's important, not to be embarrassed or humiliated. Both of my girl friends are totally humiliated by their husbands—because of the macho thing. *They* have to go out with the guys, to prove something to themselves. Angelo is mature. He's from a broken home. He was hurt very young in life, maybe that has something to do with it. He's always been with his mother. First, they lived with his grandmother, then they had their own apartment. It was a struggle for them.

The people who live across the street just moved in. It's important for them to try to make friends, while we already have our family and close friends nearby. My girl friend Debbie and I have been friends since we were eight years old. We get together as couples.

I have a friend who just went back to work. When her husband called my husband to help cut down a tree, I found out she wasn't home from work and hadn't cooked. So I made dinner and brought it over there, because she just started working. I knew it was tough for her. This way I made sure that when she got home, she would have something. She would do the same for me. We're real close that way.

I hate it when we have friends over and the men separate from the women: the women in the kitchen, the men in the basement. The men always make an excuse to go out together for a while, to pick up cigarettes or something. I think this is a carryover from when they were teenagers and their street-corner days. When I go down to the basement, their conversation always changes. My husband doesn't like it when I go down to the basement and try to join in the conversation. He says that this embarrasses him.

When it comes to religion, I'm not a fanatic. I'm a Christian and believe that you should live a Christian life, but not get wrapped up in this Roman Catholic dogma, because I've read a lot. The Renaissance. Medieval history. Church history. We don't attend Mass. We don't even get envelopes anymore. I feel guilty and terrible, but I just don't like to go. You stand up, you sit down, you say certain words, it just doesn't do anything for me. If I could just sit there by myself and pray, I'd feel better. I've tried the Baptist Church, and even Black churches. I got more out of them. I try, but I don't seem to get anything from the Catholic Church.

The Bible is fascinating. The Catholic Church should do more with it. They never stressed the Bible in school. And as a young girl I had a positive attitude toward nuns and priests. But now they're not bending. They live in their own world.

Godparents are important to me. I would always choose a family member, instead of a friend. I still call my godmother, Godmother Rosa. My uncle is my son's godfather and my sister is his godmother.

I love the Feast of Lights. I have a party each year. My friends come over. We're getting ready for the feast now. I'm so glad it's back.

* * * *

SANDY

In the ethnic enclave, social attitudes toward females and their respectability prevented personal choices and retarded goal attainment for some. Sandy explains how her mother's views influenced her personal aspirations:

> When it came my turn, my mother thought a woman's place, once she got married, was in the home and she didn't see the need for an education. Instead of going for my Bachelor of Science Degree, I started working in a medical laboratory and never achieved my bachelor degree. But she felt it was important for my older bothers to get a formal education.

And Sandy further explains that she never achieved her goal to become a nurse because of family pressure in regard to what was considered respectable for a female:

> My goal was always to become a nurse. I was also interested in the medical profession. However, I was discouraged many times on that point. My mother was raised to believe that you don't walk into a room with a patient disrobed or anything like that... the thought of my studying to be a nurse really bothered her. She couldn't deal with it.

* * * *

GIRLS AT A CATHOLIC HIGH SCHOOL

A group of senior high school girls from the urban ethnic enclave discusses the behavior of its members at a suburban Catholic High School. They all agree that they are different from the other students—in that they are more concerned for their families and that they *stick* together.

Other kids, they're more into their friends and going out and partying, where we're more into the family. We all stick together . . . and we're loyal. It's a tradition in our family backgrounds. We stick up for each other. It was the same way back when our grandparents came here. It's a kind of remembrance of when they came over.

* * * *

Our parents want us to have everything that they didn't have. Our grandparents, then our parents . . . they worked so hard. They don't want us to have it like they had it.

* * * *

Everybody knows each other in the community. There's somebody you know on every corner . . . it's like being part of a big family. One big family. Somehow you're all related, in some blood way. I can go down the street and say—that's my third cousin, that's my second cousin.

* * * *

We stick together. Everybody here. We argue with one another—right? Well, we can be arguing, or mad at somebody, but if someone else bothers them, we're right there to help out.

* * * *

When we were freshmen, instead of mingling with other people, we just stayed with the people we knew.

* * * *

When it comes to going to college, our parents usually recommend you stay close to home. All my brothers and sisters went to State College or Community College. It seems your parents, and even your grandparents, want to protect you.

* * * *

If we move or not, we're still going to have our neighborhood in our hearts, because we're still going to be coming back—like from the suburbs or anywhere else.

* * * *

Anywhere you go, you'll still come back, because this is where you grew up, and there's still a lot of community things happening in the neighborhood—like the Feast of Lights.

* * * *

When you go to college, you'll be away; but when the Feast of Lights comes, you'll come back. . .

Connie A. Maglione received her *Doctor of Education Degree* from Rutgers University, New Brunswick, NJ where she completed an ethnographic study of a New Jersey community entitled *"Current Patterns of Socialization and Adaptation in an Italian-American Community."* She also holds a *Bachelor of Science Degree* and a *Master of Education Degree* from Trenton State College.

She has varied experience in public education and is currently the supervisor of a Gifted and Talented Program for the Academically Gifted for a large New Jersey school district.

As a member of the *National American Italian Historical Association,* she has presented papers at Providence, Rhode Island (1985) and Chicago (1987); and is also the vice president of the *Central Jersey Chapter of the AIHA.* She is currently listed in three Who's Who directories; American Education, Women Executives and U.S. Executives.

Carmen Anthony Fiore is a graduate of the Trenton, New Jersey public school system, and he holds a *Bachelor of Science Degree in Commerce* from Rider College as well as a *Master of Education Degree in Guidance and Personnel* from Rutgers University Graduate School of Education. He was a social worker for the State of New Jersey and taught sixth grade in an elementary school for the City of Trenton. Recently retired from a New Jersey civil service career, he now devotes full time to his literary pursuits. He is the author of **THE BARRIER,** a novel of social commentary and **VENDETTA MOUNTAIN,** a novel of suspense set in southern Italy, while his most recent fictional work, **LITTLE OSCAR,** is yet another return to his social worker and ghetto school teacher days.

He is a member of *AIHA, National* and the *Central Jersey Chapter of the AIHA,* and is also the editor of its newsletter.